AF505756

NORTHWEST HISTORY

Jerome Peltier
4/10/96 (Age 85)

NORTHWEST HISTORY

Articles from the Pacific Northwest Quarterly

BY

Jerome Peltier

YE GALLEON PRESS
FAIRFIELD, WA. 99012
1996

Errata:

The cover and title page should read *"Ariticles From the Pacific Northwesterner Quarterly."*
Page 74: "Good Genes and a Bit of Luck", appearing on the same page, was penned by a different author.
Page 92: The article "Timberlodge" appearing on the same page was penned by a different author.
Between pages 126 and 127, photo pages, Seth Woodard and Howard Stegner, photo identified with names reversed.

Library of Congress Cataloging-in-Publication Data

Peltier, Jerome.
    Northwest history : articles from the Pacific Northwest quarterly
/ by Jerome Peltier.
        p. cm.
    ISBN 0-87770-602-6
    1. Northwest, Pacific--History--Sources. 2. Northwest, Pacific--Biography.
I. Pacific Northwest quarterly.
F851.P436 1996
979.7'37--dc21
                                                        96-52910
                                                        CIP

Jerome Peltier, Author-Historian

by Florence Boutwell

If you're driving along Trent Road, looking for home cooking with a dash of local history thrown in, slow down when you come to a cross street marked ELLA. On the corner is this sign:

Marlene's Restaurant
Revisit Old Spokane
Courtesy of Jerome Peltier

Inside the door to the left is the Peltier Room. Jerome's pictures of

Jerome Peltier
(Picture taken about 1940)

early day Spokane cover the walls.

My uneducated guess is that Jerome Peltier is the most knowledgeable and most frequently published living regional historian in the area. Since 1933 he has lived right here among us in the Valley, just a stone's throw from Marlene's Restaurant.

Peltier has had his finger in just about every area pie that had anything to do with preserving local history. With the Rev. Wilfred P. Schoenberg and Richard T. Lewis, he was co-founder of the Pacific Northwest Indian Center, now known as the Museum of Native American Culture, the name he proposed. He is chairman of the History Committee of the Eastern Washington State Historical Society and Museum. He was the first

treasurer and a trustee of the Spokane Indian Health Center. With Thomas Teakle, he founded the Spokane Chapter of Corral, a group of history buffs known as Westerners. The International Westerners honored him signally by naming him "Living Legend #16." With Sister Mary Elizabeth Dunton and Mrs. Fabian Smith, he founded the now-defunct Fort Wright World War I and II Museum and was a founder of the Realistic Art Association.

But let's begin at the beginning... Jerome Peltier was born in Clocuet, Minnesota, in 1911. He remembers well the first book he ever read, *Dr. Rabbit and Tom Wildcat.* "I read it to pieces," he said.

The family came to Coeur d'Alene by train when Jerome was 14 years old. In his own words, "Then and there I fell in love with the West. From the train I saw Indians dancing at Mandan, N.D., and cowboys riding the range in Montana. And those wonderful, wonderful Rockies!"

Shortly after settling in Coeur d'Alene, he attended a mass at the Cataldo Mission. The great Father Cataldo spoke in the Salish Indian language to an overflow crowd of mostly Indians. After mass, those who wished to speak with Father Cataldo formed a line and Jerome was one. This contact with Father Cataldo and the Indian language awakened an interest that eventually led to Jerome's writing two books about the Coeur d'Alene Indians.

When the Paulson Building was being constructed in Spokane, his father became a carpenter on the job and after it was built, the maintenance manager. Jerome and his father at that time lived in the old (bus) Terminal Hotel across from the City Hall, then located between Howard and Wall. Jerome enrolled in Kinman Business School and found out for sure that "those were not the kinds of books I wanted to have my head in."

He got a job at John W. Graham Co. as packer in the warehouse. He remembers well the wooden packing boxes of those days. "I had to size up every shipment and order each box made to fit the goods. I became so good at it that Graham transferred me to his fourth floor sample room, a real honor. I later became

Hardly a supermarket, about 1893, the very first store in the valley, between the Spokane Falls and the Spokane Bridge. This photo was taken in 1893 on a road now known as Trent Avenue. The store building was also used as a school from 1899 to the spring of 1900. Photo courtesy of Jerome Peltier Collection.

One of the many priceless photos from the Jerome Peltier Collection is this scene showing the manager of the old Trent Railroad Depot waiting for one of the many trains with passengers and mail that stopped at the depot every day.

credit manager. I spent my spare time browsing in the book department. Those were the Depression years. I could afford only to look.

"I knew John W. Graham on a first name basis. He lived halfway up Monroe Street in a house with beautiful gardens. He loved flowers and on his European trips often bought flowers in Paris and Holland and sometimes shared them with us.

"He once told me that he had not really intended to settle in Spokane — was on his way to the coast when he ran out of money, stopped off in Spokane and found a job with book and office supply salesman, Sylvester Heath. Heath was burned out in the great Spokane Fire of August 4, 1889. He decided not to reopen his business and loaned John W. $300 to set up the business in a tent across the street from where the Review Building is today."

While at Graham's, Jerome met many book lovers and history buffs, some of whom became his lifelong friends. Among these were William D. Allen, who owned the Book Nook in Spokane across from Pete Jacoy's, and George W. Fuller, a regional historian who headed Spokane's public library system for many years.

When Fuller died in 1937, his widow sold Jerome 22 pioneer letters her husband had collected, including one by John McLoughlin

and another by Henry Harmon Spaulding. That was the beginning of his collection of original manuscripts and memorabilia.

He traded books with A. W. Patterson, a brother of Robert, who founded the Crescent. J. Howard Stegner, a historian whose mother operated a grocery store at Trent, and Seth Woodard, for whose family Millwood is named, were among his Valley friends.

In 1937 Jerome married LaVerle Boyer whom he had met at a picnic in Coeur d'Alene Park when she was fifteen. They had three children.

"I left Graham's in 1947 and in 1950 LaVerle and I bought Clark's Old Book Store at W. 831 Main. We owned and operated that business until 1978. During those years we were burned out, flooded out, and changed locations five times. In the ast move (to its present location at 118 Sprague) we moved 60,000 books."

During the '50s and '60s, Jerome's articles appeared regularly in the Spokesman-Review. The supplement that he wrote about the Spokane Fire is considered the most complete written account of that event. He has published eight books and is currently working on two others. He was named distinguished author of the year by the Eastern Washington Historical Society in

1985. The same year AARP awarded him the title Outstanding Volunteer of the Year because, along with his many other community services, he spent hours visiting local nursing homes cheering and aiding the residents.

His published books are as follows: *Banditti of the Rocky Mountains* about the Henry Plummer gang of Virginia City and Bannack, Montana, *Manners and Customs of the Coeur d'Alene Indians, Warbonnets and Epaulets* about the Steptoe and Wright Indian campaigns, *A Brief History of the Coeur d'Alene Indians, Madame Dorion,* the story of an Iowa Indian heroine who came to our Pacific Northwest in 1811; *Antoine Plante,* 1852 settler of the Spokane Valley; *The Diary of Edmund Cavileer Hinde,* his overland journal to California in 1850 and his experiences in the gold fields, edited by Peltier; *Black Harris,* famous mountain man and trail guide. The last five titles were printed and published by Ye Galleon Press, Fairfield, WA, and may be obtained from them. Jerome is hard at work doing final revision on two more books, *Felix Warren,* stage coach owner, and *The Custer Fight.*

BUCKSKIN BULLETIN

Issued quarterly (August, November, February and May) by Westerners International, a Foundation, to stimulate interest and research in frontier history. A special purpose is to serve The Westerners, founded by Leland D. Case and Elmo Scott Watson in a Chicago suburb, February 25, 1944.

BUCKSKIN BULLETINS are sent in bulk to local units (usually called Corrals) for distribution to members. Individual subscriptions for active or corresponding members are $2.50 per year; all others $5.

THE BB BUNCH: Editorial - Don W. Sigler, Dan L. Thrapp. Leland D. Case; Advertising - Larry Railing, Norman Flanders; Mailing - C.V. "Jim" Hughes.

WESTERNERS INTERNATIONAL

Donald E. Worcester	President
Jarvis Harriman	Exec. Vice President
Will K. Brown	Coordinator
John F. Marohn	Treasurer

(Location: 120 West Broadway)
Box 2304, La Placita Sta., Tucson, Az. 85702

Corral Names Sparkle with History and Geography

ALL CORRALS have one thing in common: the West. But when it comes to their names there are as many varieties as Heinz has pickles.

Three are named for heroes – Jedediah Smith (Hot Springs, So. Dak.), Sam Houston (Houston, Tex.), and Buffalo Bill (North Platte, Nebr.). The new group at Columbia, Mo. would come under this classification too, as the Corral there honors John G. Neihardt, the poet and charter member of the Chicago Corral, who once worked there.

A few ripple with rivers – such as Red River (Durant, Okla.), Potomac (Washington, D.C.), and the new Rochester, N.Y. Corral - the Genesee.

Geography is popular: Yellowstone (Billings, Mont.), Narrangansett Bay (Bristol, R.I.), Pikes Peak Posse (Colorado Springs, Colo.), Black Hills (Rapid City, So. Dak.), Santa Clara Valley (San Jose, Calif.), and Santa Catalina mountains at Tucson, Ariz.).

Five recent Corrals also are geographically oriented: Yuma Crossing (Yuma, Ariz.), Willamette honoring Oregon's famous Willamette Valley (Portland, Ore.), the Mother Lode Corral (Jackson, Calif.), the Last Chance Gulch Corral (Helena, Mont.), and the Seneca Sandhills Sidesaddler group in Nebraska.

States get the play with Dakota Midlands (Aberdeen, So. Dak.), Colorado (Denver #2), Mo-So-Dak (Mobridge, So. Dak.), and Utah Westerners (Salt Lake City, Utah).

Then there's the Indian tribal name Dakotah (Sioux Falls, So. Dak.). There's also Amerindian flavor in the Indian Territory Posse (Norman, Okla.). Add the new Corral at Pullman, Wash. to this list. It is the Nez Perce-Palouse.

Other Corral names smacking with local history include: Piety Hill (Detroit, Mich.),

Spokane Corral's Jerome Peltier Knows Indians and the Fur Trade

by Cecil Hagen
Editor of the Pacific Northwesterner

FOR MORE than a few Western history buffs who visit Spokane, Wash., stopping at Clark's Old Book Store to visit its genial proprietor, Jerome (Jerry) Peltier, is a habit. He is by far the most widely known member of Spokane's Corral, because as some of his fellow members say, "He knows more about Western history than the rest of us put together."

Without him the Spokane Corral wouldn't have been chartered No. 11 in 1955. Several years earlier Thomas Teakle, a high school history teacher, began recruiting members. He ran out of prospects after signing up six because he sought men with at least M.A. degrees. Peltier convinced him the standard was unrealistic, that they should seek men with a sincere interest in Western history. Together they rounded up a charter group of 27.

After the second meeting Peltier took over as Sheriff, and since then he has appeared on 23 programs – more than three times as many as anyone else.

His chief interests are the fur trade and Indians. He can trace his ancestry to a Frenchman who landed in Quebec in 1592. His great grandfather was a licensed trader in Minnesota Territory in 1832 – 22 years before statehood.

He attended high school in Coeur d'Alene, Ida., where he had his first contact with Indians – members of the Coeur d'Alene tribe. His interests in history were aroused during his years as a wholesale salesman for a book store, by two men he met on his rounds. One was a book dealer and the other was George W. Fuller, a regional historian who headed Spokane's public library system.

When Fuller died in 1937 his widow sold Peltier 22 pioneer letters her husband had collected, including one by John McLoughlin and another by Henry Harmon Spalding. That did it. He disposed of his first editions and has collected only original material since. He says that missionaries decrying heathen ways of the Indians are by far the best written source before they were pauperized by the whites.

Calafia (La Paz, Mexico), Llano Estacado which means Staked Plains (Lubbock, Tex.), and Bear Flag (Sonoma, Calif.). And, or course, the Yale Corral at New Haven, Conn.

And the members at Berlin, Germany, are responsible for what's probably the oddest name of all, Ten Go West!

Jerome Peltier

The author of three books, Peltier has been in demand since the 1940's as a speaker on regional historical subjects. In 1963 he helped Spokane's Fort Wright College, a Catholic women's school, found its World War I and II museum.

He made the Western history movement's "big time" in 1965 as one of the founders of Spokane's Museum of Native American Cultures - the name he proposed. Sharing founding credit with Father W.P. Schoenberg, S.J., and R.T. Lewis, a former Westerner.

This museum is one of the better ones of its type in the West, and also probably the least known. It adjoins the Gonzaga University campus not far from downtown Spokane. So far it has only one building, a unique, truncated, three-story concrete and stone tepee, which would cost over $2,000,000 to replace. Its art collection, much of which is stored in vaults, is valued at a minimum of $1,000,000, and its Indian artifacts – representing tribes from Alaska to Mexico – are valued at $2,000,000.

While some rate the museum among the 10 best in the nation, Peltier conservatively says it would be difficult to keep it off a list of the 20 best in its class. For Westerners everywhere Spokane's Corral recommends a special trip or at least a stop in Spokane to visit the cultural house Peltier helped bring into being, and at the same time meet him.

His most recent honor was being selected as treasurer of the Spokane Urban Indian Health Service. He is the only paleface on the board.

His *Manners and Customs of the Coeur d'Alene Indians* was published in 1975. *War Bonnets and Epaulets*, an account of Col. George Wright's Indian campaign in the Spokane area in 1858, came out in 1958. And *Banditti of the Rocky Mountains*, about a criminal gang headed by Henry Plummer in the 1860's, came out in 1964.

In Colville Valley of the 1860s . . .

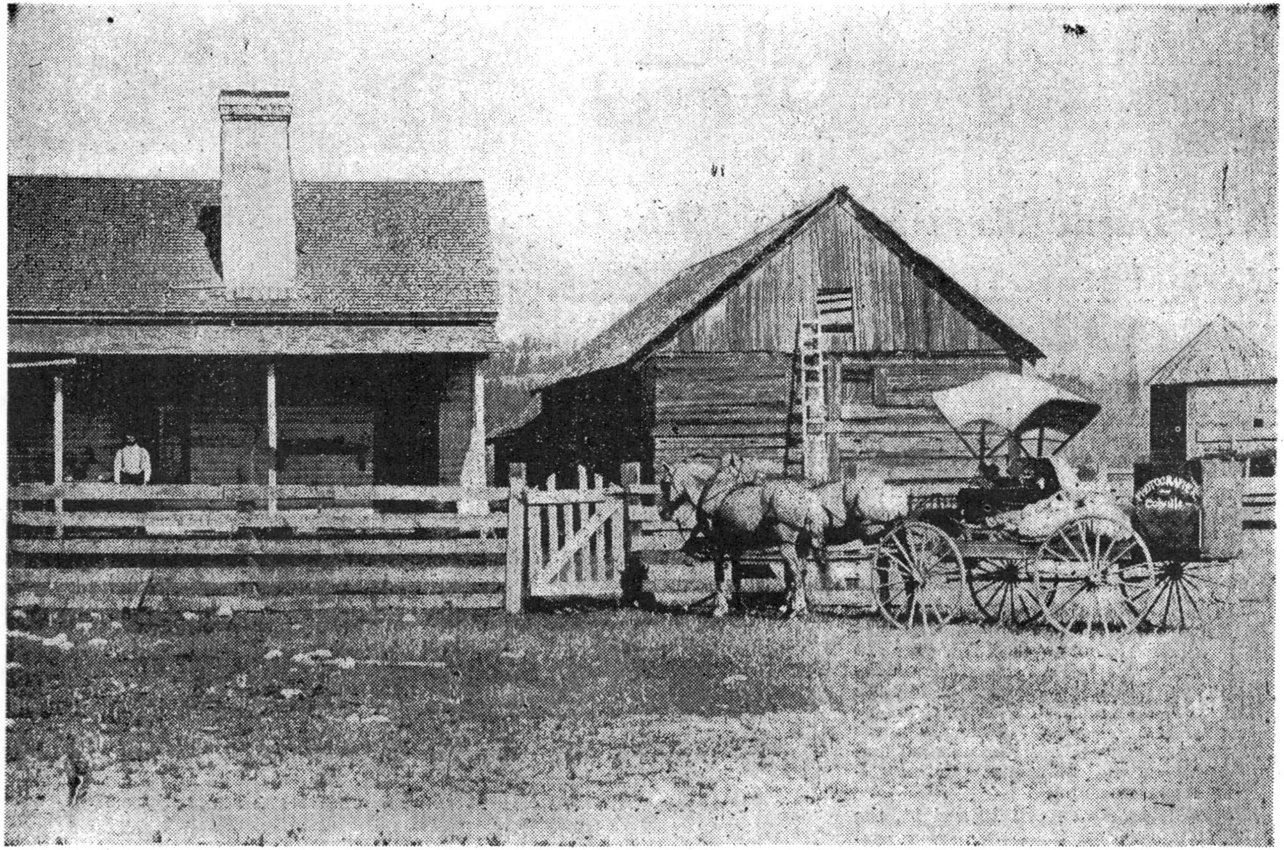

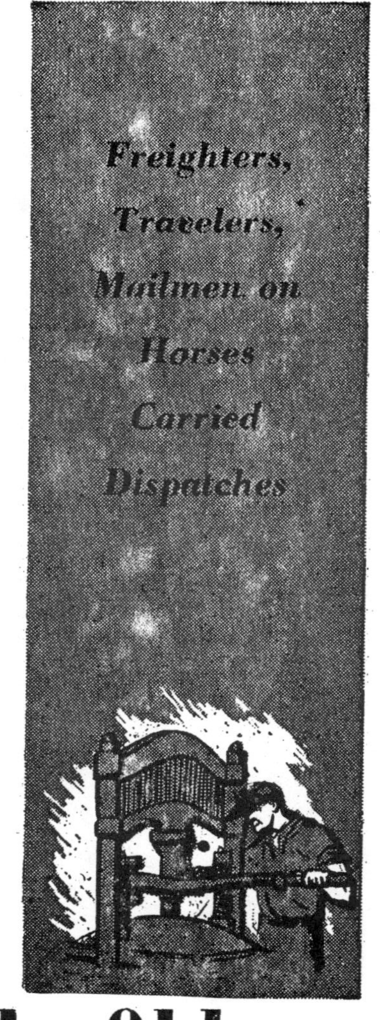

Photo of old Fort Colville, after its heyday, in the 1890s.

Freighters,
Travelers,
Mailmen on
Horses
Carried
Dispatches

. . Fresh News Was a Month Old

By Jerome Peltier

Charter Member, Spokane Posse, the Westerners, and Frequent Writer on Region History

IN THESE days of Associated Press reporting (which brings news to us from all corners of the globe within a matter of minutes) it is difficult to realize that newsgathering was once a long, slow process.

In the early days of the Inland Empire news was sent to certain centrally located newspapers such as the one in Walla Walla by correspondents from outlying areas.

This news was brought to the better known centers of civilization of that day by freighters who were on their way to obtain supplies and trading goods with which business was maintained in the outlying towns and villages. Travelers, either afoot or on horseback, carried letters and dispatches also.

The express, a faster service maintained to speed up the receipt and dispatching of news, was often used also.

Usually, the express was a man astride a fast horse whose only business was to carry dispatches to their destination in the least possible time.

When the stage routes were established they too played a prominent part in the dispersal of news, as well as bringing visitors and settlers into the area.

IMPORTANT history was being made during the 1860s in the Colville valley so the work of the correspondent was most important. There was pathos, laughter and drama (in fact, all of the elements of great news reporting) in the pages of the local correspondent's column.

The Colville area of the 1860s was much different than that of the present day. The city as we know it now was not then in existence. To the north and a trifle east of the present city of Colville was the new military establishment named Harney's Depot. It was later renamed Fort Colville. Across Mill creek from the military post was the newly built town of Pinkney City, named for Maj. Pinkney Lougenbeel who commanded the four-company post at the time it was built in 1859.

Pinkney City was county seat of Spokane county when that county comprised an area larger than that of the present state of Washington, for at that time its boundaries were the area that lay between Snake river and the 49th parallel and between the Columbia river and the continental divide. It encompassed much of eastern Washington, all of Idaho, the western section of Montana, which was divided geologically by the continental divide, and a small segment of Wyoming.

Harney's Depot took its name from Brig. Gen. W. S. Harney, who was commanding general of the military department of Oregon at the time the post was built in 1859.

IN HARNEY'S dispatch dated November 5, 1858, Fort Vancouver, Washington Territory, two paragraphs of interest to this area read as follows:

"To secure the emigrant route to this department from the frontiers of Missouri, I shall establish a post in the spring in the vicinity of Fort Boisee, on Snake river, some 230 miles from Fort Walla Walla. At least four companies should garrison this point—two foot and two of mounted force. The road is a good one from Fort Walla Walla, and it can be supplied from that point. I also respectfully recommend a post near Fort Hall on the same route, but would advise that the garrison, as well as the supplies, be furnished from the department of Utah, for reasons of economy and supervision.

"As soon as the season will permit I shall establish a garrison of at least four companies in the vicinity of Colville, to protect the interests of the citizens in that quarter and serve as a check upon the Indian tribes who were so lately hostile."

Note: The Fort Colville to which Harney refers is the Hudson's Bay post which was situated near the falls known as Kettle Falls and from which the present town of Kettle Falls derived its name. This post was in existence from 1825 until the 1870s

The excerpt quoted above proves beyond a doubt the value of Walla Walla as a supply point for the upper areas of the present Pacific Northwest, and gives the reason for building the various military outposts in the places specified in Harney's report.

The military post of Fort Walla Walla was in existence at this time.

Old Hudson Bay Company post near Marcus.

Victor's camp at Hell Gate Ronde. Pearson passed here on way to Stevens. At left: Antoine Plante's cabin many years afterward. (Henry Rust photo.)

Sidelights on Inland Empire History

The Council on the Spokane

A Fabulous Ride by William Pearson Set the Stage For Governor Stevens' Dramatic Moves and Demands At Antoine Plante's That Quelled the Angry Indians

By Jerome Peltier

S TRANGE to say, one of the most interesting sets of documents relating to the Indian war of 1855 may be found in a book that was published in 1893.

The title of this volume is "Biennial Report of the Adjutant General of the State of Washington for the Years 1891 and 1892." Printed in Olympia, Wash., O. C. White, state printer, 1893.

In addition to other interesting items contemporary to that period, of which one has to do with the Indian troubles arising from the hanging of a young Indian in the Okanogan country in 1891, are the muster rolls of the Washington territory volunteers for 1855-1856. Many names of great historical importance in the Inland Empire are mentioned. Among these were several Indians who became well known through the Indian council at Walla Walla and later, through their part (at least some of them) in the Nez Perce Indian war of 1877. These men, listed in the "Muster Rolls of the Nez Perce Indians" enlisted and served, usually, as guides.

Their services were secured by Governor Isaac I. Stevens at Craig's, which is roughly near present Cottonwood, Idaho. Among the names listed (and there are many more) are Spotted Eagle, Looking Glass, Joseph (all three being very prominent in the negotiation of the treaty at Walla Walla, and Joseph being the father of young Joseph, the leader of the Nez Perce during the war in 1877), Jason and Timothy, who was at all times a true friend to the whites and at times the butt of much mischief perpetrated upon him by some of his tribesmen because of his friendly attitude toward the whites.

Among those listed in other muster rolls were, of course, Governor Stevens; William Craig, an early Cottonwood and Lewiston area settler, after whom Craig mountain in Idaho was named; James Doty, secretary to the governor; W. H. Tappen, early Washington territorial legislator and railroad promoter; and C. H. Mason, acting governor in the absence of Stevens.

The most important muster rolls (at least in this immediate area) are those entitled "The Spokane Invincibles" and "Stevens' Guards." Both of these organizations came into being at Antoine Plante's place, which was located in the deep bend of the Spokane river near the cement plant, two miles east of Millwood in Spokane Valley.

The "Spokane Invincibles" under Capt. Benjamin F. Yantis, are listed as follows: John Crawford, 1st lieutenant; Aaron Webster, 2d lieutenant; Amasa S. Miller, 3d (!) lieutenant; Thomas Petigrew, 1st sergeant; William C. Prall, 2d sergeant; William Scott, 3d sergeant; Jonathan S. Jaqueth, 4th sergeant; Edward S. Altree, 1st corporal; Samuel K. Renick, 2d corporal; Jeremiah D. Farnham, 3d corporal; Henry C. Barrett, 4th corporal; Barney Pindred, private; John McLescue; Simon Geil; Frederick Wise; Asa Sanshoes; John Hall; James Wilson; Jacob Swartz; George Taylor and Loami Andrews, privates. The first 18 members were enlisted in Spokane Valley; the remainder of the roll in the Lewiston area.

The group called "Stevens' Guards" under the leadership of Capt. Christopher P. Higgins are listed as follows: William H. Pearson, A. Hugh Robie and Sidney S. Ford Jr., 1st, 2d and 3d lieutenants in that order; Green McCafferty, Charles Hughes, Joseph Larmier and Francis Jennet, 1st, 2d, 3d and 4th sergeants in that order; Paul Eubanks, William Simpson, John Dunn and Antoine Piller, 1st, 2d, 3d and 4th corporals; followed by Privates John Canning, Lewis Fouche, Lewis Osaugh, John Lisott, Peter M. L. Fountain, Laurance Lerongy, Charles Actor, Hazard Stevens, Capt. John (Nez Perce), Owen McGarry, Patrick O'Neil, Norby Dupre and Maxy Short. These gentlemen all enlisted at Antoine Plante's or at Spokane.

At least passing notice should be given to the name Hazard Stevens, the eldest son of Governor Stevens, for it is an unalterable fact that Hazard was only 13½ years of age at the time he became a member of "Stevens' Guard," having been born June 9, 1842. It is incredible that a boy his age could have withstood the hardships that were incident to travel in that day.

Another gentleman most worthy of mention listed in this same body of men, was William H. Pearson.

Hazard Stevens describes Pearson as follows: "One of the most remarkable men connected with the expedition was the express rider, W. H. Pearson ... a native of Philadelphia, of small but well-knit frame, with muscles of steel, and spirit and endurance that no exertion apparently could break down, waving, chestnut hair, a fair high forehead, a refined, intelligent, and pleasant face, the manners and bearing of a gentleman—such was Pearson." (Life of Isaac I. Stevens by Hazard Stevens, page 69, volume 2.)

We shall describe him in the words of one who knew him well, Governor Stevens, who, in his final Railroad report, Volume 12, part 1, page 210, wrote, "I suppose there has scarcely ever been a man in the service of the government who exceeded Pearson as an express man ... Hardy, intelligent, bold and resolute, having, a great diversity of experience, which had made him acquainted with all the relations between Indians and white men from the borders of Texas to the 49th parallel, and which enabled him to know best how to move, whether under the southern tropics or in the winter snows of the north; this year he did for the service under my supervision a labor which requires from me, at the present time, the most ample acknowledgment."

Praise indeed from his commander, and his words will be clarified soon, but first it might be well to write a few words about conditions in the territory of Washington in the year 1855.

Isaac Stevens came to Washington in 1853 with a three-fold purpose in mind. First and foremost he was named governor of Washington Territory by President Franklin Pierce; secondly, he was also Indian commissioner, with full power to negotiate peace treaties with the Indians and also place them on reservations should he see fit to do so; and thirdly, as head of a survey group, with instructions to locate the most practicable railroad route through the Rocky mountains and the Cascades to the Pacific ocean. This was to be a northern route for a transcontinental railroad.

It is, however, in his role as Indian commissioner that we shall consider him at the present time.

Governor Stevens had made several treaties on the coast above and around Puget sound, and also at Walla Walla, just previous to his visit to the Flathead and Blackfeet country. Here he had completed a satisfactory treaty between these tribes and the United States government and was on his return journey when W. H. Pearson rode into his camp on the Teton river, 35 miles from Fort Benton, in an utterly spent condition, as was his mount, which tottered as it staggered into camp.

Eager hands aided the wiry express rider from his saddle. His haggard appearance attested to the incredible adventures he had undergone.

His dispatches were turned over to the governor for his perusal, and following a short rest during which he partook of some food, he proceeded to give a verbal report of the reasons behind his fabulous ride.

In substance his report was as follows: The confederated tribes of the upper Columbia country had broken out in open warfare. Agent Andrew J. Bolon had been ruthlessly murdered approximately 15 miles north and a little west of Goldendale (not a town at that time), and similar murderous atrocities had been perpetrated against all white settlers in the area. Major Granville O. Haller with 100 soldiers of the regular army

Fort Owen and Flathead village. Here Stevens held council.
At right: Fort Benton. Governor Stevens camped near here.

In Midwinter 100 Years Ago

head, knocking him senseless. Fortunately, the brave revived, because if he had not the Nez Perce tribe would have held Pearson accountable for his death and would have possibly gone on the warpath because of it.

The storm continued for three days and although they were forced to wait until it was over, Pearson was not idle, for he spent the time making a pair of crude snowshoes for himself. These he used the next four days as he struggled through the Bitterroots carrying a heavy pack of food and supplies as well as his dispatches, after he had sent his Indian companion back to Lapwai with the horses.

The trail was obliterated by the heavy snowfall but

peace or war?" meanwhile forming a united front of seven ready guns in the hands of himself and his party. The Coeur d'Alenes declared themselves peaceful!

At this time, it was learned that four men who had brought up trade goods for a proposed council with the Spokanes were being held at Antoine Plante's place along with 15 miners who were afraid to leave the place due to the hostile attitude of the Spokanes who were camped nearby.

Stevens determined to rescue these men and have a council at the same time, if such an undertaking could be arranged.

He sent Craig along with three of the Nez Perce chiefs to Lapwai where they were

the area in a dangerous frame of mind.

It was about this time that the governor's party organized under the name of "Stevens' Guards." The miners not to be outdone, also formed a military company and named it "The Spokane Invincibles" with Judge B. F. Yantis as captain.

Perhaps the results of the council might well be told by quoting Governor Stevens. This may be found in Hazard Stevens' two volume book entitled "Life of General Isaac Stevens" on pages 134-135.

"We remained on the Spokane nine days, and I had there one of the most stormy councls for three days that ever occurred in my whole Indian experience; yet, having gone there with the most

Coeur d'Alene mission. Drawings are artist Stanley's.

had been defeated in the Yakima county and it was found that Indians west of the Cascades had arisen simultaneously and attacked many communities on Puget sound and in Oregon.

Further questioning revealed that the Nez Perce, Spokanes and Coeur d'Alenes were becoming disaffected due to the fact that some of the hostiles were taunting them, because of their non-intervention in the fight. Truly things were in a bad condition.

Following this recital, Pearson informed his listeners that he had left The Dalles, with his dispatches, on his return trip (remember, he had ridden from Montana to Olympia previously), and was on his way back), fresh and in excellent condition, and after riding all night, and reached the Umatilla river at daylight where he had breakfast at the deserted ranch of Billy McKay, a rancher who had located there. Following his repast, he roped a wild horse from a large herd which was grazing near by and had the ride of his life to remain aboard the bucking animal, after he had saddled and mounted it. His mount proved to be high caliber, because almost as soon as he had gained control of the horse, he espied some Indians coming down a near-by hill bent on his destruction and yelling insults to him. He rode as he had never ridden before in all of his highly adventurous life. He pressed on as fast as he could without ruining his horse and during the night he crossed the Walla Walla river, finally arriving at what was then known as "Red Wolf's Ground." This was approximately 10 miles west of the present Clarkston, Wash., at Alpowa. This place was also known as Red Wolf's crossing and still later, as Silcsott's ferry. It took its later name from John Silcsott, the husband of Jane, the Indian heroine who led E. D. Pierce and five others over a devious route to the area around Pierce City, where gold was discovered by W. F. Bassett in August, 1860.

But, on with Pearson's tale of his amazing 28-day ride of 1750 miles.

Pearson obtained a fresh mount at Red Wolf's camp and rode on to Lapwai where he rested a day to regain his strength. He then set out to cross the Bitterroot mountains by way of the Nez Perce trail, accompanied by a Nez Perce brave and some extra horses for use as remounts.

A blinding snow storm began and the wind arose, causing a tree to blow over and striking the Indian on the

Pearson persisted and finally arrived at Fort Owen almost dead from his exertions.

Here he rested for a short time and after being furnished with a horse and saddle, by some friendly Flatheads, set out again down the Bitterroot valley, up the Hell Gate and the Blackfoot to Sun river, finally reaching the governor's party, three days after he left Fort Owen. Governor Stevens acted quickly.

Additional arms and ammunition were secured at Fort Benton and forced marches were ordered. His group tarried for a short time at Fort Owen where additional supplies and animals were purchased.

He went back to Hellgate (near the present Missoula, Mont.) then over the Coeur d'Alene pass, even though the snow was almost impassable, to Coeur d'Alene mission (Sacred Heart mission, near Cataldo, Idaho). Here, he along with William Craig, Pearson and four Nez Perce chiefs, Looking Glass, Spotted Eagle, Three Feathers and Captain John, surprised both friend and foe alike by being in the area where Stevens could combat the propaganda being spread by Kamiakin and his hostile cohorts.

Stevens went to the core of the problem without any further loss of time. He asked the Coeur d'Alenes, "Are you friends or foes? Do you want

earnest desire to prevent their entering into the war, but with a firm determination to tell them plainly and candidly the truth, I succeeded both in convincing them of the facts and in gaining their entire confidence.

"At this council were all the chiefs and people of the Coeur d'Alenes and of the Spokanes ... and I feel that I can without impropriety refer to the success of my labors among these Indians, backed up simply with a little party of 24 men ... When the council was adjourned, the Indians gave the best test of their friendship by each coming to lay before me his little wrongs, and ask redress. ... They came in a body, ... and offered me a force to help me through the hostilities of Walla Walla valley and on the banks of the Columbia, which I declined, saying that I came not among the Spokanes for their aid, but to protect them as their father."

to make arrangements with Chief Lawyer to assemble all of the Nez Perce nation for a council. He also sent a messenger to the Spokanes with the news of his disposition of the Nez Perce.

He then set out from the mission through Wolf's lodge and along the shore of Coeur d'Alene lake and arrived two days later at the Spokane village near Antoine Plante's.

A blockhouse had been built by the men at Plante's and the employees and miners were found to be safe although under conditions of armed truce rather than actual combat.

By midnight, Stevens had dispatched Indian messengers to Spokane Garry, head chief of the Spokanes, and to Fort Colville, where the Hudson's Bay factor Angus MacDonald was summoned to Plante's for a council. The Jesuit missionaries were also asked to come.

Indians came in from all of the surrounding area. Garry and some of the Coeur d'Alenes came in November 29, 1855. MacDonald and the Colville chiefs, the missionaries and four miners arrived December 2.

The council began and a very stormy meeting followed in which Garry and several of the other chiefs gave a recital of the wrongs which had been done to the Indians in their dealings with the whites and how the council at Walla Walla had left the Indians in

The council was held December 3, 4 and 5, just 100 years ago last month, and on a spot approximately 10 miles east of the center of downtown Spokane.

As far as can be ascertained, no treaty was signed at Plante's but through the results of the council, the Spokane area had no Indian troubles for the next three years (until the Steptoe and Wright campaigns) and this was all due to the fabulous ride made by William H. Pearson.

Jerome Peltier is number 16 of 33 *Living Legends*. There are 71 active *Corrals* in the United States of America and 20 active *Corrals* internationally.

X

A BRIEF HISTORICAL SKETCH
of
FORT SPOKANE

by Jerome Peltier

General Oliver Otis Howard, Commanding officer of the Military Department of the Columbia made a searching study of the needs of his command. He came to the conclusion that the Colville area could dispense with the services of the military, that had been adjacent to Pinkney City for the years 1859 to 1879, the latter date being the year his decision was made.

He recommended in his report for 1879 that a new site for a post be located in the upper Columbia country.

Lt. Col. Merriam, who was in command of Fort Colville at that time, along with some of his command began to search for a suitable site. Winter found them at the mouth of Foster Creek so they built temporary quarters close to the present site of Chief Joseph Dam and spent the winter there. Early in the Spring of 1880 they decided to build a post near Lake Chelan but this was noted to be too inaccessible, so work on it was halted.

Later that year it was recommended that Fort Colville (U.S. military post) which was located approximately three miles north and slightly east of the present city of Colville, as well as the newly located "Camp Chelan" be replaced by a new post which was to be built at the confluence of the Spokane and the Columbia rivers. It was first referred to, as Camp Spokane. In 1881 the war department called it Fort Spokane.

This Fort Spokane is not to be confused with Fort Spokan, a post built by personnel hired by John Jacob Astor and erected in 1812 adjacent to Spokane House at the junction of the Little Spokane and Spokane rivers. The fur trade Fort Spokan was in existance under that name for less than two years but became a part of Spokane House until abandoned in 1826, at which time the operation was moved to Kettle Falls on the Columbia river.

Military Fort Spokane was established by General Order #2, February 11, 1882. This directive tolled the death knell of Fort Colville and many of its personnel came to Fort Spokane because of it.

The new post was built on the Spokane river three-quarters of a mile from its juncture with the Columbia river. It was on a plateau about 400 feet above the level of the Spokane river and about one-half mile south of the river. The entire Fort Spokane military reservation consisted of 640 acres. During a 12 year period 45 building were built on the site.

Its purpose was to protect white settlers from Indians who had recently been involved in hostilities during the Nez Perce war of 1877 and the Bannock Campaign of 1878. However, no such trouble developed and the troops were never asked to fight Indians. During its period of activity as a military facility, tropps of the 2nd, 4th and 16th Infantry, as well as the 2nd Cavalry served here.

Officers row was built of lumber brought in by mule team in 1882. A sawmill, built at the fort, supplied framing lumber for the thirty buildings that were erected on the grounds. Building continued for several years. The late Walter D. Plough of Wenatchee, Washington wrote to me that his grandfather Henry H. Plough who was a "contractor, brick mason and plasterer" built the guard house in 1893. He enlisted the services of young Walter, aged 10, in its building. Walter was told to collect broken glass to mix with cement so prisoners could not dig their way out of jail. Walter wrote:--"I took my wagon to the garbage dump and picked up old bottles, then smashed them for the floor. My grandfather paid me ten cents a load."

The above is of interest because the guardhouse has been made into a museum.

Undoubtedly many of the soldiers helped to build the post because Edward J. O'Shea claims that his father Edward, Sr., helped in its construction. He also described the difficulties of the trip from Spokane in a military covered wagon.

Ed write, "Col. Kent was post commander. 'The 4th Infantry was stationed there along with a troop of cavalry. The horses got sick for some reason and they moved out to Fort Sherman. Capt. O'Brien was also at Fort Spokane for (a)while then he, too, was transferred to Fort Sherman at Coeur d'Alene, Idaho, where the others were. The 16th Infantry came to Fort Spokane after the 4th Infantry left."

The post office for Fort Spokane was at Miles, Washington about a half-mile east of the post. Telephone and railway connections could be made at Davenport, Wash.

Dr. J.E. Gandy, early Spokane pioneer, had some interesting comments to report to William S. Lewis regarding his services as army surgeon at Fort Spokane. He began by saying that Spokane at that time was composed "principally of men and women in their prime and didn't require a great deal of medical attention". He further stated that "In the spring of 1881 Lieut. Abercrombie......was sent up here to secure a physician to attend the post surgeon and some other sick men at the newly established army post, Camp Spokane, or as it was afterward named, Fort Spokane. I responded to this call and went down to the post and attended the sick men and then entered into a contract with the medical director for this military district for my continued service as an army surgeon." Dr. Gandy continues, "During my two years army service I left my family here in Spokane. At Fort Spokane where I was first stationed, Major Smith was in command. ....Monaghan and King were the post traders. ...In 1883 I resigned my commission as an army surgeon and resumed my residence and medical practice at Spokane Falls."

An interesting sidelight illustrates the difficulties of supplying the post.

John A. Fancher, one of the earliest settlers in the Medical Lake area told William S. Lewis that in 1880 he raised some fine vegetables, especially potatoes. "James Monaghan had a contract to supply Forts Sherman and Spokane with vegetables so we sold him some of ours. That fall and winter in company with Tom Campbell, who was driving a freight team for LeFevre, I made trips to (Fort Spokane) hauling potatoes in bulk, packing them in wild hay to prevent freezing, in the built up wagon boxes. We thought it no great hardship in those days to camp out and sleep under the wagons, even in cold weather, but felt sorry for the poor horses that had to stand tied to the wagon wheels and shiver through the night!"

There are few contemporary accounts of Fort Spokane extant so it is a pleasure to quote Col. John C. Tidball who was aide-de-camp to General William T. Sherman when the general of the army visited the northwest in 1883. Tidball described the post as follows, under date of August 3, 1883....

"The country as we approach Fort Spokane becomes more rolling---in fact quite hilly---and gradually rises until within a mile or so of the post, where it suddenly breaks off in a steep descent of almost 1,000 feet to the river. ...Down this descent the road winds to the post, which is situated on a plateau at the junction of the Spokane with the Columbia. ...The plateau is a level bench about 400 feet above the river, and is inclosed by high hills which, circling around to the river above and below, restrict the plain to a length of about three miles, and a width of about three fourths of a mile. ...The country here is curiously terraced; on the opposite side of the Spokane six distinct steps can be counted. ...The site of the post is on one of these terraces. Another still lower, is next the river, and one several feet above, has a spring affording a copious supply of water to the post. It also furnishes water for the steam saw-mill of the post, which is located on this terrace. A beautiful birds-eye view of the post is obtained from this point. The post at present consists of three barracks, six buildings for officers' quarters, a hospital, a building for quartermaster and commissary stores, stables, bake house, and other buildings, all frame, and neatly and conveniently constructed. Some of them however, were at the time of our visit unfinished, and more are required to accomodate the garrison without crowding.'' Col. Tidball continues, ''The garrison consists of four companies of the Second Infantry and troop F of the First Calvalry, all under command of Lieutenant-Colonel Merriam. ...The soil upon which the post stands is fine and light, overlying a deep stratum of gravel. ..The post has the reputation of being hot in summer and cold in winter, and exceedingly dusty! To the latter we can testify, for in the evening of our arrival a squall came up which raised such clouds of dust as to make it almost impossible to tell where the solid ground ended and the dust in the air commenced. ...At a short distance below the post are the remains of a bridge over the Spokane. ...A bridge here is of importance as it gives access to the country lying in the direction of the Colville and Spokane Indian Reservations. ...The Columbia is seen from the post at the point where the Spokane enters it. The terrace formation before mentioned is due no doubt to a lake formerly occupying all this country. ...At that epoch it was bounded on one side by the Cascade ranges of mountains, and in bursting at successive periods through this range at the Dalles, left deposits in the form of successive benches. ...In other parts of our journey, further on, we saw a great deal of this singular geological formation.''

General Sherman, General Nelson A. Miles and Col. John C. Tidball had visited Fort Coeur d'Alene July 27 through August 1, and had passed Horse Slaughter Camp which the latter called the ''Bone-yard'', on their way to Spokane Falls and from there had visited Fort Spokane.

When they left Fort Spokane they traveled northward. Fort Colville (military post) was their objective.

Affairs did not always proceed smoothly as is evidenced by the Report to the Commissioner of Indian Affairs of Benjamin P. Moore, U.S. Indian Agent of the Colville Reservation, dated August 12, 1886.

Mr. Moore is referring to ferry service on the Spokane River between the fort and the reservation in the above mentioned report, which we quote in part:--....''Upon this river the military have a cable ferry, which over a year ago broke away, going over the rapids about a mile below, drowning several people. ...Last May it again broke away, the water being very high, this time causing no loss of life. ...After waiting till July, and making thorough repairs, they again tried to cross, but the boat no sooner struck the current than the rope broke and it again went over the rapids, there being on board several Indians, two of them being drowned. ...The building material is now lying, as it has been since last June, upon the banks of the river, with no possible chance of crossing it.''

Mr. Moore, after making the above complaint, suggested that agency buildings be built within two miles of the fort where ''good spring water and fine farming land are available....''.

There comes a time in the life of most military installations when they reach the end of their period of usefullness as was evidenced by a Secretary of War Report which stated that Fort Spokane was ''inconveniently situated, difficult to reach in certain seasons of the year, expensive to maintain and that it served no practical purpose.''

Major J.M. Hamilton wrote in the Secretary of War Report for 1892: ''In my opinion, ground should be acquired and a new post built thereon near the city of Spokane.'' Major Hamilton's suggestion seemed to be a good one because a concentrated effort began to put it into effect.

The Secretary of War gave it his heartiest commendation because in his report for 1895, he wrote: ''In my last annual report I recommended Forts Spokane and Sherman, Idaho, be concentrated in or near the city of Spokane.... and those posts be abandoned.''

An excellent opportunity to put this idea into effect presented itself when the Spanish American war broke out, because when all of its troops were withdrawn to fight in that campaign the post was closed April 17, 1898 when those men were marched off to war. It was formally abandoned the following year in May.

General Order #163 in 1899 called for transfer of the post to the Interior Department. It then became housing for Indians of the surrounding reservations. Soon after this it was turned into a resident school despite the fact there were five schools (in 1891) on the reservation: one which was maintained by the government and four others which were contract schools.

The school at Fort Spokane seemed to answer a desperate need, as is shown by the following letter dated August 1, 1900 by Sarah C. Ream, Acting Superintendent of the school. Excerpts follow:

''School formally opened April 2 with an enrollment of 33 pupils. By the end of the month the enrollment was 75. School closed June 30 with an enrollment of 84 and the average attendance of 74. ....The average attendance is low owing to the late enrollment of some of the pupils, one as late as June 9.''

Sarah Ream wrote that ''If the pupils enrolled were a fair sample of the others on the different reservations, they are far above the average Indian in intelligence and ability to speak English....The work of the schoolroom was quite well done in spite of the many hindrances to good work. There were no blackboards, chalk, or pencils, for some weeks after school opened and no books to speak of until about three weeks before school closed.''

She described the physical appearance of the school before it was opened --following two years of abandonment: ''The amount of debris, broken down fences, gates and sidewalks, tumble-down outbuildings, etc., that had to be removed or repaired, can only be imagined!....There are many buildings, but not one but needs repairing or remodeling before it is in proper shape or conditon for school purposes.''

Prospects for a good vegetable farm were excellent. The water system was good but the sewage system, although extensive, was in bad condition. Despite these many deficiencies, Sarah Ream felt that there ''will be no difficulty in opening school with 200 children or more, if so many can be accommodated.''

In 1903 the student body was 200 and the ages of the children ranged from 6 to 20 years. The agent at the time the school was begun was Major Albert M. Anderson. Mrs. Clara Jensen Meyers (now of Spokane) was his stenographer. Nellie Miller (now Mrs. Wm. Sewell Smith of San Diego, Calif.) was his secretary the following year in 1902.

Mrs. Franz Culp was Anderson's cook. Her first husband was a private when the fort was occupied by the military. She remained for a short while after the fort was turned over to the Interior Department.

There are so many accounts of experiences of pupils who attended school at the old fort that space does not allow their inclusion here, except for some brief remarks. Mrs. Florence O'Hara Hanes and her sister Mrs. Lulu O'Hara Bauer remember when their father was a soldier at old Fort Spokane. They have particularly vivid recollections of school days -- as does Mrs. Isabel Arcasa.

The late Bay Buck told of the type of punishment meted out to incorrigibles. He, and others, also told of the games played by the pupils, vis: baseball, tag, hide-and-seek, rope skipping - as well as other childhood games.

Many of the children trained at Fort Spokane went on to Carlisle where they received their higher education. White children of the surrounding country went to school with their Indian friends.

It has been said that many of the Indian children had tuberculosis upon arrival at the fort -- which was skillfully treated in the hospital there.

As the Indian population decreased and interest waned, many of the buildings were vacated. Several of them were moved to other areas. In 1913-1914 Cleve Hanes helped move materials from the fort buildings to Creston. The fort was being dismantled at the time. One large building was left - it was to be used as a hospital. The school was closed permanently in 1914 but the Bureau of Indian Affairs continued to operate the hospital -for both the Spokane and Colville reservations. This operation continued until 1929 and then it also closed.

The fort is presently the property of the Coulee Dam Recreation area of the National Parks Service.

More than $250,000 has been spent recently on roads, sewers, water works, beaches, a boat landing and camp sites. It is now an excellent tourist and recreational attraction. The guardhouse has been made into a museum. Along with the guardhouse there are the stables, a powder magazine and another structure remaining of what was once a fine fort. Ther is also a reservoir building midway up the hill, south of the post. The quartermaster stable was erected in 1884; the powder magazine in 1888; the reservoir and house in 1889; the storehouse in 1892 and the guardhouse, the same year. Now that they are being preserved, they will be a vivid reminder of the past -- of a time when the fort was a living thing and not the ghost it is today.

Club devoted to Old West lore ci

The shootout at the Spokane Corral took place on the evening of April 16.

When the gun smoke cleared, Sheriff Bill Kelly counted 23 bodies on each side of the great divide.

The tie vote meant that the local branch of Westerners International — a history club devoted to Old West lore — would maintain its sexist membership traditions.

In other words, no womenfolk allowed.

DOUG CLARK

Columnist

"We needed a two-thirds majority to rewrite the constitution and join the 20th century," says Bruce Harding, who led the charge to let women join the 100-member club. "Knowing we were going to have a vote on the issue really got out the old-timers, some of whom hadn't been to a meeting in ages.

"They came in everything but stretchers and wheelchairs to defeat my motion."

It was too bad, considering the woman who'd like to join is Lynne Harrison, curator of collections for the Cheney Cowles Museum. With master's degrees in history and museum studies, one might postulate that Harrison would have something to add to a history club.

"They want to keep their boys' club," she says. "I would like to be recognized and respected for the work that I do in the field.

"But I guess it's their last bastion and they don't want to lose it."

I should say not.

And from some heavenly plateau, you can bet that an old cowpoke named Thomas Teakle was watching over the vote and grinning ear-to-ear.

Teakle was the Lewis and Clark High School history teacher who <u>founded</u> the Spokane Corral of the Westerners (that's its full name) back in the 1950s. He taught from 1919 to 1946 and was the first to teach Northwest history in Spokane's public school system. He was an authority on the subject and amassed a 2,000-volume collection of rare western and Native American history.

He also never cottoned much to members of the opposite sex.

"He didn't like it when a woman was hired on as director of the Eastern Washington Historical Society," says Harding. "So Teakle left his entire collection to the Montana Historical Society."

The confirmed bachelor also coveted his privacy, an

J. Peltier wins AARP citation

Jerry Peltier, N2719 Center Road, vice president of the Spokane Valley chapter of the American Association of Retired Persons (AARP) has received a national award for his outstanding volunteer service to the community.

The award was presented last week by Bob Clemens, W2909 Holyoke, Spokane, president of the Valley chapter.

The special award was given as part of AARP's 25th anniversary celebration, and to emphasize that the group of 50-and-older people work together to further AARP's motto, "To Serve, Not Be Served."

Peltier has been making a

cles wagons, fends off womenfolk

ccentricity he carried to the grave. When he died in
969 at the ripe old age of 91, Teakle's will instructed his
ttorney to have him buried in the middle of his three
emetery plots.

He wanted to make sure that nobody, especially any
emale types, would be edging into his eternal space.

"He was a character," agrees former Superior Court
udge Ralph Edgerton, a Westerners member and good
iend of Teakle's. "And he was always opposed to
aving women in the membership."

That was pretty much the norm back in Teakle's day.

In fact, the Westerners International organization was
ormed as a Chicago men's club back in 1944.

It has always been a group devoted to things Western.

For instance: A club is not a club, but a corral. A
hapter president is not a president, but a sheriff. A
reasurer is not a treasurer, but a tallyman . . .

"When it started, the club had the nature of a
Victorian smoking club," says Don Reeves, secretary of
he board, which is located in the Oklahoma City
Cowboy Museum. "You drank a little brandy. You ate a
ittle food. And one of the members would present a
ormal paper."

Today, attitudes have mostly come a long way.

Few chapters have maintained their male exclusivity.
The latest corral to form is the Pony Express in Prague,
Czechoslovakia, where the American flag is waved and
women are welcome to join.

The president of the international body is a woman
named Reba Wells, the former chief curator for the
Arizona Historical Society.

Wells concedes men-only chapters like Spokane's are
silly and archaic, but there's little she or the international
body can do.

"We've always let the local corrals maintain their
autonomy. They can do whatever they want."

Although Harding's motion ended toes up in Boot Hill,
there have been some startling developments in the
Spokane club, developments sure to disturb old Teakle's
slumber. From time to time, women have been allowed to
come in and lecture and at the annual Christmas party,
members may now bring — oh, no, not this! — wives and
girlfriends.

With such rampant liberalism going on, you can bet
that blazing ballots will ride again.

"I'm sure we'll vote on it again," says Randall
Johnson, a 25-year member who admits he likes the
newfangled notion of having women around.

"It's one of those recurring issues that cements a
group. It gives you a reason to come back and complain."

Mamas, don't let your babies grow up to be sexists.

---

career of visiting local nursing homes to cheer and aid the residents.

He also helped to found the Pacific Northwest Indian Center in Spokane, and the Spokane Realistic Art Association.

Peltier helped found the Spokane Corral of the Westerners, the 11th such chapter in the nation. That organization now has 110 units throughout the world.

The recipient operated a book store in Spokane for many years, and has written several books on the history of the West, emphasizing the contributions of the Indians here.

Peltier spends some of his time giving lectures on these subjects in local schools.

AARP members in more than 3,300 local chapters serve their communities through their volunteer work in legislative affairs, projects that help local citizens, and in educational recreational programs.

Antoine Plante Cabin
Picture taken by Henry Rust of Coeur d'Alene, Idaho

The PACIFIC NORTHWESTERNER

VOLUME 5   SUMMER, 1961   NUMBER 3

Neglected Spokane House

By JEROME A. PELTIER

*A*FTER THE WAR OF 1812, when scattered Canadian and American fur traders were the only white men in the region, a notable oasis of civilization in the vast Pacific Northwest was an interior post named Spokane House.

It did business for 16 history-packed years under three flags — Canadian, United States and British — at the confluence of the Spokane and Little Spokane Rivers 10 miles northwest of what now is Spokane, Wash. It was the first permanent commercial establishment in the present states of Washington and Oregon. Despite its out-of-the-way location, it was the North West Company's most important interior post until Fort Walla Walla had to be built in 1818 to help service its ever widening territory. It continued in importance until 1826 when the Hudson's Bay Company abandoned it in favor of Fort Colville at Kettle Falls on the main Columbia waterway.

Although no definite date may be found in scanty records of the time, the accepted date of its building is 1810. Its actual construction was delegated to Jacques Finlay and Finan McDonald by David Thompson, Canada's great explorer-geographer.

Spokane House had been in operation nearly two years when the Pacific Fur Company built a rival post, Fort Spokan, a half mile from it. The two posts competed with each other for less than

AUTHOR PELTIER is an antiquarian who operates Clark's Old Book Store, Spokane. He is a charter member of the Spokane Corral, and as its first deputy sheriff, completed the elected sheriff's barely begun term.

a year, at which time the Northwesters acquired all Astorian holdings for a mere pittance, in a treachery-beclouded liquidation of company property. Tardy news that the United States and Great Britain were again at war, and fear that a British ship of the line was close by with orders to destroy Fort Astoria, forced the quick sale.

For eight golden years, 1813 to 1821, Spokane House rode high in the fur trade as headquarters for the North West Company's interior operations. Its last four years were spent under the flag of the Hudson's Bay Company after its coalition with the North West Company in 1821. Due to its poor location, Sir George Simpson, one of the Hudson's Bay Company's greatest governors, finally ordered that Spokane House be abandoned.

It is a strange fact that Spokane House still is haunted by poor location. For although it is commemorated by a state park, a granite marker erected by the Spokane County Pioneer Society and highway signs that tourists stop to read, all are placed on or near the Pacific Fur Company's Fort Spokan site which the North West Company purchased in 1813. The site of the original Spokane House is not even within the boundaries of Spokane House State Park. It is the purpose of this paper to produce convincing proof of this latter day historical error as well as to tell the thrilling story of this famed trading post.

Three principal companies vied with each other for the lucrative fur trade. There were other smaller companies, but these three titans dominated the field.

The
**PACIFIC
NORTHWESTERNER**

VOL. 5   SUMMER, 1961   NO. 3

Published quarterly during the calendar year by The Spokane, Washington, Westerners Corral, at P. O. Box 1717, to further its purpose of creating and promoting an interest in the cultural background and development of the American West. Subscription-membership is at the rate of three dollars the calendar year.

OFFICERS
Julian S. Marshall ....Sheriff
Willard T. McLaughlin ....Deputy Sheriff
William J. Powell ....Roundup Foreman
Ralph R. Reid .... Tallyman
Thomas Teakle ....Registrar of Brands
John R. Fahey ....Chuck Wrangler

PUBLICATIONS COMMITTEE
Thomas Teakle, editor; Lowell H. Noll, Harold R. Boyd, Cecil Hagen, Harvey Erickson, Robert Showacre.

GUEST EDITOR THIS ISSUE
Cecil Hagen

The Hudson's Bay Company, London, the oldest commercial organization in America, was and still is pre-eminent in the business of fur trading. Its official title is "Gentlemen Adventurers of the Ancient and Honorable Hudson's Bay Co." It was "chartered by the grace of God and royal favor of Charles II, in the year of our Lord 1670."

Its most persistent rival between 1780 and 1820 was the North West Company with headquarters at Fort William on Lake Superior.

The third member of this triumvirate was the Pacific Fur Company founded in 1810 by John Jacob Astor of New York. Astor planned to create a chain of trading posts stretching from the Great Lakes to the Pacific Coast with headquarters at Fort Astoria.

The North West Company was first of the three to contribute to the history of Spokane House. David Thompson, a bourgeois (meaning partner), was prominent among its traders who came into the Saskatchewan region of western Canada. He crossed the Rocky Mountains through Howse Pass, in present Jasper National Park, early in 1807, and established Kootenae House on Lake Windermere. On June 30, 1807, he dis-covered Columbia Lake, the source of the Columbia River. Using that place as local headquarters, he and his men traveled southward into the Pacific Northwest.

Thompson was the first white man to travel the entire length of the Columbia River, although it was not done in one continuous trip or in one stream direction. His men transacted the first business in the Inland Empire. They built Kullyspell House, in September 1809, on Pend Oreille Lake, near East Hope, Idaho. This was the first business venture by white men in the entire Oregon Country. November, 1809, saw the erection of Saleesh House on the Clark Fork River near the present city of Thompson Falls, Montana.

Exactly when Spokane House was built is not known, but 1810 is the generally accepted date. The only record to the contrary is a map drawn by Alexander Ross in 1821 and revised in 1849 on which he erroneously notes Spokane House as having been built in 1809. Its builders were Jacques Raphael Finlay and Finan McDonald. Finlay, more commonly known as Jaco (also Joco and Jocko), would later have been called a Metis, for his parentage was mixed French, Sauteur Indian and Scotch. He was an excellent free trapper and boat builder.

Finan McDonald, who also had an Indian wife and halfbreed children with him, was a bonny, red-headed Scot who stood six feet four inches in his moccasins. His prodigious strength astounded everyone, and his flaming temper brought him into many difficulties. When a man of his own ample proportions insulted him, he invariably challenged him to a duel.

Spokane House must of necessity have been a small post. It consisted of possibly two or at the most three cabins: one for furs and trade goods and one or two for living quarters.

Much of the most reliable information available on the early history of the fur trade in the Pacific Northwest we owe to Alexander Ross. He was a Scotch gentleman who deserted a life of teaching and farming for the more rigorous and dangerous fur trade. He left New York, in the employ of John Jacob Astor, aboard the ship Tonquin (Jonathan Thorn, captain), on September 6, 1810. After landing at the mouth of the Columbia on April 12 the following spring, he helped locate and build Fort Astoria. As a member of a party sent into the interior, he helped build Fort Okanogan on the tongue of land where the Okanogan River joins the Columbia.

It was at Fort Okanogan, the first

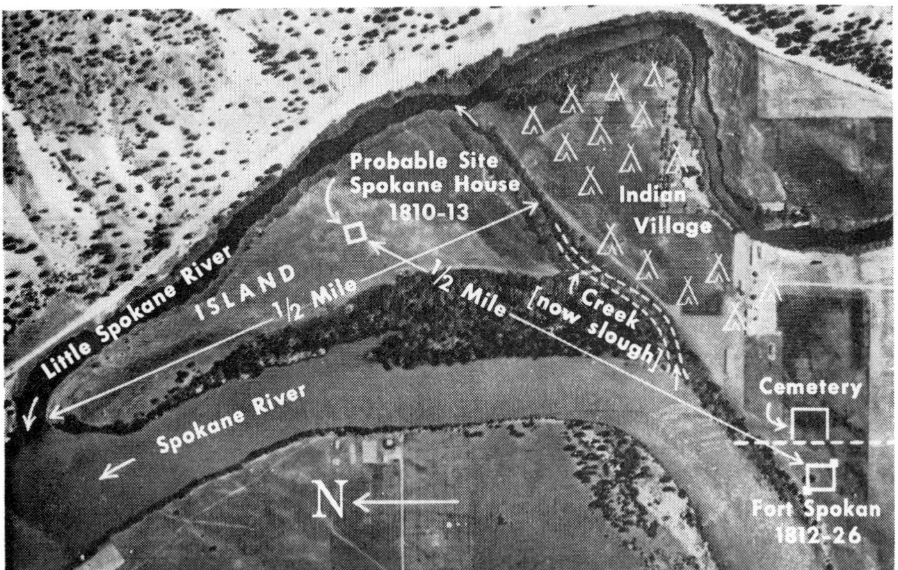

This 1945 aerial photo substantiates the island location of the original Spokane House which the author documents from David Thompson's and Ross Cox's journals.

American settlement in what is now the state of Washington, that he kept accurate notes which he later used in his two standard books on the fur trade of the Pacific Northwest.

Ross often visited Spokane House, and it is from personal knowledge that he drew a map pin-pointing its location. It shows Spokane House built on an island. He emphasized it by printing the word ISLAND under that section of the map, plus the notation, "Spokane House built in 1809."

It would be understandable, after a lapse of 24 years, for Ross to have made an error in the date but it is very unlikely that he could forget a geographic feature such as an island, when modern photos and pioneer accounts prove his statement that one existed and still does exist during high water at the point of land between the Spokane and Little Spokane Rivers.

Aerial photos show that the two rivers and a water-filled slough form a triangle-shaped island about a half-mile long and half that wide at its base. The once connecting channel, now a slough, flowed from the Spokane to the Little Spokane River.

For earlier verification, the writer corresponded with Mr. Oswald A. Burnett, son of the Reverend Charles Compton Burnett, who homesteaded the land in question in 1885. He answered as follows in a letter dated June 24, 1945:

"You speak of the slough. I mention the creek. Before the (backwater) was formed by the Washington Water Power Company (Long Lake) dam the creek was shallow, clear and ran fast.

"At times when the Big river (the Spokane) was high it formed a creek swift and 2 or 3 ft. deep, but in low water the creek was shallow."

Mr. Burnett told the writer the reason he remembers this so vividly is that when he was a youngster he was climbing one of the trees along the edge of the creek when a limb broke, dropping him into the cold, running water.

The Spokane House literature is sometimes confusing to beginners because the present Spokane River is mentioned variously as the Skitswich, Skeetshoo, Sketch-hugh, Coeur d'Alene, Pointed Heart, Schahoo and Schuihoo, and the Little Spokane as the Spokan, Trout Brook and Beaulieu's Brook.

The first mention of Spokane House that the writer has been able to locate is in David Thompson's journals. Thompson came south by way of the Kootenae and Pend Oreille Rivers from the headwaters of the Columbia, bringing trade goods from the East with which to supply his posts. Finan McDonald met him by prearrangement June 11, 1811, with pack horses at a small camp of "Kullyspells" on the Pend Oreille River, either near Albeni Falls or Box Canyon.

The party arrived at Spokane House with their loaded horses on Friday, June 14. Thompson mentions reaching the

9

"House of the N. W. Co'y. Thank Heaven for our good safe journey, we found Jaco etc. with about 40 Spokane families."

After a rest of three whole days, Thompson left for Kettle Falls, or as he calls it, "Ilth Koy Ape," which in Selish means a place "where fish were caught in the net or basket kettle." First building a cedar canoe, he set off down the Columbia, planning to establish a North West Company post at its mouth.

Near present Pasco, where the Snake River joins the Columbia, he erected a pole to which he attached a half sheet of paper with the following notice:

"Know hereby that this country is claimed by Great Britain as part of its territories, and that the N. W. Company of Merchants from Canada, finding the factory for this people inconvenient for them, do hereby intend to erect a factory in this place for the commerce of the country around. D. Thompson. Junction of the Shawpatin River with the Columbia. July 9, 1811."

Continuing on his way, he reached Fort Astoria where he surprised the people there with his sudden and dramatic appearance. He must have been dismayed to learn that American competitors had arrived at the strategic trade site 94 days earlier.

Alexander Ross recorded the incident thus:

" . . . On the fifteenth of July we were rather surprised at the unexpected arrival of a North-West proprietor at Astoria, and still more so at the free and cordial reception given to an opponent. Mr. Thompson, North-West-like, came dashing down the Columbia in a light canoe, manned with eight Iroquois and an interpreter, chiefly men from the vicinity of Montreal. McDougall received him like a brother. Nothing was too good for Mr. Thompson. He had access everywhere, saw and examined everything, and whatever he asked for, he got, as if he had been one of ourselves." Such fraternizing offended Ross' sense of loyalty.

Thompson attempted to dissuade the Astorians from trading in the upper country. His diplomacy was ignored and he was accompanied on his return trip, part way, by some of the Astorians who planned to establish a trading post in the interior. The combined parties travelled together upriver as far as Wallula Gap, where Thompson sent a letter to Jaco Finlay, at Spokane House, ordering Jaco to meet him with some horses. He also issued demand notes on the Company for horses while on his way overland. This is the first record of commercial paper being used in the Inland Empire.

He travelled up the Snake River, and crossed it at the mouth of the Palouse River. Fifty-one years later, the Mullan Military Road was to cross the Snake at this same spot, a short distance upstream from present Lyons Ferry. Thompson followed the Palouse River about a mile and then veered northward, passing the mouth of Cow Creek. His route from there into the Sprague area roughly approximated that of the later Colville Wagon Road. From Sprague he went through the Four Lakes and Deep Creek areas.

He camped a short distance from Spokane House not knowing how close he was to it. He arrived at his destination on Tuesday, August 13, 1811. His journal entry reads:

"A very fine day. At 5½ A. M. set off and at 6½ A. M. arrived at the House Thank God for His mercy to us on this journey. Found all safe but Jaco was with the horses sent to meet us. Late in the evening he arrived."

Thompson's itinerary during the next 10 weeks is a fine example of his ability to cover astounding distances in a hurry leading a party of men. His posts needed supplies. That meant paddling up the Columbia River to its northernmost point, at Boat Encampment, crossing the Rockies at Athabaska Pass and taking to canoes again on the North Saskatchewan River to Rocky Mountain House, 100 miles southwest of present Edmonton, Alberta.

After this round trip of at least 1000 miles, over some of the most rugged terrain on the North American continent, he was back at Spokane House on November 3. When he arrived at Kettle Falls, he found no one there to meet him, as expected, so he hiked the remaining 60 to 70 miles. His men and many packs of trade goods and supplies were all at Spokane House a week later.

On Sunday, March 29, 1812, when Thompson left Spokane House for the last time, he gave us an excellent record of the location of the post. His entry reads as follows: "Sunday. A sharp morning, ther 18°. Early set off 6:38 a. m. went to the top of the bank, where I set the Co. (compass) to the Ho. (House) S. 55 E. 1½ m. The Skeetshoo River passg. the Ho. runs to the north to the meeting of the Trout Brook" (Little Spokane).

There is only one place where the Spokane River (Skeetshoo) runs north, and that is directly opposite the island site described earlier in this paper. Consequently, this entry is of tremendous value when attempting to ascertain the site of Spokane House.

The late J. B. Tyrrell, acknowledged to be the greatest authority on David Thompson, wrote a letter to the writer dated August 13, 1947, in which he evaluated the entry made by Thompson as follows: "It is quite true that Thompson in making his final survey in March 1812, which is recorded in great detail in his Note Book, with Latitudes, longitudes and variations of the Magnetic Compass, discarded all his earlier observations, including those of November 1811. This final report, combining his conclusions as to the geography of the district up to that date, was used by him in the preparation of his great map of North Western America. . . . Almost all his surveys were corrected and tabulated by him in the same way on very many pages of his note books for use in constructing his map."

In August 1812 a party of Pacific Fur Company men from Astoria brazenly began building a post of their own, Fort Spokan, about a half-mile southwest of Spokane House. The Astorians called their establishments "forts" in contrast with the "house" suffix usually used by the Nor'westers. The Americans seemed to enjoy challenging the Canadians, and by Christmas had completed their larger and better buildings. Ross Cox, one of the clerks at the new post, noted in his diary:

"The spot selected for forming our establishment was a handsome point of land formed by the Pointed Heart and Spokan Rivers, thinly covered with pine and other trees and close to a trading post of the N. W. Company, under the command of Mr. McMillen one of their clerks, who had ten men with him."

Cox, along with Russell Farnham, was sent to build a subsidiary post in opposition to Finan McDonald, who was stationed among the Flatheads, but was unable to leave until he had aided in "cutting timber for the fort" and "did not set out until the 17th of October."

When Cox returned to Fort Spokan, January 1, 1813, he wrote:

"During my absence Mr. Clarke (in charge at the time) had constructed a snug and commodious dwelling-house, containing four rooms and a kitchen, together with a comfortable house for the men, and a capacious store for the furs & trading goods; the whole surrounded by paling and flanked by two bastions with loopholes for musketry."

Alexander Ross recorded how keenly the Astorians and Northwesters vied with each other for the Indians' business. He also gave the approximate distance between Spokane House and Fort Spokan in the following statement: ". . . The opposition posts of the North West Company & (the Astorians) were built contiguous to each other."

Another reference by the same writer elaborates upon the final statement in the previous quotation: "Mr. Clarke established himself at the corner of the opposition post, and being formerly a North Wester himself he was up to the rigs of his opponents." Astor had hired many former Northwesters so they were familiar with their former employer's methods.

Ross informs us that as soon as John Clarke had completed his post and had seen to it that all of his goods were under cover, he followed the North West Company system by giving a grand ball.

Anticipating the fact that some muscle-men might be needed to quell disturbances during the festivities, Clarke named three or four of his men as bouncers. It is not difficult to imagine what a riot could take place after these rugged fur traders had downed a few shots of trade whiskey — straight alcohol cut with water.

As soon as it was feasible, Francis Pillet, an Astorian, was fitted out with goods and went among the "Kootenai" Indians to oppose Nicholas Montour, a Northwester in charge of a post already built there. Competition between them eventually became so bitter that they resorted to a duel. Fortunately there were no casualties, and what started to be a serious affair ended humorously, if not to the principals, at least to the spectators.

Ross Cox described the fight beautifully in one short paragraph: "Mr. Pillet fought a duel with Mr. Montour of the North-West, with pocket pistols, at six paces, both hits: one, in the collar of the coat, and the other in the leg of the trousers. Two of their men acted as seconds, and the tailors speedily healed their wounds."

Violence, vicious and bloody, was the order of the day in the fur trade. The Indians were debauched with liquor and opposing traders were not above murdering their competitors to gain an objective. Such was not the case in the Pacific Northwest. There was a spirited rivalry for the trade without bloodshed. The Montour-Pillet duel was the closest thing to violence recorded while Spokane House was headquarters. A mutual compact was made between the rival companies to desist from trading or selling liquor to the natives. This humane policy was to the everlasting credit of both.

In its heyday Spokane House offered

many cultural inducements and physical allurements to the fur trader. Liquor, women, horse races and good food as well as supplies for the next season's trade were available.

In the spring of 1813, John Clarke received a letter from Russell Farnham, who headed a party trading among the Flatheads. Farnham wrote that he and his party, along with his North West Company rival, McDonald, were at Flathead Portage (present Albeni Falls) and that both parties were out of supplies, particularly tobacco, a much desired commodity. To further thicken the plot, a large party of Flatheads had arrived with valuable skins and wanted to trade. It was absolutely necessary that the weed reach him that night; otherwise the natives would move over to McDonald's camp because of a longer acquaintance with him.

The news reached Fort Spokan at 11 a. m. Clarke considered it an impossible request because he felt that no horse could go the distance of 72 miles in such a short space of time.

Ross Cox offered to make the ride if he could use LeBleu, a celebrated race horse owned by John Clarke. The animal was Clarke's most prized possession, but he decided to sacrifice his private feelings for the good of the Company. The seven-year-old animal, which stood between 15 and 16 hands high, was "dappled white and sky-blue." He had never been beaten in competition. Cox, along with two companions, set out at 12 noon. The three men rode at an easy canter for two hours, then Cox rode ahead at a hard gallop through the Coeur d'Alene country. After making over 60 miles, he found himself lost at night in heavy timber. His horse, using that indefinable sense that animals have, extricated him from the woods. Shortly after that he spied campfires along the banks of the Pend Oreille and knew he had reached his goal.

Cox had brought "a few fathoms of thick twist tobacco" along with him. The Indians crowded about and an animated trade began. Soon the tobacco was put to use and clouds of smoke enveloped each man's head. Such prompt service was rewarded by a promise that the Indians would trade all of their furs to the Astorians as soon as the remainder of the tobacco made its appearance. The other two riders arrived with it at midnight.

Meanwhile, McDonald's men appeared with their newly arrived supply, and upon being refused trade, scolded the Indians for their disloyalty to old friends, all to no avail.

The trade was made, thanks to LeBleu, who recovered perfectly in less than a week. Later in the summer he beat the fleetest horses of both companies on Spokane's first race course.

Ross Cox told of how he passed the summer days of 1815 at Spokane most pleasantly "hunting, fishing, horse-racing, and fruit gathering . . . " He continued, "Reading, music, backgammon, etc., formed the evening pleasures of our small but friendly mess."

Fort Spokan, or Fort Jacob as it was sometimes known, was in existence under the flag of the Pacific Fur Company for less than one year. Duncan McDougall, Donald MacKenzie and David Stuart, as partners in Astor's venture, sacrificed his Oregon interests to the North West Company June 13, 1813. It was their contention that because of the War of 1812 Astoria and its interior posts would surely be lost without hope of salvage. The sale could almost be considered a treacherous act for it is likely that much of the Astorian enterprise could have been salvaged had proper judgment been exercised.

The agreement read in part: " . . . we will give them up (meaning to the North West Company) the Post of Spokan House and the establishment of the Coutenais & also supply them with these few article of goods for which they have already made application; payable next Spring in horses . . . "

As good sense would dictate, the Nor'-westers moved from their smaller quarters to the larger American post. But they followed North West Company custom and called it Spokane "House."

As proof of the statement just made, we quote Alexander Ross who gives us a very vivid description of the post after the move was made. "Spokane House was a retired spot, no hostile natives were there to disquiet a great man. There the bourgeois who presided over the Company's affairs resided and made Spokane House the center of attraction. There all the wintering partners, with the exception of the northern district, met. There they were all fitted out. It was the great starting point, although six weeks' travel out of the direct line of some, and more or less inconvenient to all. But that was nothing: These trifles never troubled the great man.

"At Spokane House, too, there were handsome buildings. There was a ballroom, even, and no females in the land so fair to look upon as the nymphs of Spokane. No damsels could dance so gracefully as they, none were so attractive. But Spokane House was not celebrated for fine women only, there were fine horses also. The race-ground was admired, and the pleasures of the chase often yielded to the pleasures of the race. Altogether Spokane House was a delightful place and time had confirmed its celebrity."

In 1818, Fort Nez Perces (or as it was to be later known, Fort Walla Walla) was built near the confluence of the Walla Walla and the Columbia Rivers and became headquarters for the district. Despite this change, Spokane remained headquarters for the Snake River district.

The year 1821 brought about the merger of the North West Company with the Hudson's Bay Company, making a third flag under which Spokane House conducted business.

The latter half of the year 1822 and the first part of 1823 saw much building activity going on at the old post. New palings were set and some of the buildings were rebuilt or at least renovated. A new store was erected of lumber cut in a saw-pit built for the purpose; new quarters were built for the men; parts of the large dwelling house were renovated, and its chimney was rebuilt so there would be no further danger of fire. A new two-story bastion was built, with a stairway to the upper level; a gallery was built around the upper section of the palisades so that a guard could view the surrounding area without obstruction.

Just outside of the palings, to the southwest, lay the garden which had furnished and was still supplying potatoes, melons, cucumbers and other vegetables. It was surrounded by a fence and thorn bushes were planted there in an endeavor to discourage pilfering by natives who lived a third of a mile away to the east.

The Spokane cemetery lay between and equidistant from the post and the village. Quoting a passage from Cox, "The spot where the 'rude forefathers of the hamlet sleep' is about midway between the village and the fort, and has rather a picturesque effect at a distance."

The post was whitewashed until it could be seen from a great distance. The mere sight of it must have given many a weary voyageur or trader a lift when he saw it, at the termination of a trip from the far reaches of the Spokane district.

George Simpson, the new governor of the Hudson's Bay Company, visited Spokane House on Thursday, October 28, 1824. "Here we found Messrs. Finnan McDonald & Kittson Clerks and a large concourse of Indians of the Spokane and Nez Perces Tribes encamped about the Fort."

Simpson's next comments give us an idea of the magnitude of the area serviced by Spokane House. "The Spokane District comprises of the Posts of Spokane House Coutenais & Flathead Rivers the former about 8 Days and the latter 7 Days march from Spokane House with Loaded Horses. The Snake Country Expedition is likewise attached to this District."

He continues with the report of the number of beaver traded in the district the previous year. "The aggregate returns were about 9,000 beaver pelts of all sizes; a half of which were obtained from the Snake Country" (southern Idaho and northern Utah).

In all, five officers and 28 men handled the trade in the Spokane district. Peter Skene Ogden was superintendent with headquarters at Spokane House.

Simpson ruefully noted that the people in the Spokane district were living too high and using luxuries which had to be transported overland or by sea at great expense. He pointed out that two boatloads of supplies should be enough to run the district's three posts a year, but that they actually had been using five or six per year between 1821 and 1824, "principally loaded with Eatables, Drinkables and other Domestic Comforts." He indignantly added: "About 35 to 40 (extra) men have been kept merely to transport this superfluous property."

He offered a remedy by enumerating the natural foods that could be found in the district. " . . . they have abundance of the finest Salmon in the World besides a variety of other Fish within 100 yards of their Door, plenty of Potatoes, Game if they like it, in short everything that is good or necessary for an Indian trader; why therefore squander thousands uselessly in this manner . . . "

Simpson had not, as yet, contemplated abandoning Spokane House because he wrote, "I mean to send some Garden and Field seed across next Season to be tried at Spokane House and I feel confident that they will thrive. Indian Corn cannot fail."

Despite this statement, Simpson ordered the move to Kettle Falls. He realized this might anger the Spokane Indians, staunch friends of the Company, but he balanced this risk against the "very heavy expence and serious inconvenience in transporting the outfits and returns between the Main river (Columbia) and the present Establishment by Land a distance of about 60 miles will be avoided."

Simpson's journal entry for April 8, 1825, notes that "the Spokan and Flat Head Chief put a Son each under my care to be Educated at the Missionary

Society School Red River . . . " Four days later he wrote: "Baptized the Indian Boys, they are the Sons of the principal Spokan and Coutenais War Chiefs, Men of great Weight and consequence in this part of the Country; they are named Coutenais Pelly and Spokan Garry."

Spokan Garry was to return to the Spokane area in 1830 to teach his tribesmen Christianity and farming, and this way became the first school teacher in the Pacific Northwest.

On April 16 Governor Simpson wrote John Work: "I have lined out the site of a new establishment at the Kettle Falls & wich you to commence building and transporting the property from Spokane as early as possible . . . " Most of the winter of 1825-26 found all personnel at Spokane House building cedar longboats with which goods were to be transported during the spring high water. Many other duties had to be performed also. Firewood was cut; inventory taken; furs repacked; harnesses made and others repaired.

Work described the abandonment of Spokane House on March 21, 1826, in two terse sentences: "The Blacksmith & cook, the only two men we have now here, employed collecting all the iron about the place, stripping hinges off doors, etc. The Indians much regret our going off and frequently complain that they will be pitiful when the whites leave them."

Jaco Finlay remained at the abandoned fort, near which he had helped build the original one 16 years earlier, and played host, May 11, 1826, to David Douglas, the noted English botanist after whom the Douglar Fir was named. "As the principal object of my journey was to get my firelock arranged (repaired) by him," the scientist explained in his journal, "being the only person within a space of eight hundred miles who could do it, and being an item of utmost consequence to have done soon, I lost no time in informing him of my request . . . In the afternoon . . . I found he had obligingly put my gun in good order for which I presented him with a pound of tobacco, being the only thing I had to give."

Douglas also described the salmon fishery he found there. He explained how funnels of basket work were placed obliquely across the Little Spokane. After a large number of salmon were enclosed within the barrier, brush was placed across the openings of the funnels, trapping the fish for easy spearing. He recorded that "seventeen hundred were taken this day, now two o'clock . . . Fifteen hundred and sometimes two thousand are taken in the course of the day."

Following the death of Finlay on May 20, 1828, the next record the writer has been able to locate about Spokane House was written by Nathaniel Wyeth, who passed by the post February 25, 1833. He wrote: "At this place are the remains of the old Spokane House, one Bastion of which only is now standing which is left by the Indians from respect to the dead one clerk of the Co. being buried in it."

In 1951, archeologists found a skeleton beneath the southeast bastion of the old post. It is very likely all that remains of Jaco Finlay, for the body was buried in a coffin, flat on its back rather than as the Indians interred their dead. Three buttons were found at given distances along the upper torso signifying that he wore a shirt when buried. Five pipes were found buried with him. Two were clay (one bowl had the initial "J" filed or carved on it). The other three were of wood, stone and metal. A fragment of bone comb, some slate, a hunting knife, fragments of spectacles and part of an iron cup also were found with the skeleton. All are now housed in the Cheney Cowles Memorial Museum, Spokane, Washington.

The Reverend Samuel Parker was near the site May 26 and 27, 1836, when he was on his way from Walla Walla to Colville. He wrote: "The Northwest Company had a trading post here, one bastion of which is still standing."

We have verification in these two first-hand accounts that the final Spokane House actually was Astor's Fort Spokan because Ross Cox, in his description of the latter place, told us it was "flanked by two bastions."

Isaac A. Stevens, first territorial governor of Washington, was the next distinguished visitor to the area. He was accompanied by J. M. Stanley, the great artist who recorded under date of October 17, 1853: "Here was formerly a trading-post of the Hudson's Bay Company, but the 'house' was abandoned many years since, and but a few scattering stones now mark the foundations."

The nearby age-old village of the Spokane Indians continued to exist until the land on which it stood was homesteaded in the mid-1880's. The Indians also used and maintained the cemetery until they had to move away. The Burnetts remembered that the graves had individual pole fences and sharpened-post markers on which broken copper kettles often were impaled.

Oswald Burnett told me there were remains of "habitation" on the island when his father acquired the property. He remembered as a boy seeing rotted ruins, "about one log high," on a slight rise which would have been a logical building site. When his father plowed it, he found near it scattered loose stones which conceivably could have been used in a fireplace three-quarters of a century earlier.

The Eastern Washington State Historical Society, through its officers and interested members, has played a vital part in keeping Spokane House in the public eye. William S. Lewis, historian-secretary of the society, along with Jacob Meyers, N. W. Durham, W. D. Vincent and T. C. Elliott, kept interest alive prior to and during the 1920's and 1930's. Joel E. Ferris, Dr. C. S. Kingston, E. T. Becher and J. Neilson Barry, among others, continued the good work.

Through the untiring efforts of Aubrey L. White, late head of The Spokesman-Review's civic development department, the State of Washington acquired 200 acres of land upon which the Astorian post once stood. However, the state does not own the adjoining land upon which the first Spokane House was built.

Through the combined efforts of the historical society, the State Parks Board and the National Parks Service, which loaned Dr. Aubrey Neasham, regional historian, and Louis R. Caywood, archeologist, excavations were begun on the Fort Spokan site September 4, 1950, with a crew of seven men. Cellar holes were still identifiable. The work continued for three summers. Two thousand dollars was appropriated by the state legislature in 1950 to help finance the investigations.

Archeologists found that the outer stockade of the imposing Fort Spokan (later Spokane House) was 123 x 132 feet. Glass, guns, shot, pottery, beads, kettles, pipes and trade goods of all types, as well as burial sites were found in the general area.

Their work was magnificent, but it did not go far enough; for although they were apprized of the approximate and sometimes definite location of both the Astorian and North West Company post sites, as well as the village and cemetery areas, nothing was done about the island post. This could have been due to a lack of funds.

As a booster of the island site, it is my opinion that should two or three exploratory trenches be dug in the high ground of the island, proof would be unearthed of the establishment that was in use there for more than three years.

It is my contention that Spokane's oldest historical shrine should be located, correctly identified and honored, instead of lying in limbo as it does at present.

THE RISE AND FALL OF THE CHOCTAW REPUBLIC, by Angie Debo. University of Oklahoma Press. Norman. $5.00.

This 1961 edition is a reprint of the original edition of 1934 in which the author indicated her intention of writing a "history of the Choctaw Indians" that "reveals a political, social and economic existence as active and intensive and as closely circumscribed as any of the famous small republics of the past."

To classify the Choctaws as a "separate people" is not quite correct. They differed little from the Chickasaws and Cherokees. All had republican-type government long before the United States government was formed in imitation of the practices of the Iroquoian and Muskohegan nations, a fact acknowledged by Franklin and Jefferson among the founding fathers.

On the slender thread that "Choctaw schools and churches were copied almost wholly from the white man's society" the author hangs her statement that Choctaw history is closely interwoven with the larger fabric of American history. This puts the cart before the horse in the matter of governmental structure because American government history is interwoven with the wholly unique republican governmental form developed by the Choctaw and other Indian nations in which women had participated from time immemorial as voters and in administrative activities. Neither the Choctaw nor other Indian republics bore much resemblance to Plato's concept of a republic.

The Rise and Fall of the Choctaw Republic is undoubtedly factual as to dates, events and individuals for the period from "The Coming of the White Man" through "The Dissolution of Tribal Interests" in the first decade of the 20th century. But it lacks some of the reality that could have been given with more details on the lives and mores of Pushmatah, Moshlatubee and Pitchlynn who strove so honestly and strenuously to preserve the Choctaw way of life.

"The study of history" said Henry Brooks Adams, "is useful to the historian by teaching him his ignorance of women, for a woman known only through a man is wrong." The point of this quotation is the fact that the Choctaw or any Indian known only through the white man's records and interpretations of those records is lacking in reality. Unfortunately the Choctaw point of view on government, moral values and social customs has been lost in the white man's records that were used in writing this book.

—Reviewed by FRANK LILLY, a Chickasaw-Cherokee grandson who welcomes this reprint.

The PACIFIC NORTHWESTERNER

VOLUME 15　　　　　SPRING 1971　　　　　NUMBER 2

The Great Spokane Fire of 1889

By JEROME A. PELTIER

SPOKANE FALLS, Washington Territory, suffered its most extensive and disastrous fire Sunday, August 4, 1889. Most of the downtown business area was leveled before the disbelieving and despairing eyes of many of its then 12,000 citizens.

Although several dozen persons were within viewing distance of the place where the blaze actually started, all accounts subsequently reported were at variance with each other. Cause of the fire was never positively determined.

There are almost as many stories of how and where the Spokane fire started as there were witnesses. All who were at the scene when smoke first was sighted agree that a very few pails of water would have quenched the flames. Because water was not available during the telling early minutes, within half an hour an entire block was a mass of flames.

The "Spokane Falls Review" dated August 6, two days later, reported that "at about a quarter past six fire was discovered in the lodging house over Wolfe's Lunch Counter. Officers Smith and McKernan were promptly on hand and one ran to

give the alarm while the other went to the scene of action. Officer Smith states that if a few pails of water could have been obtained the whole fire could have been stopped at once."

An article in the the April 27, 1937, "Spokesman-Review" headed "He Discovered the Fire of '89," reads as follows: "It was a history making ride that Mr. Arnold and his young wife, the former Ellis L. Barzee of Turner, Oregon, took that Sunday afternoon of August 4, 1889. Noting smoke and flame pouring from the roof of a restaurant, Mr. Arnold stopped his carriage to give the alarm, pointing his whip at the blazing roof. The alarm was spread by another resident whose Sunday afternoon nap on the front porch of his nearby home was interrupted by the newlywed's cry."

Rolla C. Harbord, a railroad brakeman, is quoted in "The Spokane Daily Chronicle" for August 5, 1948, as saying he was the last official volunteer fireman alive.

The bell atop the fire station at First and Washington summoned the 18 men whose duty it was to protect Spokane Falls from fire. They ran to the station and got every piece of equipmen they had — a hose cart, pump and horse drawn fire engine — and went into action.

"The hose cart reached a fire hydrant in front of the Desert Hotel and the first

---

JEROME A. PELTIER has contributed more papers to this quarterly than any member of the Spokane Corral. He sells books for a living as proprietor of Clark's Old Book Store, and at home revels in what may be Spokane's most extensive private collection of Western Americana. He is a charter member and past sheriff.

The PACIFIC NORTHWESTERNER

Vol. 15   Spring 1971   No. 2

Published quarterly by the Spokane Corral of The Westerners, P. O. Box 1717, Spokane, Wash. 99210. Subscription $3 per calendar year, $1 per issue. Back copies available.

stream of water raced out to meet the flames," the article reports.

In a short while, "heavy black smoke had summoned every citizen in town to the battle line." Everyone who could carry water did so from taverns, restaurants and hotels. Practically all persons who fought the blaze had singed eyebrows, hair, mustaches, faces and hands because the heat was terrific."

Most accounts agree that the fire started at Wolfe's Lunch Counter when some grease ignited and the flames shot up the wall. This eatery was situated below a lodging house three doors west of Post Street on Railroad.

Another story attributes the fire to a cigarette flipped into tinder dry grass alongside the building. Mrs. Clara G. Knowles declared in a 500-word statement submitted through her attorney that "it was no greasy stove in a tavern. I stood right there and watched it . . . lost my trunk in the shuffle.

"That evening I was eating dinner with Mrs. Dolan, whose husband had one of the first shoe stores at the Pacific, no, Desert Hotel, where I was staying. When the fire broke out, we rushed to the second floor veranda, on the west side. It had started from a grass fire caused by a cigarette smoker, and was burning up the side of the N. P. Lodging House.

"That was before my marriage to Mr. Knowles; after that he never smoked cigarettes. He was one of the few men in Spokane Falls who had the habit at that time.

"As we were watching the lodging house burn, a man rushed up and told us we had better leave, as our hotel was on fire. We escaped through the back way when we found the front of the hotel in flames. All the trunks from the hotel were taken to what is now Fourth and Howard, but mine disappeared in the excitement."

By still another account, the fire started close to the X-10-U-8 (Extenuate) Tavern. The most unusual story of all has to do with a woman known as Irish Kate.

W. E. Atchison, a Works Progress Administration researcher who claimed he had government documents to prove his assertion, sums it up this way:

"Whiskey was the real cause of the great Spokane fire . . . In those days a couple of one and a half story frame buildings across from the N. P. depot between Lincoln and Post had been taken over by Sam Wolfe . . . one for a saloon and the other for a restaurant. Like all such places, they were pretty wild establishments.

"A woman named Irish Kate had taken over the rooms in the saloon building and later confessed her part in the big fire. It seems she had been drinking and went up to her room to 'frizz" her hair a bit with a curling iron heated in the glass chimney of a kerosene lamp. While she was doing this, a drunk entered and they began to scuffle.

"When the lamp flopped over in the ensuing battle, Irish Kate grabbed up some of her belongings, closed the door and dashed across to the other building . . . "

An open window that gave a good draft and some highly combustible lace curtains completed the work begun by the spilled kerosene that had been ignited by the

A week after the fire these merchants were doing business on Riverside Avenue across from the present post office. A. W. Siegel, tobacconist in third tent from left, announced on his sign: "Slightly Disfigured but Still in the Ring." "Dutch Jake" Goetz, Spokane's best known early day saloon keeper, was operating his beer garden in the tent at far right. Note the hand drawn hose cart at lower left which 1889 fire fighters used.

lighted lamp wick — and the great fire was on its destructive way.

Take your choice. These are the eye-witness accounts as well as legends of how the Spokane fire started, each as logical and as probable as the other.

Perhaps you wonder why the fire got out of control as quickly as it did. There had been no rains for weeks, and everything was tinder dry; second, the fire started in a row of flimsy, frame buildings that were as dry as lumber can be.

The third, and most important reason, is that Rolla A. Jones, a recently appointed city water commissioner, who most likely was the best informed man in town regarding the newly installed water works, decided to go fishing that hot Sunday.

He neglected to leave the key to the waterworks with someone familiar with its new equipment. As a result, when the volunteer firemen turned on the hydrants, the water pressure was too low for effective fire fighting.

The fire soon spread from the hotel to a building nearby, then to the Russ home and soon to the beautiful, newly erected, Pacific Hotel. Virtually deprived of water, firemen tried to create a fuel break by blasting down a row of buildings ahead of the fire.

Meanwhile, west of Post Street, the Minneapolis Lunch Room, the Coeur d'Alene Saloon, Blue Front Lodgings and the Railroad Lunch Counter were soon a mass of flames. The wind veered and the Northern Pacific Railroad depot offices of the Spokane and Palouse Railway, express offices and freight houses were soon destroyed.

Thanks to the work of firemen, the blaze was confined east of Lincoln Street, hopeless as that at first appeared.

Giant powder was used to blow up the Pacific Saddle Company's building. This

18

saved the Crescent Block, the City Hall, the Review office and the Commercial Hotel. The explosion was so severe that it blew all the window glass out of the Commercial Hotel, which stood on the ground where the present Great Western Building now stands at the southwest corner of Riverside and Lincoln.

Heavy charges of dynamite were used to blow up buildings between the fire and unburned areas but the flames jumped the open spaces. It was thought that surely when large buildings such as the Falls City Block were reached they would stop the onward rush of the flames, but by that time they were generating a heavy wind that carried them a block or so ahead.

More dynamite was used and geysers of dirt, mortar and flaming material flew in all directions, many times igniting another area. When the dynamite exploded, people nearby trying to salvage some of their belongings would run to cover so as not be struck by the flying debris. Wind carried pieces of burning shingles, lumber and other substances into the air for great distances spreading the fire with incredible speed.

Every horse drawn rig in Spokane was requisitioned to aid in salvaging business records and other valuables. Often they were not moved far enough and were consumed by the fire anyway.

George Mitchell, whose people were proprietors of Mitchell Bros., a freighting business, told this writer that his family was at home when news of the fire reached them. Their place, one block east of Division on Main, still remains in family hands.

Realizing the urgent need to transport records and merchandise out of the path of the fire, he and others rounded up all the teams and wagons they could find and quickly drove to the threatened area. Many times their services were in such demand that merchants fought each other to see whose goods would be hauled away first. Items of value were flung into the wagons and brought to the Mitchell place. This shuttling back and forth continued as long as danger threatened.

It was six months before all goods and papers were segregated. Sometimes it took great detective work to find out who had hauled what loads where.

The next account may seem to be deviating from the subject, but it will help tell the story of salvaging operations after the fire and provide needed background.

James Monaghan, early day pioneer of Spokane, interviewed by a newspaperman named Herbert Gaston, said: "In 1883 I came to the Coeur d'Alene rush and I had my second experience with steamboating after more than 20 years. I became interested in a company which put in a line of steamers on Lake Coeur d'Alene, the first commercial steamboats on that water. C. B. King, Jim Glover and other Spokane men were among the backers.

"In 1886 we sold out to D. C. Corbin and I came into Spokane where we were living at the time of the big fire. The summer of the fire Mr. King and I had a contract for the building of bridges and furnishing the ties and timbers for the Spokane Falls and Northern Railway. My family was camped on the present site of Deer Park on the line of construction of the road where I had men working, but that day I happened to be in Spokane.

"I never saw anything like that fire, the way it jumped from one block to another after it started. I was just coming out of a restaurant when I heard the alarm, and I took a run up there. It looked like nothing then, but it was not long before it was taking the whole town before it.

"We had our office on Riverside Avenue, about the location of the Sherwood Block now. When the fire began to make real headway, we got our books and other valuables out of there. The building went with everything else up to Washington Street. Our home on First Avenue and Bernard Street was out of the fire-swept district and was not injured."

The late W. G. Burch, a grandson of Rev. Samuel Havermale, early Spokane missionary, told the writer his version of the great Spokane fire story in the late 1930's. Here it is:

"On Sunday, August 4, 1889, we heard the clanging of bells which told us that there was a fire in Spokane. John W. Graham, who later married my sister Alta, came running over the brow of the hill down to our place dressed in a suit with swallow tails and a high silk hat. He was on his way to the fire, too. As my horse and I never missed a fire, we set out for town.

"At that time we lived just opposite of where the Comstock Arms now is, on the corner of Eighth and Washington. Our land was surrounded by a stone fence and our property extended up over the hill.

"My father, Benjamin Franklin Burch, told me to report what I saw. He owned what is now the Rookery Building, the Fernwell Building, the Victor Block and several other places which are now right downtown. As the fire spread, I would ride back home and report the loss of each property as it in turn was burned. I rode for several hours.

"As the fire spread, people would haul all their portable belongings up to our place, as it was out of the fire zone, leave them and go back after more. Soon the grounds were covered with heaps of household goods, store stocks, business records, etc. There were also horses, cows and other livestock there.

"The next day the entire business section of Spokane was a smoldering mass of ruins. My brother Clarence and I had to patrol our yard to protect all of the property that had been put in there. We paraded around with rifles . . .

"Shortly after, the fire adjusters came to Spokane Falls in droves, to pay for the losses caused by the fire. My father got his fair adjustment. There was a great scrambling for good property locations which were sold by owners discouraged by their losses. A stock of newsprint was shipped into town along with some equipment, and we again had a newspaper.

"John W. Graham started business by buying out Sylvester Heath, for whom he had been working just previous to the fire. He had a small stock of journal and ledger sheets, glue, ink, tablets, general office supplies, and a few magazines. In all, his stock amounted to about $300. He built this up to the present business which now serves the Inland Empire and some of Alaska . . ."

All statements agree that the fire burned in a northeasterly direction and fanned out until it eventually burned everything north of Railroad Avenue to the Spokane River between Lincoln and Washington Streets.

One item of special historical interest is the fact that the Pioneer Block, a two-story brick building on the southwest corner of Front (now Trent) Avenue and Howard Street and the Windsor Hotel on the northeast corner, rebuilt a year earlier from the ruins of the famous California House, both fell before the blaze.

It was in the Pioneer Block that James N. Glover, founder of Spokane, built his store, and above which many early day social functions were held. The California House was Spokane Falls' first hotel worthy of the name. It had an excellent reputation up and down the West Coast.

The "Spokane Falls Review" for Tuesday, August 6, 1889, reported the final stages of the fire as follows:

"Looking upward a broad and mighty river of flame seemed lined against the jet black sky. Occasionally the two opposing currents of wind would meet, creating a roaring whirlwind of fire that seemed to penetrate the clouds as a tremendous screw, while lesser whirlwinds danced about its base performing all sorts of fantastic gyrations. In this manner the appalling monster held high carnival until about 10 o'clock, when with a mighty crash, the Howard Street bridge over the Spokane River went down.

"A boom of logs took fire and shimmered for hours on the crystal surface of the river and many times, flying pillars of fire crossed the river, igniting the mammoth lumber and flouring mills that line its banks, but by heroic efforts, its career was checked on the south side of the stream."

Nothing remained within a 30-block area but the naked walls of formerly substantial buildings standing forlornly in a sea of flames and smoke.

Mrs. Hilda Lovejoy, a long time friend of the writer, told of seeing the reddened sky the night of the fire from her father's [Carroll J. Barclay] farm 45 miles away between Oakesdale and Steptoe Butte.

Another who saw the fire from a distance was G. W. Anderson, an early day pioneer who came to the community of Alpha, now called Latah, in 1877. He described the vivid, red glow that was visible in the sky from his farm near Latah, 28 miles south of Spokane.

The late Willard H. Heath, another friend of the writer, years ago reminisced about the fire as follows:

"I saw the Spokane fire of August 4, 1889, as a boy of 11. My parents, my younger brother, Roy, and I were at Second and Post in a small buggy, which my father used in his work as a sewing machine salesman, when we saw smoke and flames in the block on Railroad Avenue and between Post and Lincoln.

"My father, a volunteer fireman, left us where we were and went to see what was happening. When he didn't come back in a reasonable time, my mother sent me to find him. It was the next afternoon before I saw my family again.

"I didn't find father but I did meet a boy I knew. He and I watched the fire spread until it took in almost all of downtown Spokane Falls.

"We found some chickens under a wooden bridge that led to Havermale Island. They had gone there for protection from the fire. We caught some of them and traded them for meals at a restaurant on Monroe Street north of the river.

"We saw several brick buildings dynamited. It's a wonder some of us kids weren't hurt the way things flew.

"We were afraid that the flames might reach a small gas manufacturing plant at Stevens and the Northern Pacific tracks. This place was known as the gasworks. Luckily, the fire was kept at a distance from the plant and its storage tank, avoiding a major explosion.

"My father learned that lawyers and others were anxious to save their books and records and came back to Second and Post where my mother and brother Roy were waiting, to get the buggy. He sent them home on foot while he started using the horse and buggy to haul books to safe places. He earned more than $100 that night.

"I made big money selling the Chronicle at 10 cents a copy. Later, I got up at 3 a.m. to deliver the Review.

"The Chronicle burned out during the fire but the printer foreman saved some type and printing equipment which he took to a small print shop on College, north of the river. It was here that the extra, telling about the fire, was printed. The Chronicle had been in a small building, where the present Crescent store now is, when it was destroyed. A makeshift editorial room was set up on a kitchen table under a wagon umbrella on Riverside.

"As soon as it cooled down enough the whole burned out section was roped off. Washington Territory guardsmen were brought in to patrol it."

Verifying what Willard Heath said in his statement, is an account by Walter B. Wilcox, early day Chronicle newspaperman, which appeared in "The Spokane Daily Chronicle" dated May 23, 1936. Here is his story:

"Monday morning I wandered through the ruins to the site of the Chronicle office. Everything seemed destroyed. Foreman McCarter was there ahead of me.

"'What are you going to do Mac?', I asked him.

"'I'll get out the paper, if you can provide some copy.'

"'How?' I asked him, looking at the ruins.

"'I saved a couple of forms when I saw the building was going to burn,' he explained. 'I've got them over across the river on College Avenue, where there's an old print shop equipped with a Washington hand press and some type. I've got five printers there now, getting the shop ready.'

"'If you will write the copy I'll get a boy with a bicycle to rush it across the river in takes.'

"There was plenty of news to be written. My editorial office was a kitchen table in front of the ruins of the old office. A cloth sign attached to the table read, 'Chronicle Office.'

"About the middle of the morning W. D. Knight, the publisher, strolled up.

"'What are you doing?' he demanded.

"'Getting out the Chronicle,' I answered.

"'You mean the Chronicle will be published today?'

"'That's it!'

"Knight was surprised. He had planned to suspend publication until a new plant could be acquired.

"The sky was clear, and the August sun was getting very hot. Knight thought for a while, then said, 'I have a big umbrella, about 10 feet across, at my house. I think I'll go get it and put it up over your table.' The editorial office soon had a roof over its head.

"Operating that old Washington press that day was a tremendous physical effort which nearly killed off two men."

"When, late in the day the newsboys appeared on the streets, The Chronicle was sold for six bits [75 cents] a copy." [Mr. Heath said 10 cents] It was the first paper to describe the fire.

"The Review published its regular issue the following day. The Chronicle used a tent as its office until a new rotary press and type were received from St. Paul, Minnesota, and the equipment was installed in a small rooming house at the northeast corner of Bernard and Riverside."

The late Charles E. Trowbridge, known affectionately to me as Ernie, reminisced with me about early day Spokane many times. When asked about the fire, he had the following to add:

"My first recollection of anything in downtown Spokane Falls other than the Commercial Hotel, where we stayed earlier in 1889 prior to finding a place to stay, was seeing the burnt out area, where they allowed people to go the day after the fire. Children, without an adult along, couldn't go near the burned area.

"Soldiers were patrolling the burned out area to keep people from looting and also from going into areas where they could get hurt. The soldiers must have come from either Fort Sherman [Coeur d'Alene] or Fort Spokane because they were there the day after the fire and everything was under military control.

"Places were roped off where old brick walls might collapse at any time. Ruins were still smoking when we went to see what the fire had done. The fire had burned out as far as Havermale Island. Logs in the river were even burned.

"The Crescent store at the time of the fire was going to open shop in the crescent shaped building next to the Review building. [It got its name from that building]. It was planning its grand opening August 5, and what a grand opening it was, because it was the only store left in town! People needed clothing and other goods badly so they had a real rush of business. Because of conditions they could have raised prices but did not do so, and due to this The Crescent is still one of the big stores in Spokane."

My next informant is an especially close friend of many years standing, The Reverend Paul P. Sauer, S.J., who came to Spokane Falls in 1884 and who was named "Pioneer Man of the Year" by the Eastern Washington State Historical Society in 1963. He wrote these reminiscences for me:

"The fire occurred on August 4, 1889. I was only 9, hence bear in mind my observations were merely those of a child.

"That year had been a sad one for my family. Two sisters had died of diphtheria within a month and my father was at death's door with typhoid for some time. (There was much typhoid in Spokane when we first got running water on Howard Street where we lived. The water was pumped from the river and was often no longer pure.) After all that sickness some kind friends, farmers at Trent in the Spokane Valley, invited our family to visit them for a break. The invitation was accepted with pleasure.

"It was a Sunday; our family went to early mass at the new Our Lady of Lourdes Church on Main Street and we anticipated a happy day. Mother had the foresight to leave a few important documents — insurance policies, birth certificates, naturalization papers — with the Sisters of the new Our Lady of Lourdes Parochial School for safekeeping. No one else anticipated any disaster but she was always cautious!

"We really enjoyed the day in the open. After supper we drove back home. The springless wagon was made more comfortable by the straw filled sacks that our hosts had thoughtfully supplied. When we reached the east outskirts of our city, at that time about where the Sperry mill is today, we all noted that the sky was red, not from the sunset but from fire. Forest fires were then a frequent occurrence and the smell of smoke was the rule, but this was different. We halted a milkman's wagon to inquire, and when the driver told us that Spokane was burning and that the freight depot which was near our house was in the line of fire, we felt sure that our home on Howard near Railroad would be destroyed. [It was.]

"When we reached Spokane we were not even allowed to visit the site of our home. One of our best friends invited us to his shanty in the emigrant flats just south of the present Northern Pacific passenger depot.

"We were, four of us, enabled to find shelter in a small house that was already crowded with a large family, but such was a general characteristic attitude of the general populace of Spokane at this time. Small towns are less selfish than large.

"When we were allowed to visit the burnt area, it was a sad spectacle to behold. What had not been destroyed by fire had been destroyed by dynamite. We gazed upon more than 30 blocks of blackened timbers and ashes, twisted iron and molten glass; an intense heat had melted a granite pillar at Sprague and Howard, where a new bank was under construction. There were three of them at the corner; one is now at Mt. St. Michael's where it serves as a monument of former men's retreats.

"After the fire much help arrived from various places, more than was needed. I do not recall that any looting occurred, but there were isolated cases of selfish accumulation of donated goods, perishable as well as furniture. This help was a godsend to us. We obtained a tent and began to build a new home, on the north side of the river. This area had not been affected by the fire, although spot fires did occur wherever the wind dropped burning singles, or two-by-fours on the prairie. I learned later that large pieces were extinguished by watchful farmers as far distant as Pleasant Prairie [nine miles from the fire area].

This old photo, looking north on Howard Street, was taken from about First Avenue. The pillars of the building at left identify it as the partially completed bank at Sprague and Howard mentioned by Father Sauer in the text of this paper (in column above).

John W. Graham Company, still operating, began business days after the great fire of 1889 tented in the yard of a private home on Monroe Street across from the Review Building, then under construction. The "fifth" held by founder Graham, right, contains ink.

"After the fire, there were souvenirs to be gathered by persons who cared. Whole kegs of nails had been welded into grotesque masses of black iron. Pyramids of these reminders later served as ornaments on the lawns of the merchants who had specialized in hardware and building materials.

"The fire was out by midnight but the inhabitants were still anxious; a spark, a bit of wind and a new breakout might occur. Fortunately, Washington Street was wide and so was Lincoln, but the wind had carried sparks across the river, which was wide, too.

"Anxiety filled the mind and heart of the pastor of Our Lady of Lourdes and the teaching nuns of the new parochial school. Miraculously, it seemed, the church and convent school were saved. Homeless refugees found shelter within their walls.

"In a few days there were shops in tents on the ground that once had houses and buildings. I remember in particular a tent that bore a huge sign, John W. Graham. Everybody needed paper to write home. Insurance adjusters and contractors were much in evidence. The wooden sidewalks were no more. The shacks had all been burnt to the ground and brick and stone were suggested as the only building material to be used in rebuilding Spokane Falls.

"Mayor Furth took a personal interest in the fire victims and visited each family to see what help might be needed. He visited us just when I came into the house crying because I had been turned away at the relief tent. The circumstances were: My father was absent, across the river building a temporary shack for his family; mother was alone with us children; she was short of food and sent me to the relief tent for a loaf of bread. An officious or let us say overzealous official turned me down for reasons of his own.

"However, when Mayor Furth found out why I was crying, he took me back to the relief depot and ordered the officials to give me an armful of bread, meat and other eatables."

The late A. A. Kelly, proprietor for many years of the Kelly Plant Gardens on East Sprague Avenue near the city limits, wrote this account of the fire for me:

"Yes, I witnessed the red devil fire destroy Spokane Falls from Washington Street to Lincoln and N. P. Railroad tracks to the Spokane River on Sunday, August 4, 1889. I answered many calls for help to save valuables. However, there were no casualties in loss of limb or life. Within a block or two of the raging inferno I overheard conversations in several small groups of leading business men verbally contracting for purchase or leases of business lots and buildings at 10 o'clock that night within sight of their flame swept holdings. There could be no greater optimism. The fire died at 11 p.m.

"I went home three miles to my garden and finished the night digging potatoes for the many people in Spokane Falls who would be without food on Monday. As soon as the rubble and debris was cold it was dumped into the ravines that yet were outlets for excessive rain drainage and temporarily erected board walks and tent covering sprung up overnight with business as usual . . . . "

Mayor Furth proved how far-seeing and how efficient he was because he must have seen clearly the necessity for military protection of property as soon as the fire became uncontrollable. Proof of this statement may be found in the Official History of the Washington National Guard, Volume IV, pages 363-364 under the heading, Report of General A. F. Curry, on Fire at Spokane Falls, W. T. The report follows:

General Headquarters
National Guard of Washington
Adj. Gen. Office, Olympia, W.T.
Aug. 4, 1889.

SPECIAL ORDERS
No. 4½

Pending the disastrous conflagration at Spokane Falls, General A. P. Curry, commanding the First Brigade, N. G. W., will order such troops of the Second Regiment as he may deem necessary for the preservation of life and property of the citizens of said city, to report to him forth-with, and he will at once tender the services of said troops to the mayor of said city for the purpose indicated in this order.

By Order of the Commander in Chief:
R. G. O'Brien, Adjutant General
Headquarters, First Brigade,
National Guard of Wash.

"Spokane Falls, W.T.
August 30th, 1889.

"Brigadier General R. G. O'Brien,
Adjutant General, N. G. W.

"Sir: [as directed above] . . . I reported to Mayor Fred Furth for orders, whereupon he instructed me to take entire charge of the city and surroundings and guard the same, as in my judgment it required . . .

" . . . The police force of the municipal government, although as efficient as of any city in Washington, was by its limited numbers, entirely inadequate to perform the multiplicity of duties which were imposed upon it . . .

"A cordon of troops was placed about the burnt district, an area of 30 blocks.

"As this patrol had to be maintained day and night, I found that the force of the National Guard was too small to adequately perform the duty, and I called for volunteers from the Posts of the G. A. R. at Spokane Falls. Forty of these noble veterans responded to my call, and these with the officers and members of the National Guard for 14 days and nights performed the efficient and arduous duty of guarding the valuable property contained in safes and vaults, prevented spoliation and plunder by the disreputable characters who infested the town, preserved order and assisted in every way at the time of general distress. Tents were obtained for the officers and men of the National Guard and volunteers from the G. A. R. Posts, and strict and perfect camp discipline prevailed during the entire time. Rations were furnished upon my requisition from the relief tent provided by the municipal authorities . . .

"I have the honor to be, your obedient servant,

"A. P. Curry, Brig. Gen., Comdg."

One peculiar feature of the Spokane fire was the fact that nearly all residences, schools and churches escaped unscathed.

The story of this disaster, publicized through the press, brought a great response from near and far. The hearts of the people of the United States have always been open when disaster strikes. Appeals for relief brought large quantities of blankets, foodstuffs, medicines and tents for distribution among the victims.

Tales of man's weakness, his cupidity and his inordinate greed have come down to us even at this late date because large quantities of these valuable supplies which had been given freely by open-hearted fellow Americans were hoarded by some and were misappropriated by others. Those doing it were punished, when found.

Rolla A. Jones, the city water commissioner, who was the recipient of much vituperative criticism, was brought before the city commissioners and asked to speak in his own defense. He was allowed to resign, pleading innocence of any wrong doing.

The beauty that glows out of the blackened remains of the fire is the story of courage and man's inimitable will to better himself in the face of adversity.

Rather than being discouraged, those who lost most through this great tragedy seemed to react most courageously because even while the embers of a life time's work were still smoking, plans were being laid for a larger and better city. Restrictions were enacted and tent and frame buildings were allowed only as temporary quarters until brick buildings could be erected. Spokane, once again Phoenix-like, arose from its ashes to attain its present place as the queen city of the Inland Empire and third largest in the Pacific Northwest.

Insurance adjusters after the Spokane Fire of 1889.

Pinkney City, Washington Territory

By JEROME A. PELTIER

*P*INKNEY CITY, WASHINGTON, was once the county seat of a 76,-000 square mile area, which is much larger than all of the New England states combined. Little today remains externally of Pinkney City. It was built due to events of a momentous nature taking place with dramatic regularity in the Inland Empire in 1858. They concerned both red and white inhabitants. News reached the native residents that a military road was to be built. It was to bisect their ancestral lands. They viewed with panic, the settlement of their most fertile lands; they were angered by the unwarranted trespass of their lands by miners on their way to the gold fields of the Upper Columbia.

White residents of the Colville valley, who had come into the area as fur traders, began sending spirited pleas for military aid to the commanding officer at Fort Walla Walla, Lt. Col. Edward J. Steptoe. They were afraid that they would be attacked by outraged natives. Two white miners on their way to Fort Colville were killed by Palouse warriors. When Lt. Col. Steptoe learned of this he set out after the miscreants. His party of 158 men were drastically defeated at or near Rosalia in the battle of To-hoto-nimme. An immediate response to this brought together 680 men under the able leadership of Col. George G. Wright. Two pitched battles, Four Lakes and Spokane Plains, against the combined forces of the Coeur d'Alene, Spokane and Palouse tribes and their allies ended in total defeat for the Indians and victory without a casualty for Wright's well organized forces.

As an ignominious anti-climax eight hundred horses were killed; fifteen Indians were hanged; several were taken as hostages and two peace treaties were negotiated with the Coeur d'Alene and Spokane tribes. Wright refused to treat with the erring Palouse. He did, however, pause when he reached the Palouse river to harangue and hang several of them, including Wyecat. The execution of the latter named Indian was due to his having instigated, in keeping with the belief of the whites, the killing of two white miners who had been caught traversing Palouse lands near the Snake river while on their way to Fort Col-

JEROME A. PELTIER is an antiquarian centering his interests in Pacific Northwest History and realistic modern art. Further, see the Summer 1961 issue of this publication.

ville to the northward and beyond to the gold placers on the Pend Oreille river sands to the north and a little west of the fort. Those Indian captives not hanged at the crossing of the Snake were being used as hostages to discourage further outbreaks and killings. When Col. Wright reached Fort Walla Walla on the return he dispersed his men to various posts all over the west according to orders but recently received — this to be determined in advance on the outcome of the northern expedition just mentioned in the above.

In a dispatch of November 5, 1858, from Fort Vancouver, Brigadier General William S. Harney announced that "To secure the emigrant route to this department . . . I shall establish a post in the spring in the vicinity of Fort Boisee, on Snake river, some 230 miles from Fort Walla Walla. . . . I also respectfully recommend a post near Fort Hall. . . . As soon as the season will permit I shall establish a garrison . . . in the vicinity of Colville, to protect the interests of the citizens in that quarter and serve as a check upon the Indian tribes so lately hostile."

The Colville mentioned in Harney's report was a trading post of the Hudson's Bay Company to the north and east of the Kettle Falls of the Columbia river. The latter day town of Kettle Falls derived its name from this well-known fishing resort and a trading post frequented in large numbers by the Indians of the area. Upon the abandonment by the Hudson's Bay Company of Spokane House in 1825, the company's main interior trading establishment of the region had been transferred to this post near the falls.

In order to control the Spokane and Okanogan Indians, it was decided that a post should be built in the Colville valley. Four companies of the 9th United States infantry were ordered there, in the Spring of 1859, under the command of Major Pinkney Lugenbeel, who located the post site on a 1070 acre flat, alongside Mill creek approximately three miles north and slightly east of present day Colville. Building on the post site began at once. The post buildings were constructed of hewn logs. Later, Major Lugenbeel, unable to reach a satisfactory deal with the operators of a nearby sawmill, leased the mill, thus producing his own needed lumber for the post.

Two of the companies were ~~early~~ sent to the Okanogan valley where they remained for the summer protecting the American Boundary Commission. All four companies wintered at the post which had been named Harney's Depot in the beginning but later was renamed Fort Colville. Meanwhile a mushroom town had sprung up nearby the post. It was christened Pinkney City or Pinkneyville thus honoring the post commandant. Built in 1859, it was just across the creek from the post. This community grew and flourished on post patronage but with the later removal of the post it withered and died. Information from the National Archives states a postoffice was established at Pinkney City, December 17, 1859. It was discontinued in 1869.

Among the soldiers who came to Harney's Depot with Major Lugenbeel was John U. Hofstetter, founder of the present day little city of Colville, which in turn is not to be confused in any manner with the old and well-known fur trading post or the military establishment. He came to the Inland Empire while serving in the 9th Infantry and fought in the Indian wars of 1855 and 1858 receiving his discharge in 1860. Following his release, he freighted from Fort Dalles to Fort Colville for several years. He built a brewery in Pinkney City in 1865 which eventually burned to the ground. The present Colville was built on his homestead and he was its first mayor.

The early history of Spokane county was somewhat unusual. It was created by legislative act four times. Twice its elected officers failed to organize it; once it had a short-lived existance and, lastly, after a number of years of non-existence, it became Spokane county as we now know it. Due to an act of the legislature in 1864, Spokane county ceased to exist as such and for sixteen years it remained in Idaho as a segment of Stevens county.

January 29, 1858, the Territorial legislature created Spokane county, an area 200 miles wide and 380 miles long, with boundaries beginning at the mouth of the Snake river, thence south to the 46th parallel, eastward on that line to the summit of the Rocky mountains, then northward by way of that summit to the 49th parallel; westward on that parallel to the Columbia river and by mid-channel of that river to the mouth of Snake river. Its first county seat was Angus McLeod's place. General laws, rules and regulations governing other counties were to serve the county.

The officials chosen remained inoperative so a second group was named by the legislature on January 18, 1859. These men met on May 8, 1860 and established an election precinct at Pinkney City. On the second Monday of July, 1860, when the general election took place, a full board of county officials together with W. H. Watson as the Territorial representative were chosen. However, when Watson arrived in Olympia he found that his office was not recognized by the legislature. The following spring of 1861 while on his way back from Olympia to Pinkney City, Watson was killed by a Spokane Indian. After a round trip of 134 miles the Indian was found and brought back to Pinkney City and held before a justice for preliminary examination. This delay in action did not meet with general approval of the spectators who took him from the hands of the sheriff, led him to the cross beam of the brewery's double gate and hanged him. The entire matter, trial and hanging, took place within two days. The cost to the county was but thirty dollars, which included the 134 mile round trip made by the sheriff.

Incoming settlers soon made it necessary to divide the county and as a result Missoula county was created to include all east of the 115th degree. This was the first marked decrease but was not the last. Whittling of its area continued. The Spokane county district court was created in January 1862, meeting for the first time in Pinkney City on July 13, 1862. In the course of its second cession, the judge granted the county's first divorce to Mrs. Mary J. Walters.

Business in the early days of Pinkney City leaned heavily toward the liquor trade. Accompanying kindred types of business activities usually associated with this business were early licensed to operate. Other types of business were also licensed. A ferry across the Columbia to the mouth of the Kettle river was licensed. Ferriage rates were $5 per ton for freight; man and horse $2.00; pack animal $1.25; loose animals $1.00; footmen 75 cents. December 15, 1860, the first road in the county was located from this ferry landing to Pinkney City and from thence southward to the Spokane river. The next public improvement was a public well costing $100 to dig.

In order to ascertain what type of business was conducted in Pinkney City, the writer located a list of licenses and to whom they were issued. A board consisting of J. W. Seaman, chairman; R. H. Douglass, treasurer; Cyrus Hall, justice of the peace; and John Gunn, assessor, met at Pinkney City, August 8, 1860 and established a list of licenses and their prices. Grocery Businesses (including saloons) were $200.00 per year; billiard tables and bowling alleys when conducted in conjunction with a saloon were $30.00 per annum. The license granting period appears not to have any time limitation on the period such permits were to be valid in operation.

At another meeting in the later portion of 1860 licenses were granted for a period of six months. Henceforth this term appears to have been the uniform period for a granted license to operate. During the early period of the terms of the licensing board there appears not to have been a time limit placed on their terms, if terms they had. Again, later in 1860, a division of term periods was provided. Terms were placed at one, two and three years for the staggering of the initial terms. After the expiration of any one of the terms selection was to be for a three-year term. This board functioned for both the village communities and for the county as well.

The following anecdote has been told by the son of an early merchant in the communities of either Pinkney City or Colville. Such an acceptance of the presumed worth of an unknown individual most certainly would not be found operating in our business attitudes of the present day. The son relates that his father met a man named Wellington who chanced to be not too well dressed but carried the appearance or impression of being well educated and did possess polished manners. There was an immediate attachment between the two. His father left orders with the clerks, after the man had been fed at the merchant's home, and then sent him to the store to be outfitted in clothing and other needs. The man refused the proffered outfitting since he had no money with which to pay. He was told the merchant would probably take care of that. Later the latter told the newcomer that he needed a man and would put him to work.

The man objected that he had no mercantile experience which met the reply — "Well, you can learn can't you?" This closed the matter with the man going into the employ of the merchant. The original unknown Wellington remained steadily in the merchant's employ for a period of two years, receiving nothing but his food, lodging, clothing and a small amount of money. When the employer withdrew from the business, turning it over to his partner, he reminded the latter that they had not taken Wellington into consideration in their settlement with each other. What about him? The partner immediately responded: "Why we'll pay him two thousand dollars for the two years he worked for us." This was done.

Wellington appears to have been a rather personable individual. Making contacts with the military men his impression was all to the good. From time to time officers put him in the way of making many remunerative contracts which later ended in making him a well-to-do man in the light of his day and time. In all he gathered together better than $80,000 in property.

One of the best known business men in the community of Colville was Marcus Oppenheimer who operated a general store. He too was notable for his considerate attitude toward others crossing his path. He and his two brothers are said to have had the largest store of its type north of the early established Walla Walla. He too has left behind him a somewhat notable memory coming down through the years as based on his business policies. The town of Marcus has been named in commemorating the part he played in the nearby areas surrounding the older Fort Colville and Colville.

The chief clerk of the Surveyor General's office for the territory, in 1862, wrote that "I passed over this portion of our Territory in 1853, and at that time there were fifteen or twenty settler families located mainly on Mill creek, . . . The valley now contains a population of more than 1,000 and over 150 land claims are now being improved . . . Colville valley is about fifty miles in length, and from one to five miles in width."

Spokane County's first public school was established in Pinkney City in 1862. The court room in the county courthouse was the schoolroom with 18 or 19 pupils attending. The first private school was at the Catholic mission nearby. Father Joseph Menetrey established it. The church, not far distant, was of hewn logs, having been built under the supervision of Father Joset, S. J., in 1865, with services being attended by whites as well as half-breeds and Indians.

Transportation business was non-existent. W. Park Winans relates that when 13,000 pounds of supplies reached them from Wallula, the charges amounted to $1,950.00 or 15 cents a pound. Transmission of news from the outside world was slow as it required thirty days for such to reach Pinkney City from Washington, D. C.

Pinkney City's lawless element went unrestrained for some little time since jail facilities were inadequate if they even existed. Eventually, by borrowing from the school funds, a jail was provided but it took several years to repay the fund. This jail was of log cabin construction and was designed to take care of not only civil but military offenders.

Militarily, matters at the post were early complicated by the Civil War raging during the 1860's. All lower ranking officers of the 9th Infantry at the post in 1861 resigned and joined their fortunes with the Confederacy. On November 17, 1861 Major Lugenbeel was relieved of his command being replaced by Major James F. Curtis commanding the 2nd California voluntary infantry. It was early claimed that members of this California regiment were largely criminals from the streets of San Francisco. Later events appeared to completely justify this assumption. Both minor and major crime committed by these infantrymen soon came to be almost the order of the day. Offenders if confined were soon released due to lack of evidence against them. Intimidation of witnesses was stated as the cause for this situation. As a crime curbing measure, the local distillery was closed and all whiskey in town was destroyed, this by the order of Major Curtis of the post command. Major Curtis was relieved of his command on July 11, 1862 at Fort Colville, being transferred to the Fort Vancouver command. His successor rescinded the former order banning liquor and once again it began to freely flow. Regular army troops once again appeared at Fort Colville on November 9, 1865 and continued to be stationed there until the fort's abandonment in September 1882.

Within a year or more following the close of the Civil War, Pinkney City and its surrounding area began to take on new life especially in the field of agricultural production. From time to time discoveries of gold, true or unfounded, began to filter into the community from neighboring mountains which reports resulted in population defections and some uneasiness in the community. Under the heading of Pinkney City, the **Walla Walla Statesman** for June 1, 1866, thusly described Pinkney City:

"This place is generally called Colville and is adjoining the reservation. It has a population of some 200 and is improving. Ferguson & Co., Abrams & Co., and Smith & Young are the principal houses. Ferguson & Co. perhaps sell as many goods as all the other firms. They are enterprising men and are branching off to all the trading points opening up there. Both other firms are extending their business and growing in favor. Mr. Shaw is fitting up a nice saloon, with billiard tables and all kinds of liquors, and in fact everything suitable for leading a fellow to the devil, and if any one has a fancy for traveling in that direction, Shaw is just as good company as he will find. . . . The merchants all have large stocks on hand, but their sales have not been as large as they anticipated."

Somewhat later the **Statesman** again opined concerning Pinkney City that "A few days since, two of the hurdy-gurdy girls, . . . got tired of quadrilles and took to themselves pardners for a matrimonial 'dance' . . . . I would recommend all hurdy-gurdy girls in good standing and who are tired of 'tripping the light fantastic toe,' to come to Colville."

Beginning with October 17, 1867, a number of successive command changes at Fort Colville were made until in the summer of 1879 Lt. Col. Merriam assumed command. Shortly he and his men went to near the mouth of Foster Creek where they spent the succeeding winter of 1879-1880. Evidently they were looking for a new site for a post. Finding this site not suitable they went to near the mouth of the Spokane river where they began the erection of a new post to become known as Fort Spokane. Following this decision by Col. Merriam, Lieut. Webster with the men left at Fort Colville were ordered withdrawn from that post in 1882. With this withdrawal came the death knell of Fort Colville and with it Pinkney City. People of the latter community moved homes and business houses from Pinkney City to the newly founded community of Colville three miles to the southwest.

In the following year of 1883, several residents of the area platted the new townsite that was to become known as the present little city of Colville. The transfer of people, buildings and businesses was necessary since there was no longer but little, if any, revenue in the community with the transfer of the soldiery elsewhere. The first person to leave was the trader with the next being the jailer and his building, the two being moved as a unit. All buildings not moved entire were wrecked or dismantled and within a comparatively brief time abandonment was complete.

As late as 1947, timbers of the last remaining building could still be seen. It had been something better, perhaps, but was then doing service as a stable but was lately converted to use as a chicken house. Such was the closing reminder of what had once been a frontier post of the national military establishment and of an accompanying town of better than one thousand people. It was truly a ghostly reminder of what had once been a scene or community of intense and, at times, near violent living. But all was now a long time gone.

The PACIFIC NORTHWESTERNER

Vol. 28   Summer, 1984   No. 3

Romeo and Juliet on the Oregon Trail

by JEROME PELTIER

THE TRIUMPH OF YOUNG LOVERS over parental objections has long been a popular theme in fiction. The story of how two sweethearts overcame this obstacle in 1853 is a romantic part of the story of settlement of the Northwest. The couple were George Snipes and Martha Imbler.

George's parents were Elam Snipes and Asenath Rawson of North Carolina, where George was born in 1832. Elam, in his constant search for better farm land, moved first to Tennessee and later to Iowa when George was fifteen. In Iowa, George met the love of his life.

Whether the fateful meeting was in the schoolhouse which George attended for three months each winter, at the village store, or at a neighbor's house is not known, but there is no question that George Snipes and Martha Imbler fell deeply in love. Equally well known is that Martha's father, David, objected to the affair.

The reason for David Imbler's objections was never stated, but he adamantly opposed the courtship of his daughter. We must assume that the lovers met surreptitiously and discussed marriage, and we can imagine the difficulties they encountered in arranging their trysts because of the restrictions that were placed on young women during that period.

I first learned about George and Martha from their daughter, Lillian Snipes Waterman of Spokane, Washington. Mrs. Waterman granted me several interviews during which we discussed her historic family.

JEROME PELTIER is a living resource for information on Northwest History Formerly a used book dealer, he has been a collector of books and memorabilia dealing with the Northwest since 1937. A distinguished author, Peltier has written six books and has presented 24 papers to the Westerners. He organized the Spokane Corral with Thomas Teakle in 1955, and was its first Sheriff. Now retired, Peltier still continues his original research in regional history through analyses of legal records, studies of old newspapers, and interviews with offspring of early settlers.

ISSN: 0030 - 882 X

| Vol. 28 | Summer, 1984 | No. 3 |

Published quarterly by the Spokane Corral of The Westerners, P.O. Box 1717, Spokane, WA 99210. Subscription $5.00 per calendar year. Back issues available, $1.25 ea. Articles appearing in this journal are abstracted and indexed in HISTORICAL ABSTRACTS: and/or AMERICA HISTORY AND LIFE.

OFFICERS

Sheriff . . . . Larry Schoonover

Chief Deputy . . . . Everett A. Sandburg

Program Deputy . . . . Lewis Sabo

Photographic Deputy. .John Ellingson

Membership Deputy. .Jerry Stevenson

Roundup Foreman
   (Secretary) . . . . E. F. "Bud" Hayen

Chuck Wrangler . . . . Joe Daniels

Tallyman (Treasurer) . . Ralph R. Reid

Registrar of Marks and Brands
   (Editor) . . . . Norman Bolker

Publications Committee. .Jerry Peltier
   Seabury Blair, Randall Johnson

In one interview on April 10, 1958, she told me the story of her parents' romance. She said that the Imblers, in an effort to prevent the marriage, abruptly packed their belongings and headed West in order to leave while George was temporarily away from home. They did so at the cost of abandoning a comfortable and productive farm in Jefferson County, Iowa.

THIS IS THE STORY as Mrs. Waterman related it to me.

"My Mother was Martha Imbler. Her Father (David Imbler) was against her seeing Dad, so he pulled up stakes in New Purchase, Iowa, and set out for the Willamette Valley of Oregon. Dad was away at the time the Imblers left and did not know about their plot to leave him behind until he got back home and was given a note that had been written by my Mother for him."

That note was given to a trusted friend who delivered it to George upon his return. It spoke volumes and stirred George, who had not planned to leave Iowa, into sudden action. It read:

> My Dearest George:
> Father is dragging us off to Oregon so that I can't marry you. He thinks that you'll never find out where we have gone. He has been very careful to let no one know that we were leaving. I didn't know until today that we were going anywhere, let alone to a place as far off as Oregon.
>
> But George dear, I am sure you'll come out to Oregon. When you do, you know that I'll marry you wherever and whenever you you catch up with us. Be very careful, George, when you come, that Father doesn't suspect that you are anywhere near. I know that he would tie me up and never let me out of his sight if he thought I might have a chance to see you.
> Hurry up, George. I'll be waiting.
>   Your loving Martha

Hurry he did, according to Lillie Waterman. "Dad set cut in pursuit the day after he received her letter. When he got to Council Bluffs, he made arrangements to leave the next morning with a light fast moving train whose speed was such that they passed several slower moving outfits, among them the David Imbler train."

THIS SYNOPSIS OF THE STIRRING EVENTS alerted me to the possibility of further details. I asked Mrs. Waterman if she had any papers or documents about her family, and at a later time she furnished me with some additional material including a typescript of an interview with George Snipes by Mrs. G. J. Crandall at The Dalles, Oregon, February 14, 1914, which was signed and authenticated by Mrs. Waterman on October 11, 1958. The account makes clear that although George was an eager swain, he was a prudent one, selecting his emigrant train with care.

The interview with George states, "The reason I came to Oregon when I did, leaving my Father's family, was because my girl was leaving Iowa for (the Willamette Valley) Oregon, with the Spring immigration with her Father's family, the Imblers. I took the next oxtrain that left two weeks later, and on April 10 I started on a stern chase. We did not overtake the Imbler train until we reached Salmon Falls, now in Southern Idaho. Then we traveled a day behind or a day ahead until we reached The Dalles, September 15, and I was a day ahead of their train in here.

"I was twenty-one years old the day we crossed the Rocky Mountains at South Pass . Our train took the north side of the Platte River. The immigration of 1853 was very heavy. As far as you could see there was a long procession of covered wagons, both before and behind. I came with the Luce brothers. About twenty-three men more than twenty years old were in the Luces' train, and six women.

"We had no trouble with Indians and saw a good many. The day before we got to Fort Laramie, one of our young men shot and killed an Indian because he was bound to have his red headed sister. This was in Sioux country. We stayed two nights and one day at Fort Laramie and left in a big company. The Indians had left the country, since it was too near the Fort for them.

"WE SAW FEW BUFFALOES, killed only one; twelve was the biggest bunch we saw. Antelope were thick. I saw thousands of them but never killed but one, they were too fleet, and I killed that one accidently. As I raised my gun to aim, it went off and broke one antelope's back. We had plently of provisions through to The Dalles.

"We stayed all night on Ten Mile Creek and the next morning, when hitching up, I found a (business) card of Dr. Shaug's. He had been our family doctor in Iowa, and I was anxious to see him. He came to Oregon the year before, had wintered in Portland and came back to The Dalles in the Spring. He had a store at the mouth of Mill Creek, then called 'the landing', and was trading with the Indians and emigrants . . .

"ON SEPTEMBER 16, (THE NEXT DAY) I went to The Dalles, and saw Dr. Shaug. He wanted me to stay and work for him. I told him I wsa going to get married and go to the Willamette Valley. I would have to steal my girl, for the old man objected. I had followed my girl two thousand miles and would not

This stone hut, probably a water-cooled storehouse or springhouse, is an outbuilding of the first Snipes home at Rowena, Oregon. It was restored by the present owners Mr. and Mrs. Gene Adkisson of The Dalles.

give her up now. Shaug told me this was the place for me to stop, for there were just as good chances for a young man here. Dr. Shaug asked me who my girl was and when I told him, he said (he) knew them in Iowa, the Imblers, my girl's name was Martha Imbler. He said he would get up some horses, and he knew two men, Jim Griffin and Jim Thompson, that he would send with me.

"So we started and when we got to Fifteen Mile Creek, the girl was gone. They (sic) had gone about seven miles to Pine Hollow and had camped there. Their name, Imbler, was on the wagon sheets.

"I stayed at Fifteen Mile and one of the two boys went to the camp and asked if there was a man there by the name of Imbler, and the old man said that was he. They were sitting on the ground eating supper and asked Jim to tie his horse to the wagon and eat with them. He sat opposite the girl and drank a cup of coffee.

"The girl got up and went to the wagon where Jim had tied his horse and when Jim went to get his horse, he slipped a letter up under the wagon cover, and the girl, Martha, took it. She called her sister and they got a candle and read the letter. She told Jim that as soon as they were in bed, she would be ready.

"B Y THIS TIME, MR. IMBLER had discovered the other man below camp and he told the family he did not like the way they talked, and to guard their cattle, so they put guard out and built a big fire, and one of Martha's brothers was the guard. When his back was turned, she got out of the wagon and left them. It was not until the next morning that the old man knew that one of his girls had 'flew the coop' and he was good and wrathy.

The cornerstone, at the lower right side of the front aspect, is part of the original structure. According to local tradition, Lt. U.S. Grant drew the plans for the barn and sent enlisted men from Fort Dalles to build the barn and this stone hut. Richard Campbell, who owned the Snipes property in 1920, is believed to have inscribed the legend on the cornerstone.

"They (sic) came to Fifteen Mile and I had gone to bed. I got up and dressed and (we) rode to The Dalles . . . It was about 2:30 in the morning when we got there, and one of the boys told me a Methodist preacher arrived in the emigration that afternoon while I was away, and that he was in that tent over there.

"I called to the tent, and asked if there was a preacher in there, and a voice said, 'Yes. What do you want?'

"I replied ' I want you to come out and marry a couple.' . . . Our marriage took place in that tent, not far from where the Umatilla House is now, on the bank of Mill Creek . . .

"This part of Oregon, now Wasco County, was then a part of Clackamas County, and Oregon City was the county seat. Our marriage record is among the earliest filed in the County Court House at Oregon City. No license was needed then. The preacher or justice filed a notice at the county seat that he had performed such a marriage in that county, and that was all there was to it.

"When we married, all the money I had was $1.60, but when we were standing up to get married, Dr. Shaug slipped twenty dollars into my hand and I gave the preacher ten of it. That was Sunday morning, September 18, 1853."

DAVID IMBLER REACTED JUST as one would expect when he learned that his daughter had run away. According to Granddaughter Lillie, "Grandpa Imbler flew into a rage when he heard how he had been outwitted, and rode his fastest horse at a gallop all the way to The Dalles. He tried to separate the young couple, but they would have none of it. He attempted to take Mother away bodily, but the crowd that gathered would not allow him to do so because they admired the young bride and groom for their cross-country courtship and wanted them to be happy . . . Grandpa Imbler was told at this time that if he had guarded his daughter as well as he did his cattle, she would not have been able to make her escape from him.''

After staying briefly in The Dalles where George worked for Dr. Shaug, the newlyweds moved to nearby Rowena, where they built their first home, called Snipe's Pocket. Lillie was born there six years later. She was one of fourteen children.

As soon as he could get the ground broken, George planted a garden and sowed some grain, using a yoke of oxen that one of the Luce brothers had left behind when he went down the Columbia to the Willamette Valley. George planted fruit trees which he bought from Lewelling's nursery at Milwaukie, Oregon - apple, pear, and cherries. He also planted peach seedlings which he grew from pits. His trees were among the earliest planted East of the Cascades in Oregon.

Martha died in 1890 after a brief illness. Her death devastated George, but he eventually recovered from his grief and went on with the business of living.

George died at his home in The Dalles on July 16, 1922, at the age of ninety. He and his beloved Martha had raised a large family and had helped pioneer The Dalles area where he lived for seventy-nine years.

His brother, Ben Snipes, had a meteoric career as a cattle baron and banker in Washington Territory, with a spectacular rise and fall. Steady cautious George never made or lost a fortune, but he garnered his prize in life.

His daughter, Lillie, lived to be 103, dying in Spokane on July 23, 1964. I feel fortunate to have known this woman who was intimately associated with people who experienced some of the history making events of the Northwest.

The

PACIFIC NORTHWESTERNER
SPOKANE CORRAL

| Volume 29 | 1985 | Number 4 |

How It All Began

by JEROME PELTIER

LONG BEFORE THERE WAS A SPOKANE CORRAL, I was the proprietor of Clark's Old Book Store at 831 West Main Street, Spokane, Washington. The store, established in 1910 by Reba Knight, a retired school teacher, was sold a year later to John Clark, formerly of Denver, Colorado. Clark had visited Spokane with no intention of becoming a book dealer, until he met a close friend of Knight's named Agnes Davis who wanted to run a book store.

Clark fell in love with Mrs. Davis who said she would marry him only if he would buy Reba Knight's store. He agreed, and they ran it until 1930, the year of his death. After that, Mrs. Clark ran the store with the assistance of her two daughters, and later, with her son-in-law. My wife and I bought the store from Mrs. Clark in 1950, operating it until my retirement in 1979.

Clark's Old Book Store enjoyed a good reputation as a source of old and rare books, and after we bought it we specialized in Western Americana. We dealt with history buffs from all parts of the nation. We soon had a nucleus of customers with special interest in Western history.

Book stores are natural gathering places for people interested in intellectual discussions, and fans of Western history are no exception. The concept of the Westerners organization originated in the book store of Leland Case and Elmo Scott Watson who co-founded the Chicago Corral. Book stores have figured in the creation of every Westerner's group I know of. History enthusiasts in Los Angeles congregated at Arthur Clark's in Glendale and Dawson's in Los Angeles, leading Paul Galleher, Arthur Clark and Glen Dawson to form the Los Angeles Corral. Both Paul and Glen told me of the part they played in its founding, and I told them of my services toward starting ours.

In this first hand account, **JEROME PELTIER** describes the problems encountered while organizing the Spokane Corral of the Westerners. Jerry, a charter member and de facto first Sheriff, delivered this address March 21, 1985, on the thirtieth anniversary of the founding of our Corral.
Author of six books on Northwest history, Peltier has presented twenty five papers to our group over the years.

Published quarterly by the Spokane Corral of The Westerners, P.O. Box 1717, Spokane, WA 99210. Subscription $5.00 per calendar year. Back issues available, $1.25 ea. Articles appearing in this journal are abstracted and indexed in HISTORICAL ABSTRACTS: and/or AMERICA HISTORY AND LIFE.   ISSN: 0030-882 X

OFFICERS

Sheriff .... Alfred Butler
Chief Deputy .... Lewis Sabo
Program Deputy .... Alexander Joss
Photographic Deputy..John Ellingson
Membership Deputy ... Byron Barber
Roundup Foreman
    (Secretary) .... E. F. "Bud" Hayen
Chuck Wrangler .... Joe Daniels
Tallyman (Treasurer) .. Ralph R. Reid

Registrar of Marks and Brands
    (Editor) .... Norman Bolker
Publications Committee..Jerry Peltier
    Seabury Blair, Randall Johnson
Honcho for Journal
    Distribution ....Frank Knox
Distribution Committee..Byron Barber
    Joe Daniels, Tom Corcoran,
    Harry Kellogg, Alexander Joss

Paul Galleher started the conversational ball rolling when he asked me why I wasn't mentioned in a booklet about Westerners that his Corral published. Paul had received his information from Fred Mark, one of our members, and I knew that the information was incomplete.

Paul continued, "I thought it was odd that no bookman was mentioned in the founding of the Spokane Corral, because all of them have had bookmen associated with them, such as Peter Decker in New York, Bill Kelleher in New Jersey, and Jeff Dykes in the Potomac Corral."

TEN CORRALS HAD BEEN FORMED before ours. Thomas Teakle, who looms as a central figure in starting ours, was a constant visitor to our book store. He was a tireless reader and researcher of the lore of the Western cowboy. Through our shop he obtained many fine books that he bequeathed to the Montana Historical Society in Helena.

Our discussions were long and varied and became a daily habit. I would deal with other customers, and then return to our discussion. I soon learned that "Tommy", as my wife La Verle called him, had a large collection of literature published by some of the first Westerner Corrals, and when I commented that I would like to read this material, Teakle brought me some of his quarterlies and Brand books, which are compilations of articles by Corral members. I found the reading fascinating, and the idea of having a local Corral occurred to me

I brought up the possibility several times to a group of my friends who met each Saturday at the Chung King Restaurant that used to be at the West 700 block of Sprague Avenue. The group, comprised of James Cormana, who now lives in St. Maries, Idaho, Leonard Veeder, now deceased, and Finley Johnson, a coin and stamp dealer, were all knowledgeable in Western history. I rounded out the quartet. Jim and I met often, and our discussions brought out the fact that Spokane would be a great place in which to launch a new Westerner's group. This strengthened my personal convictions, so one Monday as I handed Mr. Teakle the Brand books and quarterly booklets he had loaned me, I remarked that I could see no reason why we shouldn't be able to start a Westerner's Corral here in Spokane. I suggested that it be named the Pacific Northwesterner's Corral because there was no other such organization in the entire Northwest. Teakle then told me the story of his abortive attempt to start a Posse here previously. He commented that he had

Courtesy of Jerome Peltier   Courtesy of Jerome Peltier

Thomas Teakle — He was the first to think of the idea, but dropped it.

Jerome Peltier — He revived the idea and brought it to fruition.

arranged with six men with wide educational backgrounds to join the group. His plan ended when one of his prospective members died, and Teakle did not pursue it later. He became fully occupied for the next six years with research on the history of Idaho, Washington, Oregon, and Montana based on material taken from early area newspapers. His typescripts, amounting to seventy books of about three hundred pages each, are now in the archives of Whitman College in Walla Walla, Washington.

Teakle seemed to think that the failure of his previous attempt settled the matter. I didn't think it did, so I asked him what type of men he had approached as possible Westerners. He answered, "All college men, preferably those with Master's degrees, so that they would write scholarly papers."

I retorted, "Perhaps that is why you had only six people who were interested. Why didn't you broaden the concept and ask people who had wide historical interests?" He replied that he wanted a first class organization that could stand up to the level of any of the currently existing Corrals.

I told him, "Don't tell me they have only college men and educators in their memberships. I think that interest and enthusiasm should be the criteria. Hobbyists always do great research work and they should be approached. Let's try to organize a group with these ideas in mind."

Finally he agreed that together we would probe among our friends, acquaintances and my customers to find a group that would qualify for membership. We had many discussions regarding this and the type of organization we wanted. I told him of my experience with a group with which I was then associated, **Friends of Northwest History**, meeting in the Campbell Museum under the auspices of the

39

Eastern Washington State Historical Society, that had started with 125 members but now had only twelve members because they became a bunch of sitters and listeners. We agreed that our strength would lie in the presentation by members of papers that they had written.

TEAKLE AND I FELT strongly that ours should be an all male group. I'm afraid that Tommy wouldn't have stood still for the Christmas parties that our wives attend, which started in 1974. We felt that slide shows were not appropriate presentations unless they contributed to a paper. We both agreed that we should have a quarterly publication as soon as we could staff and finance one, because only then could we reach out to people all over the country. We believed that a corresponding membership should cost three or four dollars a year, depending on the cost of the publication. Lowell Noll, a printer, was invited to join our Corral, and his knowledge and expertise were invaluable when we eventually began producing our journal.

Meanwhile, Teakle was working like a beaver contacting people for membership. He brought in a daily report of success or failure. My wife was most kind because she ran the shop while Tommy and I discussed Westerner business. If any female deserved to be an honorary founder, it is that good patient woman. I talked to customers I thought would make good members. Tommy wrote to the Chicago Corral for permission to use the bison skull insignia, which is the recognized symbol of all Westerner groups, and they acquiesced.

When we had eighteen prospects who agreed to become members, Tommy reported that he had reached the end of his recruiting. He wanted to quit, but I wanted him to continue. I gave him the names of twelve more prospects and asked him to search his mind for more friends or former students, cautioning him not to be so stringent in his requirements. He agreed that there were others that he could ask, so he started on another search. He was indefatigable in his pursuit of members.

I talked and how I talked to possible members among our customers. Many out of town people liked the idea but couldn't join us because of the distance they lived from Spokane. Eventually we got twenty eight who agreed to go with us. Our goal had originally been fifty, but as I told Tommy, "We can start with a lesser number, because we will soon have the number we want when our members go out and talk about our group." We later enlarged our membership to seventy five, and currently, it exceeds one hundred.

During this time, I was gathering data for my book on the great fur trader, Moses "Black" Harris, writing letters to authorities of the fur trade like Dale Morgan and Charles Kelly. I was also arranging for an interview with Jerome Drumheller, son of pioneer Mayor of Spokane, Daniel Drumheller.

This was a busy time, but I still found time to make diary entries about plans for the Westerners. Although we had talked about it long before, on February 8, 12, and 22, 1955, I wrote, "Ate lunch with Jim Cormana and we talked about Westerners."

An entry dated March 28, 1955, reads, "Mr. Teakle and I discussed Westerners again. We are nearing the time for organization. We tried to figure out which day would be best (for meetings) and I said to be arbitrary and name one and they would come. Teakle and I decided that the third Thursday of March (17th and St. Pat's) would be O.K."

Tuesday 3/8/55. Went out at noon to find out which hotel could accomodate our Westerners group for a dinner meeting. Went to the Ridpath and the Secretary said the lowest rate they had was $2.50 per plate. Next I went to the Spokane Hotel where I talked to my old friend, Sheila Symmes, who arranged a nice meal for $1.75 per plate. This looks like the best deal! Following this, I talked to some people at the Desert Hotel. They had a $1.75 meal but not as good as at the Spokane.

I CHECKED AT THE DAVENPORT HOTEL and found that the prices were far beyond what I thought the prospective members would be willing to pay. At the Spokane Hotel, I found everything to my personal satisfaction, the menu was great, facilities were good and there were several nice rooms available for our use. Sheila who was in charge of the banquet rooms, assured me that we would have the best of care if we decided to give our business to them.

On his own, Teakle sent out the letters of invitation to the first meeting, and the contents disturbed me. This was mine:

West 1917 Riverside Avenue
Spokane 11, Washington
March 7, 1955

Mr. Jerome A. Peltier
East 8009 Liberty
Orchard Avenue, Spokane

Dear Peltier:

        The organization meeting of the Spokane West-
erners, for charter membership in which I solicited you
some time since, will be at 6 o'clock the evening of
Thursday, March 17th at the Spokane Hotel.

        This will be a complimentary dinner for which
there will be no charge. However, it will be necessary
to know in advance what the attendance may be. Use the
enclosed postal card for notification, mailing it so that
it may reach me no later than March 14th.

        Enclosed is a list of those who have accepted
the invitation to become charter members of the Spokane
Westerners.

                Most cordially yours,

                Thomas Teakle

I had expected to be mentioned as a co-founder of the organization. Further I hadn't planned on paying for the dinners, and could hardly afford to do so.

The great night came, and all of us met at the Spokane Hotel. Again, from my diary:

Thursday, 3/17/55 . . . After half of the members came, I led the group up to the Stone Room while Teakle waited for the rest. All came by 6:30 and we were seated — all twenty eight of us. Judge Edgerton, Thomas Teakle, Dr. Edgar Stewart and I sat at the head table. After eating I got up and made some comments about our purpose for attending the meeting, and introduced Mr. Teakle as pro-tempore President — all agreed. He called roll, then gave a short sketch of the aims of Westerners' movements in other areas. Election of Officers followed. I nominated Judge Edgerton and someone else nominated Ed Becher. Becher won the office of Sheriff (President in other groups). Edgerton nominated me as Deputy Sheriff, another did the same for Father W. L. Davis. I was elected. Louis Livingston was elected Roundup Foreman (Secretary), Cecil Hagen, Registrar of Marks and Brands (in charge of publications, in other words, Editor), Lowell Noll, Chuck Wrangler. He arranges for a banquet each monthly dinner meeting. Mr. Teakle then read the New York Westerner Constitution (in part) and made comments that would aid our organization.

At no time during the meeting did Teakle give me any credit for my part in starting the Posse. He made no mention of the many hours I had devoted to the organizational work. It is my feeling that he could have been charitable and say something like, "Without Jerry's help, this organization would not be starting tonight." I was hurt because there was no attempt even at a later date to rectify this oversight.

The diary continues: After the meeting was over, the officers were asked to stay and two committees were selected as follows: Constitution and Program Committee. I walked with Cecil Hagen to within a block of the store. We talked all of the while. I'm supposed to give the first talk because Stewart has the proofs of his **Custer's Luck** to go over. These have to be sent to the University of Okla. Press . . .

The Constitution Committee was composed of Judge Ralph Edgerton, Father William Lyle Davis, S.J., Joe Baily, Thomas Teakle and Joel Ferris. Publications Committee was headed by Cecil Hagen and he was to be aided by Joe Baily and Seabury Blair.

A few days later, Teakle came to me and asked if I would mind exchanging program days with him so that he could present the Corral's first paper. I had no objection, so I took the third meeting date for my presentation.

Our organization had been progressing smoothly, but problems soon developed. Two clinkers went into the machinery within twenty four hours. My diary tells the story which begins the night before our second monthly meeting.

Wednesday, April 20. Worked. Got home, ate part of dinner, then got a call from Noll informing me that he had set up a dinner for the Westerners for tonight. I informed him that the meeting was not until tomorrow night. His call upset me a great deal. It made a very bad night for me.

I imagined that we would have to pay for another meal when we met the next night, if the hotel would be willing to arrange another one for us. Fortunately, the hotel forgave our mistake, set up again on the correct night and charged us only once.

Thursday 21. Day off. Helped L. for awhile. Told Teakle about the wrong night set up. He went to the Spokane Hotel to see if everything was O.K. for our meeting. It was and I made a date to meet him at 5:30. I did (meet him) and we (the group) all met in 2A, a nice room. Becher brought Ella Mc Carty in direct violation of all the rules of the organization which is **no women.** He had her speak to us. She didn't get a good reception. The evening was spoiled by Becher's attitude. He tried to resign and the vote came out 8 to 8, although there were 21 there. Teakle gave a wonderful and humorous paper on "Some Aspect of Frontier Montana Journalism." An outstanding piece of writing and compilation. The evening was ruined by Ed Becher. Home at 10:45. Imagine that — and the meeting started at 6 p.m.

Friday 22. Dr. Edgar I. Stewart was in (the store) and offered to inscribe copies of his forthcoming book on Custer — **Custer's Luck.** He also gave his opinion about Becher which agreed with Teakle's and mine. He left after about 10 minutes because his wife was at the Dr.'s Teakle came in about 15 minutes (later). All of us are upset over Becher and his attitude. Teakle is going to try to have him removed because nothing was proved by the vote last night.

I BEAR NO MALICE, TOWARD ED BECHER, but these remarks are made for the sake of the record. I am sure that Becher meant well when he invited Ella Mc Carty to speak at our meeting, but he had violated our rules regarding women at our meetings. Furthermore, presenting two lectures at one program would prolong the meeting to the point of discouraging members from attending. Becher and Mc Carty had great knowledge and interest in the history of our region and contributed to it by teaching and lecturing. Ella spoke before many classes and groups about Spokane history and legends. She also made tapes of her stories. Ed, a high school teacher of Northwest history, led field trips for his students. He wrote a text-book that was used in the high school curriculum. He later wrote a fine book intitled **Spokane Corona,** and a pamphlet on the city. Becher had much to offer the Corral, but I feared his actions could ruin it if he continued to disregard the rules.

I do not know what happened during the second meeting at which time I was in the midwest with my wife on a long-planned vacation, but I know that Ed Becher never came to another meeting.

For my presentation, I had planned to deliver a paper on Spokane House, but when several members told me they would drop out if papers were as technical as the first two, I said I would keep mine simple. I then assembled a paper on the notes and writings of an old friend of mine, Eugene Carlton Sampson, who had made the run into the Cherokee strip in 1893, and had witnessed the executions of several men sentenced by Judge Parker, Oklahoma's famous hanging judge.

As Deputy Sheriff, I presided in the absence of Sheriff Ed Becher. My diary of Thursday, 6/6/55 reads: "Jittery today. Gave my paper on Eugene Sampson to 20 members on the Spokane Westerners. I think it created interest because there was animated discussion following it."

We took our first field trip Sunday, July 17, 1955. Twelve men and one woman met at the Spokane and Eastern Bank. We visited Plante's Ferry, Spokane Bridge, Horse Slaughter Camp, California House, Indian Hanging Site, Four Lakes and Spokane Plains Battlefield, Camp Washington and Spokane House.

The following year, Judge Edgerton was elected Sheriff, I was re-elected Deputy Sheriff, and Louis Livingston re-elected Roundup Foreman. The Registrar of Marks and Brands was once again in the competent hands of Cecil Hagen. Ralph Reid was Tally Man, a job that he has held since that time. Lowell Noll was re-elected Chuck Wrangler. By December 1956, our Registrar of Marks and Brands, Cecil Hagen had published the first issue of our quarterly, **The Pacific Northwesterner.**

B Y THIS TIME ALL MAJOR ASPECTS of the Society were established and have continued along similar lines since. This account would not be complete without a final note. At a meeting held during Lowell Bradford's term as Sheriff, I was referred to as co-founder of our Corral along with Thomas Teakle. I took my bow with other past officers, happy that at long last, I was receiving some recognition for my work. Teakle looked balefully at me all during the remainder of the evening.

The following morning, he came into our shop, and I knew that finally we would reach an understanding. He asked me how Bradford had gotten the background information. I answered, "It is perfectly obvious! You didn't give it to him, did you? And there were only two of us at the beginning."

He replied, "That's right! I had forgotten all about those talks we had and how it all started."

I was amazed at his statement. Perhaps he had a mental block in this regard, due to his desire to be recognized as an authority on Western history. Who knows? At any rate, he was more charitable in giving me credit for our teamwork after that. He even reminisced about it with my wife and me. She reminded him of the work she did, too. I'm glad our misunderstanding was resolved gracefully, because I admired Mr. Teakle and his high degree of scholarship.

He was the first high school teacher in the Spokane school system to teach a course in Northwest history. A native of Iowa, he was the author of a book **The Spirit Lake Massacre,** relating the events surrounding the Sioux Indian outbreak of 1862.

Those of us who were fortunate enough to be charter members can look back on many years of accomplishment and many excellent papers given by our members. These papers and our publication are among the best in the International Westerners. I'm sure that the other charter members join me in urging Corral members to continue our tradition of high quality recording of Western history. ☐

The PACIFIC NORTHWESTERNER

SPOKANE CORRAL

Vol. 30   No. 3   1986

Milroy and the Council At Kettle Falls

by JEROME PELTIER

TREATIES THAT THE FEDERAL GOVERNMENT MADE with Indian tribes have often been tarnished by broken promises, and the one made with the Colvilles and allied tribes is no exception. The treaties, ratified in good faith in the Nation's capitol, were administered locally by Indian Agents who, exposed to local pressures, frequently altered the original intent to the disadvantage of the Indians. When this happened to the Colvilles and allied tribes, the government sent General R. H. Milroy, Superintendent of Indian Affairs for Washington Territory, on a fact finding mission in 1873 to determine what had gone wrong with a previously satisfactory agreement. On this journey he was accompanied by his fourteen year old son, Robert Bruce Milroy.

As a collector of historical documents, I had the good fortune to discover an account of Bruce Milroy's recollections of this trip. The manuscript, written as part of his memoirs, is in pencil and is smudged and nearly illegible in places, but I have attempted to reproduce the text faithfully, including the errors in spelling and grammar. Although the trip was serious business for the General, for the boy it was a grand adventure.

Robert Bruce Milroy was born in Rensselaer, Indiana, on September 23, 1859. He was the son of General Robert Huston Milroy, who served in the Civil War as a Major General in the Armies of the Potomac and Tennessee, and is known as the hero of the Battle of Winchester, Virginia.

I

THE TRIP TO KETTLE FALLS

OUR PARTY LEFT PORTLAND, Oregon, in the early part of July, 1873, on a steamboat for the upper Columbia River. The party consisted of the General, who was ordered by the government to locate the site for the Agency of the Colville Reservation. With him was the Agent for the Reservation and

---

Jerome Peltier is a human encyclopedia of knowledge of Northwest History. He carries the information in his head or is able to find it in his extensive library of original manuscripts and books. He has written numerous articles and six books on Northwest History and has presented twenty-six papers to the Spokane Corral over the past thirty-one years.

Volume 30   No. 3   1986

Published quarterly by the Spokane Corral of The Westerners, P.O. Box 1717, Spokane, WA 99210. Subscription $5.00 per calendar year. Back issues available, $1.25 ea. Articles appearing in this journal are abstracted and indexed in HISTORICAL ABSTRACTS: and/or AMERICA HISTORY AND LIFE.   ISSN: 0030 - 882 X

OFFICERS

Sheriff . . . . Lewis Sabo

Chief Deputy . . . . Seabury Blair

Program Deputy . . . . Douglas Olson

Photographic Deputy . . . . John Ellingson

Membership Deputy . . . . . . William Kelly

Roundup Foreman . . . . . . Robert Brown

Chuck Wrangler . . . . Joe Daniels

Tallyman . . . . William Papesh

Registrar of Marks and
    Brands . . . . Norman Bolker

Publications Committee
        Jerome Peltier, Seabury Blair,
        Randall Johnson

Honcho for Journal
    Distribution . . . . Frank Knox

myself, acting as messengers for the General. A young Jew, whose uncle was the trader on the reservation, started with us.

The steamers on the upper Columbia run in those days were woodburners and were not the fastest boats on the river. So the trip was monotonous and only broken by the portage at the Cascades and embarking on another boat which took us to The Dalles. Another portage from The Dalles to Celilo, and another steamboat took us to Wallula. Here we took a stage for Walla Walla. The weather was hot and the dust so bad, the 40 mile trip to Walla Walla was very disagreeable.

While outfitting in Walla Walla for the overland trip, news of the Portland fire was received so the young Jew hurried back to Portland.

The General, learning that an old military friend of Civil War days, and who was now a Congressman and Chairman of the Committee on Indian Affairs of the House of Representatives, was at Lewiston, Idaho, took the stage from Walla Walla to Lewiston intending to get the Congressman to accompany us to Collville. They were to come down the Snake River on the steamer from Lewiston and would meet us at the point that the military road crosses the Snake river.

WE LEFT WALLA WALLA with two light hacks loaded with provisions and camping equipage for the trip. The first night out we camped on the Touchet at a ranch and placed our horses in the barn, leaving the wagons in the corral. As the ranch house was small there was not sufficient room for all of our part to sleep in it, so I concluded I would sleep out. I spread my blankets in one of the hacks with my head to the back end. At supper we had been told that a big cougar had been killed down on the creek close to the corral and they were expecting that its mate would be around. I had just come out from the East and had never seen a live cougar, but to my young imagination they were just as ferocious and blood-thirsty as the worst of maneating lions and tigers. I got into bed feeling that in the hack I would be safe from attack from cougars or other wild beasts.

Sometime during the middle of the night, I was awakened by a warm, wet substance passing across my face and I felt the hot breath of an animal on my face. In my sudden awakening I had no doubt whatever but that it was a cougar licking my face and preparing to make a meal and I was to be the meal. But on attempting to further renew its familiarity and assurance by continuing its carressing and licking my face, in my desperation I struck out with my fist and yelled as loud as my young lungs would allow. I struck the animal on the nose and my hair gave a further stiffening as I heard a jump and a bawl, but I immediately discovered that it was a young steer that was trying to carress me instead of a cougar.

We got to Snake River crossing the next day and it was here that I had my first experience with "fools gold." I saw so many of the apparent gold particles in one place in the water that I thought I could get enough with my hands to make it worth while. After a thorough test of these particles with a knife and by mashing on rocks I became convinced that "everything is not gold that glitters."

WHEN THE STEAMER CAME DOWN THE RIVER the next morning, she swung into shore and the General, the Congressman and his son Jim, a boy of about my own age, got off.

We loaded up and were ferryed across the river and started on our road again. We went by Palouse Falls and had a good view of them.

That night we camped at a place called "Camp Louginville", where we expected to find plenty of water, but found that the springs and stream had gone dry. The ground was wet and marshy in places but we could find no water. The mosquitoes however were in evidence and insisted upon our acquaintance. I never saw mosquitoes worse that they were there, any place outside of Alaska. Suffering for water and annoyed by mosquitoes the night was one long horrid torment. The Congressman swore and fought mosquitoes all night and by morning his tongue was so swollen for want of water that he could not talk. We got out at first break of day and had to travel until 10 o'clock A.M. before we came to "Big Lake" (Sprague Lake?) and got water. The immagination does more to cause the misery and suffering under such circumstances than actual need of water. The Congressman's tongue was swollen so much that he could not shut his mouth. All of the party suffered greatly from thirst, but those who were most loud and constant in fretting and complaining, were worst off.

ON COMING OVER A RISE and seeing the lake we were all greatly relieved and when I saw a short cut to the lake I jumped from the wagon and ran toward it. On getting down to the shore I came into a trail and ran along it a short distance—when I saw it ended at a spring. I threw myself down flat at the edge of the spring and drank all the water I could swallow, then raised up to get my breath. Looking into the spring, I saw it was full of "wiggle tails", but feeling that I had to have more water, I shut my teeth and strained the water through them, until I got enough. In fact, I got too much for between the overload of water and the thought of the wigglers, I had swallowed, I turned side and threw up all the water and wigglers I had loaded up with.

Our road took up across the Spokane river some distance below where the Falls are and where the present city of Spokane now is, but we went up to see the Falls and saw the salmon trying to jump up the Falls and the Indians spearing them.

Kettle Falls when the Columbia was a free-flowing river.

. . . The Congressman's son and I became great chums before we arrived at Fort Colville. We hunted and fished together and got into the usual amount of boyish devilment and trouble, as long as we remained together.

When we arrived at Fort Colville, we found it a small frontier post, intended to have one full company of soldiers stationed there. But it was such a lonesome out of the way place that the soldiers deserted so fast that there were but sixteen privates left and half of them were in the guard house for trying to desert. At guard mount a drummer and fifer and four soldiers turned out and on dress parade on Sunday morning seven privates turned out in line.

ON THE COLUMBIA RIVER some fourteen miles from Fort Colville is the old Hudson Bay Trading Post, (known as Colvile) where the Boundary Commission wintered while making the survey of the international boundary between Canada and the United States. There was a trading post there and the old Hudson Bay factor (Angus McDonald) lived a mile or so from the post in a large log house. This was just above Kettle Falls on the Columbia.

A Council was called of all the Indians that belonged to the Colville Reservation and runners were sent out to notify all the tribes and sub-tribes and bands to be present on the day appointed. It required some time to get word to the Indians scattered over the reservation as it covered all the northeastern part of the territory of Washington. While waiting for the Council, Jim and I ammused ourselves with hunting and fishing and riding around the country on horseback. One day the Congressman, Jim and I went down to see the Kettle Falls. It was a grand sight to see the great Columbia making two big leaps downward, the lower one being the greatest. The salmon run was on and the Indians were lined along the rocky shore spearing them. The salmon would try to leap the falls. They would make surprising jumps and if they struck the falling water before they commenced to fall back, they could generally get up over the falls. Immense numbers were successful in thus running the Falls, but far more wore their lives out in futile attemps to surmount them.

48

The water around the foot of the Falls was a mass of seething salmon constantly jumping at the Falls. Quite a way out in the river, close to the Falls was a rock just large enough for a man to stand on. The Indians would paddle out in a canoe to this rock and one Indian would get on it and spear salmon there.

WHILE WE WERE AT THE FALLS an Indian was standing on the rock facing the Falls with spear raised ready for instant throwing, when a large salmon jumped from the water behind him and struck the Indian in the back of the neck, knocking him off the rock into the raging river. The Indian must have been so surprised and scared that it caused him to give a terrified yell as he went plunging into the water. A canoe put out from shore and caught him.

Having come lately from the East, I had the natural feeling that Easterners generally have regarding the Indians of the West, i.e. I thought they preferred my scalp to anything else about me, and would willingly take it if opportunity offered. While walking alone one day from McDonald's, the old Hudson Bay factor's, to the trading post, I had to pass through some timber where the underbrush grew quite close up to the trail. I noticed quite a number of Indians gathering for the Council, camped in the timber, but saw nothing at all to arouse my suspicions in the least. I saw some squaws digging roots around and passed one who was quite close to the trail. I had just passed her when my moccasined foot was grabbed firmly in such a way as to throw me flat on the ground. My first thought was that I was going to get a knife into my heart. I turned as quickly as I could and saw the squaw I had just passed; she was holding my foot firmly in the air and was measuring the length of my foot with the first two joints of her middle finger. As I did not see any knife, I let her finish measuring, then she let go of my foot and turned around without a word and went to work digging roots. I tried to get her to explain what she meant, but she would not say a word. Nearly two months later I received through the Post Trader, one of the finest pair of moccasins I ever saw. They were made of fine, half smoked fawn skin, beautifully decorated with colored silk thread work.

There were over 3000 Indians present at the Council; it was held in front of McDonald's big log house. Poles were planted in the ground and cross pieces strung along these and then covered with green branches.

(The manuscript ends at this point.)

II

THE REPORT TO THE COMMISSIONER

THE REASON FOR GENERAL MILROY'S visit to the Kettle Falls area may be found on pages 294 through 297 in his report for the year 1873 to the Commissioner of Indian Affairs. The report, "The Colville Reservation," reminded the Commissioner of the original scope of the reservation proper, which included the Colville Valley and "lands east of the Cascades" that had been set apart by Executive Order of the President on April 9, 1872. The allied tribes, consisting of the Columbia tribe of Chief Moses, the Kettles, the Colvilles, the Okanogans, Kalispels, Spokanes and San Poils, accepted the designated territory. The tribes, having the Salish language in common, were willing to live together on their ancestral land.

The problem was that the terms of the agreement had been changed by the Executive Order of July 6, 1872, through the chicanery of some unscrupulous land hungry white settlers,

49

a compliant Indian agent, W. P. Winans, and a Federal government that unwittingly ratified the change. This order placed the reservation to the west and north of the Columbia River, east of the Chenagan (Okanagan) River, bounded on the north by British Columbia. The order would have moved the allied tribes from a fertile valley to cold dry highlands that white settlers had abandoned because they were unsuitable for croplands. It would also have displaced the tribes from the salmon-rich Spokane and Columbia Rivers and deprived them of the right to fish there. These changes, made without their knowledge, were now the law.

AS A RESULT OF THIS LEGAL ENTANGLEMENT, Milroy had been ordered to talk with the tribal members involved, to soothe their feelings and to locate a reservation that would please most of the injured parties. For this important meeting, he enlisted the services of John P. C. Shanks, a special Commissioner (who had been sent with T. W. Bennet and H. W. Reed) to meet, confer with, and finally place on reservations, Indians in several parts of the West. Milroy and Shanks spent three days, from the 7th to the 11th of August, traveling over and evaluating as much of the new reservation as possible in that short length of time. The next two days the two men met the non-treaty tribesmen in Council.

On August 13, Shanks returned to Idaho to conduct further business with his two companion commissioners, Bennet and Reed. As a result of the previous talks, John Shanks compiled a list of twenty-two facts concerning the tribesmen involved in the projected reservation. Several of these items were complaints made by the natives against white people who wanted the land in the first suggested reservation. There was wholesale condemnation of W. P. Winans, who had been the agent prior to the current one, John A. Simms. It was reported that Winans not only had helped settlers change the boundaries of the reservation to the west of the Columbia River, but that he had sold Indian property in his trading store in Colville, and also paid his personal bills with Indian goods.

The Indians claimed that Winans permitted some immoral Indian women to conduct a house of ill repute in Colville, which Agent Simms closed as soon as he became aware of it.

The twenty-two items that Shanks listed may be found on pages 161 through 163 in the "Report of the Commissioner of Indian Affairs" for 1873. They are contained in a letter from Colville, Stevens County, Washington (Territory) dated August 14, 1873, which Shanks wrote to his Co-commissioners, T. W. Bennet and H. W. Reed.

General R. H. Milroy, Civil War hero and Superintendent of Indian Affairs for Washington Territory in 1873.

MEANWHILE, THE GENERAL AND HIS SON rode over the reservation to evaluate its potential. Except for three days, he and Bruce were in the saddle from August 20 to September 11. During those three days, the General met with members of the allied tribes at the Council at Fort Colville, that Bruce referred to in his memoirs. Following the

50

Council, General Milroy asked that a new Executive Order be issued defining the boundary lines of a territory that appeared to be agreeable to the Indian tribes.

"Beginning the middle channel of the Columbia River, two miles below the mouth of the Okanogan River; thence up the middle channel of the Columbia River to the mouth of the Big Spokane River; thence up to the south bank of the Spokane to a point where the northerly line of the lands granted to the Northern Pacific Railroad intersects the same; thence northeasterly with the line bounding said grant to a point where it intersects the boundary line between the Territories of Washington and Idaho, thence north on said boundary-line to where the same intersects the boundary-line between the United States and British Columbia; thence west on said last named boundary-line to a point two miles west of Sooyoos (Osoyoos) Lake; thence southerly with the course of the Okanogan River, but two miles therefrom; to the point of beginning."

MILROY PLACED THE LINE OF THE BOUNDARY two miles west of the Okanogan River, because he knew that the valley of the Okanogan was the ancestral home grounds of the Okanogan Indians.

At approximately the same time, Commissioners Shanks and Bennet and Agent for the Nez Perce J. B. Montieth entered into an agreement with the Coeur d'Alene Indians for their reservation. After hearing of Milroy's proposal but without his knowledge, the three recommended cancelling their just completed agreement in favor of including the Coeur d'Alene and Pend Oreille tribes in the reservation that Milroy had proposed for the seven tribes. They did not consult any of the Indians involved. Shanks' explanatory letter to the Commissioner of Indian Affairs at Salt Lake City, dated November 17, 1873, follows:

"Under the instructions to the Commission to visit the Indians in Idaho, Shanks and Bennet, in company with J. B. Montieth, agent (Nez Perce Agency), met in Council the Coeur d'Alenes at Hangman or Lotah (sic) Creek, on the 29th day of July 1873, and entered into a written agreement with the Coeur d'Alenes for a reservation, conditioned that it should be approved by Congress. This agreement is in the hands of J. B. Montieth, and perhaps has been reported to you. The Commission did not desire to go beyond its authority in this matter, and only joined Mr. Montieth as there seemed to be a necessity for it at the time. But the Commission, after an investigation of the whole subject now recommends that the agreement entered into with the Coeur d'Alenes be not confirmed, but that the reservation recommended by the Commission for the nine tribes, including the Coeur d'Alenes, be adopted. All of which is most respectfully submitted. (Signed John P. C. Shanks, T. W. Bennet, Henry W. Reed.)"

When the Coeur d'Alene chieftains learned about the change, it must have made them angry as well as disillusioned, because the reservation that lay within their ancestral lands had been taken away from them, seemingly at the whim of the Commission.

THE PROBLEM WAS FINALLY RESOLVED more or less to the satisfaction of the White settlers, and was accepted by the Indians. The Coeur d'Alenes now have a small reservation on their traditional land in north Idaho. The Pend Oreilles have their own reservation in northeastern Washington State; the allied tribes have theirs north of the confluence of the Columbia and Spokane Rivers. Their reservation is less than half that proposed by Milroy, but it lies within the southern portion of the region he had recommended.

Commissioner Shanks thought that Agent Winans abused his position, although Winans, in an unpublished manuscript entitled "Steven County Washington," disputes that. This document is remarkable for Winans' acknowledgment of the tragedy in which he played a part.

III

AGENT WINAN'S STATEMENT

WAS APPOINTED JANUARY 1ST, 1870 Special Indian Agent for non-treaty Indians in Eastern Washington by Colonel Samuel Ross, Superintendent of Indian Affairs . . . Serving . . . until the Colville Reservation was set apart and John A. Simms was appointed Agent by the President, who requested me to continue under him, which I declined to do, having decided to move to Walla Walla. During the time I was Indian Agent, I superintended the taking of the census in 1870 of the non-treaty Indians in Eastern Washington, and from that and subsequent reports, the reservations for the Colvilles, Lakes, San Poells, Spokane, Okanogans and Coeur d'Alenes were set apart. I was instructed by Col. Samuel Ross, Superintendent in November, 1870 to find Kamiakan, the ex-chief of the Yakimas, and endeavor to have him accept 20 bales or 600 blankets, his due under the treaty made in 1855 by General I. J. Stevens. Having received the blankets and learning his location, I went with my interpreter to Rock Lake where Kamiakan with his immediate family then lived. I found his camp in the morning just after he had had his bath. I was invited in his lodge, and there stated the wishes of the United States Government to make good its promises and live up to the treaty as made by Gen. Stevens and as an evidence of it I had at his door a four horse load of blankets that I wished to deliver to him. He listened silently to all I had to say, and when he saw I had completed my statement he arose, standing erect, with his left arm extended, pointed with his right hand to the ragged sleeve of his grey woolen shirt, said: "See, I am a poor man, but too rich to receive anything from the United States." No persuasion on my part to influence him to change his mind had any effect. Kamiakan felt and believed that he had been deceived and wronged by the United States, deserted by his own people, and wished no favors from either. About two years after this the settlers crowded around his camp and although he had resided at Rock Lake for years, the filings on the land by the white man finally deprived him even of a camping place, on land the home of his father. He believing himself wronged by the United States, deserted by his people, robbed of his home by the settlers, died a few years afterward on the Palouse River, a broken hearted man.

The blankets that were intended for him were hauled to Colville, and during the following winter were distributed to the destitute Indians by order of the Superintendent of Indian Affairs.

I closed out my business in Colville in 1873, moving to Walla Walla in the spring of 1874, where I have since resided.

IN ALL OF THIS STATEMENT, there is no mention of the problems that were brought forth in the report by Shanks, nor any acceptance of responsibility.

Young Robert Bruce Milroy went on to attend the Territorial University of Washington at Seattle and took more work at Hanover College in Indiana. Later, he went to the University of Michigan at Ann Arbor, where he earned his law degree.

In 1885, he and his brother W. J. Milroy began the first law firm in Yakima, Washington. In 1892 he was Assistant Attorney General for Washington State. He later was Superior Court Commissioner from 1918 until his death January 9, 1940. He was given many honors, both when he was alive and posthumously. □

Seth Woodard,
Spokane Valley Pioneer

by JEROME PELTIER

SETH WOODARD WAS A PIONEER who deeply influenced the development of the Spokane Valley. He helped establish public schools there and assisted in its commercial development. Because we were friends, he granted me interviews in which he told me of the part he played in the history of the area.

He was born in Pottowatamie County, Kansas, where his father had been a carpenter, surveyor and farmer. After several years of crop failures, his family joined the westward migration in search of better opportunities when Seth was nine years old. On April 9, 1882, the Woodards loaded their family of eight children and their household items into two covered wagons, joined a caravan of several other wagons and headed for Oregon.

Woodard related his memories of the trip West:

> As far as (we) the youngsters were concerned, the trip from Topeka, Kansas, was a lark, but I can see now it was serious business for the old folks. We started in April and got to Spokane in October. The Oregon Trail was only about three miles from my Dad's homestead (in Kansas). We would often walk up the hill when I was a kid, and see many wagons traveling on that trail that folks told us was the Oregon Trail, so we children got the idea that everything west of Kansas was Oregon. We got interested in those wagons but didn't ever think that we'd get to travel in one, but we traveled with the others on the road to Oregon. Some place along the road, I believe that it was near Salt Lake, my mother developed a bad case of sore eyes. The sand was putting her eyes out. We stopped there to get medical care, and the doctor told Dad that if he went on in the wagons with my mother, she would go blind. So they compromised by leading my mother and some children onto a train. We went to San Francisco by train, took a steamboat up to Portland and on up the Columbia by steamboat by transporting around rapids until we got to old Fort Wallula and were met there by a stage of some kind which took us to a little place near Walla Walla.

WOODARD'S "FORT WALLULA" was actually the original Fort Walla Walla. Fur traders of the North West Company had built a post in 1818 on the Columbia River where it joined the Walla Walla and named it Fort Nez Perce. It

JEROME PELTIER, a frequent contributor to this journal, has been called "a living legend" by Westerners International, the parent organization of this chapter, for his accomplishments in gathering historical material. He has acquired numerous diaries and original manuscripts of early settlers and a significant collection of oral histories of local pioneers. Jerry has published eight books of Northwest history, his latest concerning the life of Moses "Black" Harris, a Northwest fur trader.

was a wooden structure. When the Hudson's Bay Company took over, it was renamed Fort Walla Walla. This structure was burned to the ground by Indians during the 1850's, and replaced by an adobe structure. This adobe fort should not be confused with the later military establishment which bore the same name. After it was abandoned as a fur trade post, the adobe walls stood for many years. A railroad community named Wallula, was built on the same site. Two moves later, the town still serves the area as a railroad station.

Woodard continued:

We waited there for the wagons. Most of the wagons we traveled with went down the Columbia River, but Dad with one or two other wagons went North. We landed in the Spokane country in the fall of 1882. That first winter, one of my mother's brothers had taken a homestead below Farmington, right on the Idaho line, and he persuaded my father to take his family down there and live with him through the winter. We came back the following spring.

Dad went to look the country over, and as he looked over this valley and saw such wonderful bunch grass on it, he imagined that this was the place to stay, so he settled here. Raising cattle had been his hobby in the east. He had raised thoroughbred Durham cattle of the beef type and Percheron horses. He thought the grass would be a good place for (grazing) stock so he bought 170 acres of land from the Great Northern Railroad, right here where Millwood is at five dollars an acre. The plot extended from present Argonne Road west to Park Road and north to Buckeye. We kept stock there but (usually) moved to Spokane in the winter so us kids could go to school, since there weren't any other schools out here.

SETH TOLD ME that "Many times I walked three miles to school and back since the only school at one time was at Edgecliff."

Vacations were spent working, as may be deduced from Seth's comments: "Father was a stock raiser so I spent most of my vacations in the saddle looking after my father's stock. I rode the range from the Spokane to the Snake River in search of strays. The open range in those days covered from the Canadian border to the Snake River. When we moved out here in the Valley in 1883, there wasn't a fence in sight. Cattle and horses used to wander to the southwest, following the line of least resistance. We used to carry a six shooter in case we ran into rustlers, and we ran into them alright, but I never got into a shooting scrape. On the long rides we used to carry two blankets, a slab of bacon and some coffee, depending on our rifles to bring down game."

Seth recalled that when his family came to this area, it took the better part of a day to go to Spokane for supplies. He said, "The first general store was opened in 1890, about where Edgecliff Road joins Sprague Avenue."

When the Woodards first arrived, their land was in the Trent School District. "The land across Argonne Road was in the Carnhope District. There was a spirited rivalry between the two districts to get pupils to attend their respective schools because there were so few children of school age in the area. My Dad's land was in the Carnhope District and my oldest brother had taken up a homestead in the Glenrose District. We lived there (in Glenrose) to take advantage of that school. Dad got a permanent home built on his land and we lived there and walked to school, so I started to get interested in schools before I was grown up.''

When Seth was twenty, he and some other people circulated petitions in the early 1890's to start another school closer to what subsequently became Millwood, but they did not obtain enough signatures to get a hearing.

Several more attempts were made prior to 1900, but all were unsuccessful. Meanwhile romance came into Seth's life and he married Cordelia Larson, formerly of Michigan, on January 31, 1897. Their first child, Viola, was born in October 1899. This responsibility made Seth realize more fully the importance of having a school close by, as he put it, "I pitched in and headed the petition to show them that we really needed a school up here. Finally we got a hearing before the County Superintendent of Schools and he allowed (us to start) the District.''

THE BATTLE WAS NOT YET WON, because people living near Alcott School objected so strenuously to the Superintendent's ruling, that they were allowed to have a hearing on the subject. The County Commission listened carefully to all of the witnesses, considered the testimony and then sustained the Superintendent's ruling. Seth and his group of concerned parents were allowed to organize a school district, and soon they had named a School Board and had built a schoolhouse in time for the September term.

Photo by Frank Palmer from the Jerome Peltier Collection.
Courtesy of the Eastern Washington State Historical Society

Stacking sheafs of wheat in the Spokane Valley, about 1910.

Seth said:

> I took a school census at that time, and in that first district there were only thirty-four (children) between the ages of five and twenty-one. When school opened, they averaged eighteen pupils a day for the term, and a teacher was hired for a three month term only. In all that territory, there are now several thousand. By 1904, we had outgrown the one room schoolhouse and so we built a four room schoolhouse which still stands on the corner of Park and Mission. (This is now a Grange Hall.) Two years after that we built another school at Parkwater which is still standing (in 1954). Another was built in Dishman two years later, and the following two years after that, I built another grade school in Millwood. About that time Pasadena Park had joined our district by petition and we built a grade school across the river in Pasadena Park and then an annex was built on the school in Millwood for high school purposes and about that time I resigned from the Board and refused to run any longer.

J. Howard Stegner, Seth's friend of long standing, noted that Seth was Clerk of the Board when Orchard Park School was organized in 1900. He also gave the dimensions of the building (24 by 40 feet) which was erected at a cost of $600. Howard added that Seth served on the Board for eighteen years before retiring. It is obvious that Seth Woodard was intensely interested in the education of youngsters in Spokane Valley.

DURING MY INTERVIEWS WITH SETH, his comments veered to the religious aspects of life during the pioneer days. Seth told of the difficulties overcome by priests and ministers in bringing religion closer to home.

> I don't know of any organized church in the valley when we came here. There were traveling ministers who would hold meetings any place they could get a chance. My father's house was always open to any minister of any denomination or faith coming through who was willing to talk on the spiritual side of the affair. I remember old Father Cataldo, Father Jacques and others in the Catholic ministry going through, would stop at our house or some other house and hold a meeting. All of the neighborhood would come to that meeting.

> Some Methodist ministers might come through and if they could get a suitable place, they might hold meetings every night for a couple of weeks. After we got schoolhouses, they were used for churches. Not only were there church services, but soon we commenced to organize Sunday Schools, which were taken care of in private homes for a long time. When we had room in the schoolhouse, we began to have regular Sunday School services. For instance, the old schoolhouse located on Mission and Park Road was the first Sunday School in this immediate area that was organized. Mr. Warren, who had retired from the ministry of the Southern Methodist Church, came out and organized the Sunday School and I was appointed the first Sunday School Superintendent. A school was started on Orchard Avenue (now Park Road). By that time the Presbyterian Church at Millwood was getting started.

RELIGIOUS MEN DID NOT DISCRIMINATE when giving aid to neighbors who were in trouble. Seth continued reminiscing:

> I remember one time during an extra hard winter, my father's family had a siege of typhoid fever. The snow was so deep that no one could get

to us, hardly, and one day there was a knock on the door. My mother opened
the door and there was a Catholic Father. He said, 'I heard there is a family
here that is sick and in distress.' My mother did not want to deceive him
and she said, 'Yes, we are sick but we are not Catholic and I see by your
garb that you are Catholic and I don't want you to be deceived.' I was in
bed but I remember hearing him say, 'I am not looking for Catholics. Father
Cataldo sent me out here to find someone who was in distress and see what
I could do for them.' He sized things up for awhile and went away and the
next day a whole wagon (load) of provisions came, and folks stopped and
everything that was needed came to us. Ever since then I have had a tender
spot in my heart for Catholics even though I am not a Catholic by profession.
We got on our feet and were able to finance ourselves again. Then my father
went to their church and tried to repay them for their kindness and they
wouldn't take it, saying 'No, just pass it on and do good for somebody else.'

During an interview I had with him in October 31, 1954, Seth told me about
his part in improving transportation in the Valley:

When the Coeur d'Alene-Spokane Railroad Company had an electric
line, which was built after the turn of the century (1903), it was first surveyed
along a route following Mission Street of today, and the people over here
thought it would be better to come further north because there was a lot
of vacant land between here and Dishman and we wanted it over on this
(the north) side of the river. After they got their stakes in, we got together

1910 was a good year for the apple crop.

Corn in the shock, Spokane Valley

with them and I showed them over this country and told them the advantages of this country, of the improvements we expected to make. To make it more attractive to them, Dad and I offered them the donation of a strip of land sixty feet wide through the entire mile and a half of our ranch as their right of way. Then I took the field with a Notary Public to see what we could do the rest of the way up the right of way. When we explained things to somebody and they (the landowner) would agree to let us go through, we'd sign them up immediately, and I engineered the getting of the right of way, and they put a station here called Woodard's Crossing, by which it was known for several years. The dairymen and farmers brought and received goods at the Crossing.''

SETH TOLD A REPORTER for the Spokane Daily Chronicle in March 1949, "We didn't ask or even get as much as a pass on the railroad, but the company built a station at the townsite and called it Woodard Station. In 1909, a steel bridge was built across the Spokane River near Woodard Station connecting the newly organized Pasadena Park Irrigation District with the electric car line. In 1910, after the Inland Paper Company purchased much of the townsite, Woodard Station was renamed Millwood. According to Seth:

When I sold some of my land to the paper mill, they naturally wanted their mill advertised. Someone started to give it the name of Milltown and that didn't set well, and the railroad company wouldn't change the name

58

without Dad's permission because they had named it for us and we gave them the right of way. Mr. Brazeau, the first superintendent of the paper mill, suggested the name of Millwood. 'We'll call it mill to advertise our mill and we'll call it wood after the Woodards.' Dad said it was alright with him if it was alright with me and I didn't care what they called it anyway.

The townsite of Millwood was laid out in 1911 and a water system was installed. A large hotel, some stores and a post office created a commercial center. In 1921, a second bridge was built across the Spokane River at Millwood. It was named the Argonne to honor the soldiers who lost their lives in a battle in France during World War I. Woodard Road then was renamed Argonne Road. The bridge was made of reinforced concrete and was so well constructed that it is still in use in 1987.

Seth's family had grown. Mrs. Woodard bore eleven children during the twenty years from 1899 to 1919. The oldest son died in 1911 when he was only nine years old.

Seth became superintendent of the newly built water system when the south branch of the Corban Canal was constructed. He held this job from 1932 until his retirement in 1959. In 1915, he joined the Spokane County Pioneer Society. As usual, he was a driving force in its projects. He served on the Historical Monument Committee during which time the Society erected several monuments. He was a man of many talents. While attending school in Spokane in 1891, he joined the Salvation Army Band and people could hear him playing his cornet with his fellow musicians on Main or Front Avenue. He was still a member of the band when the Salvation Army held their fiftieth year celebration in 1941.

HOWARD STEGNER, HIMSELF A VALLEY PIONEER, told me a story that illustrates Seth's courage and concern for the public welfare. "My first recollection of Seth was in June of 1894. This was the year of extremely high water in the Spokane River and it soon became apparent that the Trent River bridge was in danger. Seth, a lad of twenty-two, decided that something had to be done about it. When driftwood and logs began to pile up against the truss rods, he had the bridge closed to traffic. The river banks are high here, so from the deck of the bridge to the water was about forty feet. They (some of the men) took up a couple of planks from the deck and a windlass was rigged up . . . Young Seth, with an axe, was lowered down through that hole on the end of a forty foot rope. Sitting in a sling . . . Seth swung and swayed as he chopped away at the key log in the jam against the bridge. When he succeeded in breaking the jam, much pressure was relieved. He soon had a cable fastened to the center of the span and the other anchored over near the Northern Pacific Railroad fill. At that time, the Trent Bridge was the only bridge between Spokane and Spokane Bridge and the Idaho line, a distance of twenty-five miles."

After a lingering illness followed by a stroke in 1958, Seth Woodard died on June 9, 1960. He was eighty-seven years old. He was survived by five sons, five daughters, twenty-six grandchildren and twenty-eight great grandchildren.

He was honored by having a school named after him in September 1953. Howard Stegner presented a photograph of Seth Woodard to the school in February 1960. It was a privilege to have had Seth for a friend. He was a man who did not have to be told where problems lay. He saw them and did what he could to remedy each situation as it arose. He was a do-er! If we had more like him, we would have a better world.

Billy Norman—Frontier Capitalist

by JEROME PELTIER

THE WAY MOST PEOPLE picture an empire builder is far different from the appearance of the short, soft-spoken, dapper gentleman that I once knew named William S. Norman. It is easy to understand why most of his friends called him "Billy," for he was easily approached and generous with his time and ideas. His smile was infectious. He was born in Cheltenham, Gloucestershire, England, January 8, 1858. His father ran a printing and lithographing shop and was also the editor and publisher of two newspapers in Cheltenham. Billy worked for his father before coming to Washington Territory in February 1883.

On arrival, Norman settled on land at Dragoon Creek, north of present day Spokane, while he worked on farms on Moran Prairie. He soon left to embark on a more exciting project. The Canadian Pacific Railroad was completing construction of the western part of its transcontinental line. Tracks were being laid from the first crossing of the upper Columbia River on the east to Revelstoke, B.C., situated at the second crossing on the west, where a bridge had to be built.

H. H. McCARTNEY AND COMPANY held the contract for supplying all of the grain, hay and foodstuffs for the construction gangs and horses. The supplies came mainly from Washington Territory and Oregon, and Joseph and Marcus Oppenheimer, Spokane financiers, had the contract for getting them to Revelstoke. Transporting them presented a formidable problem as there were no roads north of Northport, W.T. The Columbia River ran by Little Dalles, ten miles east of Northport. The Oppenheimers elected to build a warehouse at Little Dalles and a river boat to carry the supplies up the river. They hired Joe Vogel to supervise the job, and Vogel hired Norman as timekeeper. When Vogel learned that Norman could transcribe dictation and write letters, he made him his secretary and raised his salary from twenty-five dollars to sixty dollars a month.

Building a lake steamer in the middle of a wilderness was a difficult task. To get lumber for the boat, a sawmill had to be freighted in and assembled. Norman wrote me in a letter, "All of the lumber employed in the building of the boat except for the ribs, was cut out and dressed at a sawmill plant established for that purpose on Onion Creek a mile and a half above Little Dalles . . ." The ribs had to be brought in from Portland, Oregon.

OBTAINING MARINE ENGINES was even more of a problem. Bringing new engines to the building site would have meant shipping them from the East Coast via Cape Horn to Portland, then up the Columbia to Wallula, with several

JEROME PELTIER, historian, author and frequent contributor to the Pacific Northwesterner, obtained much of the material for this paper from interviews and correspondence with Norman. The last interview with this pioneer industrialist occurred in 1950, four years before his death. Through his far-sightedness, Peltier has preserved a valuable first person account of regional history.

portages en route. The time and expense would have been excessive. Two years earlier, a lake steamer, *The Katie Hallet,* had sunk in Lake Pend Oreille. The Northern Pacific Railway had used *The Katie Hallet* to ferry trains across the lake before the railroad bridge had been built at Sandpoint. To save time and money, the contractor decided to salvage *The Katie Hallet's* engines. With great effort, the boat was raised and the engines removed. Then a road had to be cut through virgin forest to deliver them to the building site.

Norman's letter recounted:

> Work was begun on the steamer, *Kootenai,* February 19, 1885 . . . Joe Vogel, a German, one of the roughest, toughest bosses ever, was placed in charge of construction and had the sawmill as well as the boat finished in the incredibly fast time of three months. He was a great driver and organizer of men.

> Our *Kootenai* boat was 150 feet long, equipped with powerful double engines, Corliss, the engines driving in parallel to the stern wheel . . . We hauled the engines from the Sandpoint location on the Washington side of the Pend Oreille Lake or River, about two hundred miles to Little Dalles with a string of fourteen oxen—huge beasts better than fifteen hundred pounds . . .

After the oxen had completed their labors, they were slaughtered to feed the workmen.

THE KOOTENAI WAS COMMISSIONED in late April 1885 and Billy Norman became the purser. Captain Pingstone, an old Hudson's Bay man, assumed command. Earlier he had been captain of *The Fortyniner,* the first boat to ply the upper Columbia River, beginning in 1865.

Norman wrote:

> . . . I made twenty-six trips up and down the river between May first and the end of October, (1888) carrying all the supplies needed for crews building the railroad bridge at Revelstoke and building the grade . . . to meet the incoming rail heads from both East and West. This operation and the tonnage handled by the boat enabled the Canadian Pacific Railroad to complete the connection of the transcontinental road in 1888, or a year earlier than would otherwise have been possible.

> During that year, the steamer carried fifteen hundred steers, fifteen hundred tons of hay and a great quantity and variety of foodstuffs. Burns and Cranston got cattle from Judge Haines in the Okanagan (B.C.) country and drove them up the Dewdney Trail to the loading corrals, where we got them. (Burns and Cranston were cattle buyers for the Canadian Pacific, and Judge Haines was the owner of the largest cattle spread in British Columbia. The trail was named after Edgar Dewdney, a civil engineer who built a road that went from Hope, B.C. to Rock Creek and from there to Salmo and Fort Steele, to accommodate the flood of miners following the gold strikes in that area.)

> One time after we had taken on a load of 150 sheep and five hundred pounds of powder, we struck a rock in the river and lodged there. In spite of our most vigorous efforts, we could not dislodge it, so we decided to try

to raise the boat by freeing the sheep, thus lightening the load. The sheep were turned loose and thereafter gave a great deal of enjoyment to the men on board the boat who used them as targets during the tedious days that followed, for we were stuck in the center of the river for a week until a jack arrived from Portland.

Our ride through the Little Dalles when the job was done in the fall of the year (1885) was indeed a memorable recollection. The boat went down stern first, without mishap but at great speed and was duly tied up and placed under the guardianship of Marcus Oppenheimer who ran the store at the Marcus river crossing (of the Columbia). When (Daniel Chase) Corbin (the Spokane entrepreneur) started expanding the S and P (Spokane, Portland and Seattle Railroad) to Nelson, B.C., he bought the boat, and it was used for transportation on the river from Little Dalles to the Kootenai (river) junction, including Trail, B.C.

As mining developed in the Nelson area, the river boat became an indispensable part of local commerce.

WITH THE END OF THE SHIPPING SEASON, Billy Norman returned to Spokane and became a stenographer at the Spokane County Court House, then at the county seat in Cheney. He had learned stenography as a reporter while working on his father's newspapers in Cheltenham. Spokane was about to enter a period of rapid economic expansion fueled by numerous discoveries of mineral wealth nearby and the coming of the Northern Pacific Railway. Sagebrush covered land was being developed into farms and a rapidly growing Spokane became the trade center for the region. It was at this time that Billy was presented with a number of opportunities that led to his meteoric rise in the world of business.

Early in 1886, Norman formed a real estate partnership with A. A. Newberry who represented the interest of the Northern Pacific Railway. Norman suddenly found himself in the company of the movers and shakers of Spokane. He noted that "A. A. Newberry had much to do with fashioning the railroad situation in the Inland Empire (a region comprised of eastern Washington, northern Idaho and Montana west of the Rockies). He was a great friend of Corbin and it was through his (Newberry's) efforts that the Spokane and Northern railroad was built by Corbin." Norman became assistant secretary to Newberry, A. M. Cannon and Paul F. Moore, all pioneer bankers, during the organization of the Spokane and Northern.

BILLY LEARNED LESSONS in high finance from these men and had ideas of his own that he wanted to explore. Charles Hopkins, owner of a newspaper and a telephone company in Colfax, Washington, gave Billy his first big break. For undisclosed reasons, Hopkins offered to sell the telephone company to Norman. The offer was a surprise, but Norman seized the opportunity. His letter to me of May 10, 1949, says, "My memory is pretty clear still as to the happenings of those early days, especially the successful start of the W. S. Norman Telephone System and its ramifications of long distance lines throughout the Inland Empire. The original investment as a starter was $565 which was given to Charles B. Hopkins to release the equipment—a switchboard for fifty lines, thirty telephone boxes under rental lease from the Bell Company and sundry diverse equipment required in the installation. In selling this equipment, Charlie Hopkins threw in part of the system from Spokane County through to the Montana line via the Wallace and Kellogg (Idaho) area."

Courtesy of Jerome Peltier

Telephone and telegraph offices in Spokane shortly after the fire of 1889. Presumably the wire and cable piled in front of the spectators was used to replace the burnt lines. The telephone company is believed to be part of the W. S. Norman Telephone System.

Norman could not provide the entire cost of the system himself, but brought in his friends who made up the difference. His partners were S. Z. Mitchell who later became one of the executives of the General Electric Industry of America, now known as the General Electric Company, Burt Nichols, who later built the Nichols Block on Riverside Avenue in downtown Spokane, and Lieutenent Fred Spalding. Mitchell and Spalding were both engineers with the Edison Electric Illuminating Company, one of the early electric utility companies in Spokane. Eventually S. Z. Mitchell became president of the Electric Bond and Share Company, a large electric utility holding company.

A S SOON AS THE TELEPHONE EQUIPMENT reached Spokane Falls, it was placed in the front room of the Norman and Newberry real estate office in the Hyde Building. When the company began business, it had thirty-five telephones available and only fourteen subscribers. Billy was not dismayed. During the next few months, he bought out his partners.

N. W. Durham, Spokane historian, states that Norman influenced the U.S. War Department to condemn its telegraph line between Coeur d'Alene City and Fort Sherman to Spokane.

During an interview I had with Norman, he gave me a different version:

I paid twenty-five dollars for the telephone line from Spokane to Fort Sherman. This line ran from Walla Walla to Missoula, following the old Mullan Road. It was government owned and operated at this time. Towns through which they (the lines) ran were the eventual owners of the lines, with the stipulation that the lines be maintained in good order.

The lines had been down three days when I went to Coeur d'Alene to see Colonel Carlin . . . We were introduced and I said, "Colonel, I would like to buy the telephone line." He said he'd write and ask permission to sell. He got permission (to do so) and advertised it in the newspaper as required, and I eventually bought it, after signing an agreement to the effect that I would keep it in good running condition.

Apparently Norman misspoke himself in describing the telegraph line as a telephone line, as he later changed this statement.

Norman related in a letter:

A Montana syndicate, headed by D. C. Corbin had secured a contract to move 50,000 tons or more of ore from the recently discovered Bunker Hill mine. The tonnage was handled across Lake Coeur d'Alene in lake boats and then transported over a spur track from Fort Sherman to Hauser Junction (Idaho) to East Helena (Montana) for smelting. Afterward, as other mines were developed, the Corbin road gridironed the Coeur d'Alenes as far as Burke and Mullan on the east. At that time and before the Corbin road was built, I had purchased the U.S. Military telegraph line, from Coeur d'Alene City through the Fourth of July Canyon to Cataldo Mission and thence to the Montana Line. In 1886, it was repaired and equipped with telephones. The lines were extended as Corbin extended his rail lines. My telephone company gave free use of service on all of its lines in exchange for right-of-way and the transportation rights for a rail velocipede for repair purposes.

AFTER COMPLETION OF THE FIRST NATIONAL BANK BUILDING in 1887, on the corner of Riverside and Howard Streets, Billy rented the third floor and basement for the telephone office. By this time 250 subscribers were using the company, and connections had been made with telephone exchanges in Wardner, Murray, Mullan and Burke, Idaho, in the Coeur d'Alene mining district. This was only eleven years after Alexander Graham Bell had invented the telephone.

In 1884, the Edison Electric Illuminating Company had built a hydro-electric power station on the site of the present Upper Falls plant of the Washington Water Power Company. Billy Norman bought stock in the company in 1887 and became active in its management. At the time he joined the company, the power plant was small and the water supply uneven in quantity, so he immediately tried to improve the situation. In 1888 he got an option on all of the water power rights on the Spokane River west of Post Street and east of Monroe by paying $485,000 for the C and C Flouring Mill and the Post Mill which held the rights. The Washington Water Power Company was formed as the entity to buy the rights and to purchase the Edison Company and its power station. To raise capital for further expansion, the company enlisted the assistance of merchant bankers in Brooklyn, New York. The company then built a dam across the Spokane River and a power station at the foot of Monroe Street, completing the planned project.

THE JOY OF ACCOMPLISHMENT was overcome by the great fire of 1889 which destroyed the Spokane telephone system. Fortunately, the small Edison power station was not burned. Unfortunately, the fire destroyed all of the Washington Water Power poles and distribution system.

SPOKANE FALLS.—VIEW OF ROSS PARK ELECTRIC STREET RAILWAY, MAIN STREET.

Courtesy of Eastern Washington State Historical Society

An etching of Main Street, Spokane Falls in 1890, showing the Ross Park Electric Street Railway, from the Northwest Illustrated Monthly Magazine, April 1890.

The fire was a great economic leveler and resulted in consolidation of some local businesses. Norman and Hopkins sold one-half of their interest in Inland Telephone and Telegraph Company to Sunset Telephone and Telegraph Company which at that time represented a large part of the interests of the Bell Telephone Company in the Pacific states.

The street railway system needed help at that time of crisis too. The city was fragmented and each part had its separate system. J. J. Browne and A. M. Cannon owned a horse-car system and G. B. Dennis was the principal owner of a partially completed electric street railway known as the Ross Park Line. The Spokane Cable Railway was also partially completed. All of these lines were acquired by the Washington Water Power Company which proceeded to unify and electrify the entire system. The power company also monopolized all of the city's lighting system.

THE PANIC OF 1893 stopped any plans for further business expansion. Most businesses strove merely to survive. Washington Water Power was able to stay afloat, but in so doing, many of its promoters lost heavily. Norman was one of these and he had to sever his connections with the company in 1898 because he could no longer pay his required assessments.

He told me, "Crops, mainly wheat, failed in the agricultural area around Spokane and many people went bankrupt. Conditions were terrible through the years 1893 to 1896 until the (mining) camp at Rossland started working. The Depression continued in the Puget Sound area until 1898 when it became a beehive of industry due to the discovery of gold in Alaska. While the Depression was at its height, the Vice President of the Northern Pacific Railway wanted to go by rail through Spokane and Coxey's Army tried to stop it, but everyone, including myself, got out shotguns and saw the train go through."

Even during the hard times there were some business opportunities that later proved to be very profitable for those who had the vision and the money to act on them. Billy took advantage of one such opportunity when owners of the Spokane Hotel declared bankruptcy, and he took control of the stock and refurnished the hotel. Four months later the bottom fell out of the business, and the mortgage company threatened to close the hotel. The creditors, hoping to rescue part of their investment, leased it to Billy and his brother Ben in 1894 on very lenient terms—no rent for the first six months and only five hundred dollars a month for the next two years.

SPOKANE'S ECONOMIC PICTURE BRIGHTENED considerably with the opening of the Le Roi mine in the Coeur d'Alenes. The hotel business improved and in 1899, the two Norman brothers along with James Breen, the manager of the

Photo by Ernest Belger   Courtesy of Eastern Washington State Historical Society Museum

Looking north at the middle falls of the Spokane River in 1910. At this time, the Washington Water Power Company had access to more water power than it could use, and was offering "INDUCEMENTS TO MANUFACTURERS, EITHER ELECTRIC OR WATER, AT LIBERAL TERMS."

Le Roi smelter, bought the land, the building, and later an adjoining piece of property from John N. Finch, a prominent Spokane investor.

In 1900, they remodeled the building and made it the finest hotel in Spokane until the coming of the Davenport. The dining room was famous for its Silver Grill, designed by architect Kirtland Cutter. It featured a fireplace complete with spit where one could watch his beef being roasted.

The Normans developed a chain of hotels, among them the North Yakima Hotel and the Tacoma Hotel, which they purchased in 1905. Billy organized and was an officer in the Rossland, B.C. Water and Light Company. He was also a director of the C and C Flouring Mill, a business employing as many as two hundred people. He made time for civic activities as well. He served three years as secretary of the Spokane Board of Trade, the forerunner of the Chamber of Commerce. He was a member of a pro-business club that among its programs succeeded in convincing Congress to build Fort George Wright west of Spokane.

IN ADDITION TO HIS HOME at West 644 Seventh Avenue, Billy Norman owned property on the Little Spokane River. When I walked over the grounds with him in 1950, he showed me some huge trees with patches of bark hacked away. They were growing along a well marked path. The marks were eight to ten feet above ground level and resembled blazes. We thought they might have been cut to mark the trail for fur traders of the Northwest Company or the Pacific Fur Company who had travelled to the trading post at nearby Spokane House more than a hundred years earlier.

I questioned Billy about old settlers who might have lived near his property and he answered me in a letter dated June 4, 1947:

> . . . My recollection is that an old settler's home was very close thereto. It was one of those double long buildings with a roofed gangway between two sections, one in which the settlers lived, the horses at night being in the other. No white man ever slept away from his horse or his boat if he happened to live on a stream, and this station must have existed for many, many years off and on, for it was on the road to Colville, which is much older than Spokane, and the trail up the Little Spokane River, which passed through the Norman ranch was part of the route to the early day gold fields in British Columbia at the Columbia's headwaters.
>
> My early day record of the trail through the beautiful woods on the ranch is very vivid and many, many times in all succeeding years from my first visit in the spring of 1884, I have shared in its delights. It was then quite well traveled by Indians in their annual pilgrimage from the North for their winter supply of salmon, for the Little Spokane was a great spawning ground before the dams interfered. The east side of the trail was then a mass of bushes, and I remember well that the clematis and the honeysuckle were much in evidence in this charmed area . . .

He was ninety-six when he died August 12, 1954. He died in the same home in which he had lived since the year of the great fire of 1889. Billy Norman had the gift of grasping opportunities when he saw them, benefitting not only himself but at the same time, benefitting his community. □

A Young Man Goes West

by JEROME PELTIER

GEORGE WASHINGTON SUTHERLAND'S GRAND ADVENTURE began in 1872 when, as an 18 year old, he felt the urge to see the wide open spaces of the American West. He had read letters from William Purington to his father, Captain George Purington, of Bowdoinham, Maine, that described in glowing terms the fertile grasslands of Washington Territory and the opportunities available to anyone daring to leave home and start again in a new land. At the time, George had been working as a farmhand for Purington, who had been a Captain in the Union Army during the Civil War. When the Captain mentioned that he and his family would soon be leaving to join William at his cattle ranch, George asked if he could go with them.

Unfortunately, George had a serious problem. He had only $15 to his name. Somehow, George convinced the Captain to lend him $140, and his father chipped in $25 making a total of $180. The Puringtons were leaving on Friday, so three days before that, George asked his mother for permission to go. After much hesitation, she reluctantly agreed. In the meantime, Captain Purington had gone to Boston and had purchased George's train ticket to San Francisco for $122. George was on his way on August 20, 1872, with $58 that had to last him until he reached the Purington ranch somewhere in the southeast part of Washington Territory. This is the story that George Sutherland related to me as he sat on his bed at Sacred Heart Hospital in Spokane in 1941 when he was 87 years old. He later told me of many other events that happened to him during his long and active life, but exciting as they were, all were but an anticlimax to his trip west.

The Puringtons had first class tickets and George was traveling second class, so George didn't see them again during the entire trip. For the first time in his life, he was alone without friends or family. The train did not have a diner, so for the entire nine day trip, George ate from a large basket of food his mother had packed for him. At night, he slept on his stiff uncomfortable seat in the unheated car, covered by a pair of blankets that his mother had insisted he take with him.

HE CROSSED THE MISSISSIPPI at St. Louis over the Eads steel bridge, an engineering marvel for its time. At Council Bluffs, Iowa, he walked across the bridge over the Missouri River to Omaha, where he boarded a Union Pacific train. He stopped over in Cheyenne, Wyoming, for a day and a half. Wyoming was the first state in the nation to grant women the right to vote and he noted that many women in the town were voting. He continued his trip through Rawlins, Wyoming, and Ogden, Utah, passing bands of antelope as the train chugged along

Over the years, **JEROME PELTIER** has had the foresight to collect important historical data from this region's pioneers in the form of interviews and holographic accounts. He has been a prolific source of original material contributing to the history of the Pacific Northwest.

the plains. Once a herd of buffalo thundered down the tracks, almost destroying them. Finally the train crossed the deserts of northern Nevada and reached Sacramento. He arrived in San Francisco on August 29 to be met at the station by a confidence man who tried to swindle him out of his meager funds. George ignored him and hurried to the steamboat office where he bought a third class passage to Portland, Oregon, for $20.

About 4 p.m. the next day, he left on what he called "the old tub, the Oroflame, a side wheeler. No one would travel on such a boat today. When we got outside the Golden Gate, the boat began to pitch and wallow for four days until we got to Astoria."

At that time, Astoria consisted of a cluster of huts on pilings. The boat tied up there for half a day while cargo and mail from the East were unloaded. He finally reached Portland by evening and learned that another boat would be leaving for Wallula the next morning. He hurriedly spent $12 of his rapidly depleting money for a ticket. He couldn't afford to buy meals or a berth, as they cost extra.

HIS BOAT LEFT EARLY the next morning and by 10 a.m. had reached the cascades of the Columbia River, where cargo had to be unloaded and carried by cars on a narrow gauge railroad six miles upriver to another steamer which continued the trip to The Dalles. Following an overnight stay, freight and passengers were again transported by narrow gauge railroad to another steamer eight miles upriver which went as far as Umatilla where it stopped for the night. At that time, Umatilla was a lively town of about 3,000 people. All supplies for eastern Oregon and southern Idaho came through there until the Oregon Steam Navigation Company constructed a rail line to its docks on the Columbia at Wallula. Supplies then went from there to Walla Walla, which became the main distribution point.

A steamboat on the Columbia River near the cascades below The Dalles in the early 1900's.

Walla Walla didn't look like much in 1871. The bridge in the foreground is crossing the Walla Walla River.

The day he arrived at Umatilla was windy, and sand was piling up in the streets in drifts three or four feet deep, according to George. After a night in town, he boarded another steamer which took him to Wallula where he arrived penniless and hungry. He had spent the last of his money for a berth. He made a deal with a teamster to haul his rifle and baggage to Walla Walla while he walked, arriving there about 6 p.m. after a hot, dusty hike. He went to the St. Louis Hotel and told the proprietor that he wanted a meal and a place to sleep but had no money. The proprietor said, "Young man, the world is yours. Help yourself." George took him at his word, had a good meal and a good night's sleep.

George recalled, "Every other door was a saloon. There were many teamsters. I watched some of them packing mules, as many as seventy-five to a train (for the trip to the mines), and the mule trains were strung out for miles. There were many large corrals mainly for the mules."

WALLA WALLA WAS THE SUPPLY CENTER for the region. "The mules were hitched in teams of six, eight or ten to large freight wagons. Horse-drawn stage coaches were coming and going through town. Men worked hard and played hard, and saloons had plenty of patrons. Card games were going on all of the time."

In his wanderings around town, George located a teamster who had heard about the Purington ranch and was passing by it. He agreed to transport George's belongings and guide George there if George was willing to walk all of the way. George borrowed $2.50 from his new-found friend, paid his hotel and food bill with it, and left that afternoon on the last leg of his journey. This would be a jaunt of eighty miles to the area around Penewawa on the north side of the Snake River approximately twenty-five miles due west of present day Pullman, Washington.

The man's team consisted of a small mule hitched to an unkempt scrawny cayuse pony, barely able to pull an unloaded wagon let alone a loaded one. George felt so sorry for the animals that he left his trunk behind, taking only his blankets, his rifle, a pistol and a saddle bag. He had brought the guns as protection from the Indians and badmen that he understood infested the West at that time.

The first days travel brought them to what George called Whetstone Hollow, which offered good grazing for the team. The road was merely an Indian trail showing traces of heavy use. In places, the ruts were two feet deep, while in other places, the trail could barely be discerned. Drivers often deviated from the track, going where they felt they could make the best time.

The second day, George observed that the hills were dry and parched, although they were covered with nutritious bunch grass. By noon, they reached the Tucannon River where a man named Platter ran a crude rest station. After climbing out of the Tucannon Valley, they started down toward the Snake River on a narrow hilly road, the wagon nearly tipping over several times. Finally the river came into view, glistening in the distance, and Brown's Ferry became visible. While they were hastening down the Snake River breaks, a post rider charged past them, carrying the mail from Kelton, Utah, to points north via Walla Walla, Colfax, Spokan Bridge, Rathdrum, Idaho, and by boat across Lake Pend Oreille to Missoula, Montana.

TWO OTHER SNAKE RIVER CROSSINGS existed at that time: Lyon's Ferry near the mouth of the Palouse River and the ferry at Lewiston where the Snake joins the Clearwater River. Dusty sign-boards advertised these ferries declaring that plenty of wood, water and grass was present along the road.

George described Brown's rest stop as a square box shanty and a shed in which a man could rest himself and his horse. This was the first habitation George encountered since leaving the Tucannon River. After crossing the river, George helped pull the wagon up the hill where the team found good grass and water, as the signs had promised.

By noon of September 17, George arrived at Gooseberry Springs in Whitman County and his teamster friend told him that after they reached Alki Flat, he could easily find the Purington ranch by heading south toward the Snake River. George thanked him, gave him his pistol as a pawn for his $2.50 debt, and they parted.

With a feeling of loneliness, the youth started across the rolling hills. No other human being was in sight. It seemed as if there was always a hill ahead of him, but finally, he came to a ravine that led down to the Snake River, where he quenched his thirst. He realized that he had turned south too soon and was lost, but after walking several more miles, he saw a small shack ahead of him. The sun was setting and his pack was heavy, so the hut was a welcome sight. He knocked on the door and a surprised William Purington answered with a warm welcome for the weary traveler.

A MAN NAMED HOLBROOK WAS STAYING with Purington at the time, and these two men were George's first acquaintances in Whitman County. He rested a few days and after getting a horse, went out with the other hired hands to learn how to be a cowpuncher. The next phase of his life had begun.

"My wages were $25 a month and board, and I wasn't worth that much as I was a green Easterner. I did become quite a cowboy eventually," George said. It was not long before George became fully trained in riding and rounding up cattle. Soon he was able to go on long trips in search of strays.

"There were thousands of cattle down there, and we had a huge range to cover. My employer ran a herd of from 500 to 1000 head. Our range extended from Lewiston to the Palouse, 90 miles east and west, and from the Snake River to Spokane Falls." There were no fences. Cattle from various ranches mingled freely as they grazed, and were separated by brand at roundup time.

"Spokane Falls was a poor feeding ground, so we did not give it much attention. I think that the first time I was there, there were only two houses in the place. Colfax was the same."

IN A CONVERSATION SEVERAL YEARS LATER, George described the rangeland in the Snake River country. "Along the banks of the river, large portions of the hills at the north had slid down the canyons (in the past) due to cloudbursts and the continuous flow of small streams, and had formed bars . . . which were very fertile. A number of Indians had claimed this land, but then the settlers started coming in, some of whom took squatter's rights on it. This, of course, caused trouble right away. The first place to become involved was four miles above the place that I was working — Penewawa.

"There were two brothers named Smith who were cattlemen, who were the first to settle on this land and they thought that the Indians were not entitled to such good land and should be back on a reservation, so they took it for themselves. This land is in cultivation today (1945) with fine orchards of peaches, pears and cherries, and is worth many thousands of dollars.

"There were two other bars on the river that received freight from Portland from a steamer that called once a week. One was at Almota, where Henry Spalding, son of the missionary, ran a store and a hotel. The other was at Wawawai. Senator La Follette of Wisconsin and the Holt brothers had a large orchard there and shipped quantities of fruit all over the country. There was trouble here between the Indians and settlers and one Indian was killed by the man I was working for. The trouble was finally settled by Chief (Spokane) Garry, who was a noted Indian at that time.

"During those days, the Indians became rather insulting and would come into cabins if there was no man around and (ask the womenfolk) for something to eat, tobacco or matches. Of course, the settlers were frightened by them at first, but later became somewhat used to them. The women would stand no nonsense and always kept a rifle or pistol handy. I was afraid of them at first, (but) after awhile picked up enough of their jargon to talk with them and was able to understand (them).

"At the Purington ranch, we planted peach, pear and apple trees. In the Spring of 1873 we planted all kinds of seeds and also sweet potatoes, tobacco, peanuts and cotton. They all grew well. The wind blew a gale at times so we set out a wind break of locust trees.

"The winter of 1874-5 was the worst I ever spent. Cattle died by the thousands, for the snow was deep and the springs were frozen so badly that it was impossible for the cattle to drink. It was frightfully cold. When Winter broke, dead cattle were everywhere. Great pieces of ice came down the Snake River. Some of the flows were 40 feet high."

GEORGE TIRED OF THE MONOTONY of ranch life and left for the big city in 1875. He went to Portland where he started on a succession of jobs that took him from Walla Walla to Moscow, Idaho, and Newport, Washington. Employment was readily available for anyone willing to work and George tried everything from being a waiter, a barber, a sewing machine salesman and a druggist. He even took a turn at practicing medicine.

In 1877, he was in Colfax when word arrived of the Nez Perce uprising. George provided me with a written account of his experience:

On June 15, word came that a group of the Nez Perce Indians under the leadership of Chief Joseph had begun hostilities against the white settlers in western Idaho Territory by killing in cold blood several of the settlers. On Sunday, the 17th day of June, I, as well as many others, were at a camp meeting at what was known as Chase's Mill, about 18 miles east of Colfax, when a man by the name of Joe Evans came into camp about 11 o'clock with his horse covered with sweat, and said: "The Indians are coming down Union Flat, killing and burning everything in sight." (Actually, no fighting occurred in Union Flat.) The meeting broke up without waiting for the benediction, and everyone started for home or for Colfax. When I arrived back in Colfax, I found the streets barricaded and great excitement. An old man by the name of D. S. Bowman was upon the stoop of the only store in town, and he was saying, "Gentlemen, I have lived in Indian country all of my life, and I can say to all of you people that we should organize a company of volunteers. Then you will be recognized by the government." We organized a company on the spot. We appointed officers (and) all signed the roster and were sworn in. Then we were all told to go out and get all the firearms we had or could borrow. When we returned, all we could muster was 22 rifles, shotguns, and pistols. My duty, with two others, was to stand guard at the south end of town on the hills where it was supposed that the Indians would come through.

The next morning, I was ordered to reconnoiter and report. I went first to Three Forks, where Pullman is now situated, but there was no one within 5 miles. From there I went to Palouse City. There were very few families there, but the men from town and country were building a stockade. I stopped over there to help where I could. The next day, I went on to Moscow. Only a few people were there, but they were building a stockade with a big cellar inside for the women and children. It was built on a sloping side hill, and we could see the Indians passing along the foothills, (on) the trail between Spokane and Lewiston. I stayed there for 2 days and had a chance to send a report to Colfax. Then I went to Lewiston, arriving there the same evening that General Howard arrived by boat from Portland with company of Georgia troops. They had no experience in fighting Indians, but a company was ordered out to go up Craig's Mountain to Grangeville and Mount Idaho and White Bird Canyon. They were sent down in regular formation and the Indians were up on the sides of the canyon, and as I was told by one of the company, they had no chance at all . . .

After Joseph and his band eluded General Howard and fled over the Lolo Pass into Montana with the intention of reaching sanctuary in Canada, Sutherland and the members of his company of volunteers were ordered to watch for any stragglers who might circle back. "We went to Mount Idaho, Grangeville, White Bird and many other places where we thought we might run into Indians, but we did not see any from that time on." The company was mustered out in August or September of the same year, 1877.

GEORGE'S ACCOUNT CONCLUDES, "All the records (of the company's activities) . . . were destroyed in the big fire, so we have no record of our company's doings. After our enlistment, we had to furnish all of our equipment, horse, saddle, blankets and eat where we could. After 60 years, I think I am entitled to a badge of some kind as 5 of my company were receiving pensions (and I was not). I have saved Uncle Sam quite a sum of money by not applying for one. I did not need the money and I did not think that I was doing anything but my duty. We had to protect our homes under any circumstances."

George continued traveling over the Northwest investing in various business enterprises including mining, all with mediocre success. He eventually settled in Newport, Washington. There, he was a member of the City Council, served several terms as Mayor, was County Commissioner of Stevens and Pend Oreille Counties and president of a bank. He died in 1949 after a long and active life in which he realized his ambition of being a pioneer in the American West. ☐

Good Genes and a Bit of Luck

by NORMAN BOLKER, M.D.

MERELY SURVIVING WAS AN ACCOMPLISHMENT on America's frontier, and overcoming serious illness was a personal triumph. Physicians in that milieu must have been acutely aware of their limitations; yet they did much with what little they had, and their patients appreciated them, as Daniel Drumheller, one of the pioneers of the Northwest and an early Mayor of Spokane, related in his memoirs.

Drumheller was an exceptionally durable person. When only fourteen, he crossed the plains from St. Joseph, Missouri, to Sacramento, California, with a wagon train in 1854. He promptly became a full-time cowboy in northern California, had a stint

The
PACIFIC
NORTHWESTERNER
WESTERNERS, SPOKANE CORRAL

Vol. 33   No. 4   1989

Getting Through The Depression

by JEROME PELTIER

WE ALL HAVE HEARD ABOUT THE CRASH of the stock market on Black Thursday, October 26, 1929. After three days of heavy selling with prices dropping fifteen to twenty points each day, millions of shares were offered on the New York Stock Exchange and there were no buyers. Share prices plunged, shattering dreams of wealth by large and small investors alike. Bank failures soon followed and the entire global monetary system collapsed. Exports shrank and with the loss of jobs in factories, farm income dropped severely. The American consumer no longer had buying power, and by 1932, this country was in the depths of The Depression.

I was making a mere $10.50 a week on my job at the John W. Graham and Company in Spokane. After Franklin Delano Roosevelt became President, and the minimum wage was increased to $13.20 for a forty-hour week, my salary was raised to that amount. One year earlier, I had been making $15 per week for a part-time job.

Small as it was, that amount of money bought a great deal of food and merchandise at that time. My Dad was out of work for a short time and my salary was the one that supported three of us during that period.

Our way of life was simple. My mother cooked over a hot, wood burning stove which had a water reservoir on the outside nearest the fire. This was our source of hot water. The stove had a warming oven about 2½ feet above the cooking area. I remember this Monarch stove had a capacious oven where my mother baked delicious cakes and pies. When winter came, it was pleasant to be in the kitchen near the stove, but during the summer, cooking over the stove would cause my mother to perspire freely, particularly during the fall canning season.

JEROME PELTIER is a collector of books and manuscripts on the history of the American West and a prolific writer on that subject. His latest book, *Black Harris,* published by Ye Galleon Press, describes the life and times of a Northwest mountain man.

Vol. 33   No. 4   1989

Published quarterly by the Spokane Corral of The Westerners, P.O. Box 1717, Spokane, WA 99210. Subscription $10.00 per calendar year. Back issues available, $2.50 ea. Articles appearing in this journal are abstracted and indexed in HISTORICAL ABSTRACTS: and/or AMERICA HISTORY AND LIFE.   ISSN: 0030 - 882 X

SPOKANE CORRAL — WESTERNERS
OFFICERS 1989

My wife, La Verle, faced the same difficulties in the late thirties, when she preserved hundreds of jars of foodstuffs while we were struggling to support a growing family. The girls would hot pack tomatoes, preserve peaches, pears and apricots, and make jams, jellies and pickles for the coming winter, because wage earners always had to be prepared for a long layoff from work.

DOING LAUNDRY WAS A DIFFICULT JOB during the days of the wash tubs and serrated wash boards. Electric washing machines were a luxury, so most people just starting out in married life had only the bare necessities. My wife had two wash tubs, one for the first wash and the other for rinsing. The two tubs were placed on a rack, one at each end about waist high, with a higher built-up section in the middle that had a hand wringer on it.

Water was boiled in a copper bottomed boiler and put into one of the tubs where it was used to do the first washing. The clothing was fed through the wringer into clean water on the other side. It was finally re-run through the wringer into a wicker basket, taken outdoors and hung on a clothesline to dry. Crystal White and Fels Naphtha were popular laundry washing soaps of the day.

Some women even made their own soap. During winter or inclement weather, the newly washed clothing was draped over a rack near a stove to dry. In some cases, people had clotheslines in their basement where they hung the clothes. The wooden clothes pins used to hang the clothes looked very much like stick men.

Buying an electric washing machine became our first priority, and we purchased one very soon after the birth of our first child. After the clothes dried, it was time to iron them. In the early 1930's, irons were gasoline heated or heated directly on the stove. The latter type had removable handles, generally, because metal handles would get too hot to touch. By the end of the decade, electric irons were in common use. Electric mangles were popular, too.

As there were no automatic controls on temperature of the irons, the user had to be careful not to scorch or burn fabrics. A cloth covered board with three fold-away legs usually served as the ironing surface.

Dupont did not invent nylon until the 1940's, so women wore either fine silk stockings, rayon cotton or woolen ones. Silk stockings were very expensive, so they were usually worn only on festive occasions.

MANY HOME BUILDERS could not afford bath tubs so wash tubs were used instead. Water was heated in the reservoir on the kitchen stove and in a copper or galvanized metal boiler, and when it reached the proper temperature, it was poured into the tub for the bather. It was pleasant and comfortable for youngsters, but a tight fit for adults.

Space was limited in small homes, so many families stacked bunk beds in double layers in their bedrooms. Refrigerators or ice boxes, as they were commonly called, were cooled by blocks of ice that were purchased from an ice-man who brought it by truck to the house. The housewife could indicate the amount of ice she needed by putting a card in the front window of the home. Children would follow the ice wagon to get the chips of ice that flew when the ice-man broke the required amount of ice with his icepick. Ice chips were a treat on a hot day.

The ice was placed in a metal lined chamber in the ice box, and when it melted, the water was caught in a pan beneath that had to be emptied periodically.

FOR THE MOST PART we were healthy, but when children caught contagious diseases such as measles, diphtheria, mumps, smallpox, chicken pox or whooping cough, the doctor would immediately put a quarantine sign on the door as a warning to others. No one was allowed to leave the house or enter until all signs of the disease were gone. After the sign was removed, life could go on as before. Usually, several members of the family would get the disease before the session was over.

During the time that banks were closed in Spokane, John W. Graham paid his employees with script which was accepted by most Spokane businesses, who were confident that Mr. Graham would eventually redeem it with legal tender when it again became available. Another member of the Spokane business community who made it a point to ease the burden of the average citizen was Dr. David Cowen, who had the busiest dental office in the Northwest. It was his practice during the Depression to accept vegetables and fruit in lieu of cash for his dental work. He would then give the produce to orphanages and to the needy.

You often hear about people selling apples on the street corners. This never happened around here because the entire Spokane valley was covered with fruit orchards, mostly apples. You could buy them for fifty cents a box, or only twenty-five if you picked them yourself. Cantaloupes sold for fifty cents an apple box and strawberries for ten cents per berry basket. A person with a job could eat well during the Depression, but food lines were available for those with no money. The food came from government warehouses, and while it was not fancy, it kept families alive. Usually, the food that was distributed was cornmeal, oatmeal, lard and navy beans. Sometimes macaroni was dispensed. The Red Cross also distributed food.

The Salvation Army and other charitable institutions gave Christmas parties for children whose families were destitute. Santa Claus would enter with a big bag of goodies, giving each child one piece of clothing, a repaired toy and a stocking that

Bread Line — No One Has Starved

Etching by Reginald Marsh
From the Bolker Collection
Courtesy of Gonzaga University

was stuffed with an orange, some nuts and a small bag of hard candy. This was the only Christmas gifts that some children had. If families were better off, children might receive electric trains, tricycles, or wagons. Girls got dolls with eyes that could open and shut. Dominos, checkers, and Parchesi were popular, and Monopoly was a runaway best seller. Games provided inexpensive entertainment.

A S SOON AS A BABY WAS EXPECTED, a provident family began saving money for the hospital and doctor bills. In the later 1930's, the hospital charged from fifty to sixty dollars for a ten-day stay in the maternity ward. Mothers were expected to stay in bed that long after delivery. Doctors usually charged fifty dollars for the delivery and the pre- and post-natal care. If you couldn't pay the entire amount immediately, you paid it in installments.

Not all of the people in Spokane lived in warm houses. During those days, there was a shanty town on the north bank of the Spokane river below the lower falls. The poor habitations were made of pieces of board, large flattened tin cans and sometimes empty wooden crates. Plywood boxes were much desired in such buildings. Although the shacks were small, somehow men lived in them.

Another shanty town was located south of Gonzaga University campus in the old McGoldrick Lumber Yard close to the present Post Office Annex on Trent Avenue. This area would be flooded periodically during the spring runoff.

S POKANE HAD ITS SOUP KITCHEN and flophouse — Hotel De Gink. In those days, gink was slang for a down and outer. Hotel De Gink was located in the former Schade Brewery on the curve at East 538 Trent Avenue, just south of the Trent Avenue bridge.

A friend of mine, Frank Jones, described the workings of the hotel to me. The personnel of the place stayed on the third floor which was kept very clean. The second floor was used as a flophouse where hoboes could sleep. There were rows of bunks

78

there. If you didn't have your own bedroll, you slept on the bare floor or on newspapers or cardboard. At least you were warm and under a roof.

The men were fed on the first floor and cooking was done in the basement. Food was obtained through the kindness of people in Spokane who provided damaged or slightly over-aged food.

Many men were saved from starvation by this way station and others like it. This place was like an oasis in the desert of no jobs and little hope. It gave men a brief rest before they hitched a ride on a freight train headed out of town as they searched for work elsewhere. This shelter was only temporary. The transient was allowed to stay only one night, after which he had to go on his way.

Public schools provided education for the children of the community just as they do today. For a higher education in Spokane, one had to enroll in Holy Names Academy, Whitworth College or Gonzaga University, all private institutions that required tuition that was sometimes beyond the student's ability to pay.

If the will to learn was there, students could find a way to get their education. Many worked during the summer to supplement the money their parents could scrape together. In my case, the would-be student was the only breadwinner in his family and had to keep his full time job. For those like me, there was still a way to do it. We worked during the day and took courses at night. It took longer but we eventually earned our degrees.

MANY OF THE PEOPLE who wanted a home of their own built them themselves. They would buy a lot, excavate for a foundation, pour the cement and lay the concrete blocks, put up the joists and lay a floor over it. After covering the floor with tar paper or cheap roofing, they would live in the basement until they saved enough money to complete their home. When the building was eventually completed, they owed very little on it. Many houses started out small and were enlarged later as funds became available.

Happiness is a state of mind. In spite of the bleak economic conditions, many pleasures could be found in daily life. Most of them were inexpensive, although if one had money, there were ways to spend it.

One pleasant way to enjoy a Sunday was to have a picnic in the park. Mom fixed a nice lunch and everyone had fun eating, talking, swimming and sometimes listening to the town band as it played nearby. Potluck dinners and church or club get togethers were great entertainment and brought people closer together. Church bingo and Grange Hall dances also brought out a great many people. There was usually food and drink at these functions, and a good time was had by all. On special occasions, a visit to Natatorium Park was a great treat.

Sometimes, the women in the neighborhood held a quilting party. One woman would have a rack set up in her living room, and friends would come in and work on her quilt. They would have a nice get-together, and many of their quilts became masterpieces of the art of sewing. I remember that my mother had one that was called The Double Wedding Ring design, and it was indeed a beautiful thing.

Although vacation trips were rare, when one came the family participated in it. A trip was limited to one that fell within the finances of the family, because in those times, you could not play now and pay later. One could go to Seattle or drive around the Olympic Peninsula admiring the beautiful scenery, or a family might go to Walla Walla during fair week, admire the fat animals, watch the horse races and see the rodeo all at a nominal price. Though not a great distance from home, it gave all of the family an outing which they could think and talk about. These and a trip to Crater Lake are outings my family remembers with pleasure.

TRAVELING IN A CAR that had tires with inner tubes was sometimes an experience that a driver did not want to repeat. Tires were not perfected and roads were not as smooth and easy to drive on as they are today. Most roads were narrow, gravelly, and in many places rocky. The rough stones caused tires to blow out or go flat. When this happened, the driver got out his jack, raised the car with it, removed the flat tire and replaced it with a spare. If you were on a fairly long trip, this might happen several times before you were able to repair your tire. Then you would be forced to dismount the tire from the rim, find the hole in the inner tube, locate the cause of it, extract it if it were a nail or piece of glass, and then patch the hole by cementing a piece of rubber over it. After the cement dried long enough, the entire process had to be repeated in reverse. Then came the job of inflating the inner tube to the proper hardness with a hand operated pump and installing the tire on the wheel, while making a fervent prayer that this would not happen again before you got home. Meanwhile, Mom was dealing with the restless children.

Gasoline was just a fraction of its present cost. I remember when it sold for eighteen cents a gallon. Oil was also reasonably priced, as were automobile repairs.

THE FOURTH OF JULY HOLIDAY was a festive occasion. At Natatorium Park, one could enjoy the carnival rides. There was usually a patriotic speech by an official, and always a beautiful fireworks display. People usually spent a little more money on entertainment this day than on the others.

Then as now, young love flourished the year round. One way of getting your girl out of her house was to go for a ride in a car. If you had a friend who drove the car, a ride with your girl in the rumble seat was very cozy. Movies, eats and necking were the order of the evening. Sometimes, dinner followed by dancing made up the evening's entertainment.

Another type of entertainment known as marathon dancing was popular for a time. This was a contest called the Walkathon in which the contestants would dance continuously to the music of a band until they were exhausted and fell asleep in their partner's arms. The partner still erect would fight to stay upright and keep the other from falling to the floor. If one fell, he or she would be disqualified and could not continue. The ordeal went on until all dancers were eliminated except for the last couple still standing. While the contest was in progress, the band would play fast music to test the endurance of the dancers. If one of the contestants was talented, he could step up to the microphone and entertain the viewers who paid admission to see the spectacle. The survivors got the cheers of the crowd and the prize money, usually $1000. The promoter got the rest of the money after paying the expenses. For the audience, it was an exciting way to spend an evening.

As a new decade approached, reports from Europe told of a developing threat to peace. Hitler began his plan of world conquest, and the conflagration of World War II would soon be upon us. As our nation beefed up its defense and that of the western world, massive government spending spelled the end of the Depression. We had faced our difficulties and triumphed over hard times. Would we be able to triumph as well over the forces of Fascism? ☐

Vol. 34   No. 1   1990

The Fur Trade Was Equitable in the Far West

by JEROME PELTIER

There is an apocryphal story, that recurs during conversations regarding the early fur trade in Canada and the United States, which relates that some fur trader, some place, once traded a long barreled muzzle loading gun for a pile of beaver pelts, laid flat as high as the weapon was long. Some raconteurs (while doing their vocal embroidery work) have added a bayonet to the length of the piece of ordnance. A trade of pelts equal to the length of the bayonet made the additional deal even more preposterous!

Some present day Indians are particularly fond of repeating this tale when discussing the dishonesty of traders who once came among their people. In this way they imply that such shoddy trading procedures were the rule rather than the exception, if such an exception really existed.

It appears to me that they do their own people an injustice when they make such a statement because the old Indian was not as stupid as his successors seem to imply. He always got value received for value given. Trades consummated during his period of existence were all a matter of economics, just as ours are today, and as a result business between them continued to the advantage of all. The native traded beaver and other pelts which were a common commodity among his people to the trader. Getting in return beautiful beads, cloth, metal objects and shells which were rare indeed to him, his wife, and fellow villagers. As an example, he had to go only a short distance away from his village, at least in most cases, to obtain beaver or other pelts which he could barter for blankets, clothing, kettles, etc. These modern objects gave him prestige and eased his wife's work load at the same time.

JEROME PELTIER is a frequent contributor to this journal. He has written on many aspects of western history. His longtime memberships in the Hudson's Bay Record Society and the Champlain Society has allowed him to study and write on North American fur trade history.

Vol. 34   No. 1   1990

Published quarterly by the Spokane Corral of The Westerners, P.O. Box 1717, Spokane, WA 99210. Subscription $10.00 per calendar year. Back issues available, $2.50 ea. Articles appearing in this journal are abstracted and indexed in HISTORICAL ABSTRACTS: and/or AMERICA HISTORY AND LIFE.

ISSN: 0030 - 882 X

SPOKANE CORRAL — WESTERNERS
NEW OFFICERS OF THE SPOKANE COUNCIL

Sheriff . . . . John Ellingson
Chief Deputy . . . . William Kelly
Program Deputy . . . . Edwin Weilep
Membership Deputy . . . . . . Joe Cochran
Roundup Foreman . . . . Bruce Butler
Post Rider . . . . Frank Knox
Chuck Wrangler . . . . Aaron Jones

Tallyman . . . . William Papesh
Register of Marks and
    Brands (editor) . . . . . . Terry Russell
Publications Committee
    Jerome Peltier,
    Randall Johnson,
    Seabury Blair

This type of trading was just one step above the bartering that took place for native items with neighbors and near neighbors prior to the coming of the fur trader. At that time common items were traded for items not indigenous to their country, just as it was done later after the white man came to trade with them. For example: dentalium and abalone shells found on the west coast reached interior tribes through a series of trades. It would be interesting to know just how many and what a variety of items were traded by various tribesmen before they eventually reached an interior tribe like the Spokanes. Tobacco, which was so important to native Americans, had to be traded from the Spokane to the neighboring Coeur d'Alene tribe. A superior weed brought in later by the fur traders replaced the native product.

Despite much extensive reading, since 1935, in fur trade journals and histories, I find that I have never seen any contemporary documentation to support the claims in the gun story. I have read stories of debauchery east of the Rocky Mountains and much about violence, but have seen no proof of a trade as outrageous as the gun story.

The Beaver Magazine (Outfit 264 #4, March, 1934), published under the auspices of the Hudson's Bay Company, contains an article by Sir Charles Piers entitled "Fire Arms of the Hudson's Bay Co." Sir Charles wrote: "The Company's trade gun is plain but eminently serviceable with the stock continued up the muzzle for strength. Its long barrel (42 inches in the longer and 36 inches in the shorter) gave range and accuracy. Its bore was a half inch and it carried the Company's trademarks on the barrel, lock plate and butt, and sometimes the Company's name." The detractors of the Company wove the fantastic story that the length of the barrel was to enable the trader to get more beaver skins from the Indians by telling him that he must pile beaver skins up to the top of the barrel with the gun standing butt to the ground if he, the native, wanted the gun.

Sir Charles set the value of guns at twenty beaver skins each, which is much higher than evaluations shown in older trade lists. He also noted that a greater muzzle velocity was built up in larger barreled guns because it gave the slow burning powder of that day more time to burn. Guns with shorter barrels, or those that were cut short for use on horseback, were used only at close range because they were not as accurate as the longer guns.

It is time that a straight forward account of the difficulties of the fur trade should be written, and by so doing, shed light on the values of items that were brought to the natives of the Pacific Northwest of the United States. I shall limit my study to the three great fur trading giants that dominated the field in the Pacific Northwest: The Northwest Company, The Hudson's Bay Co., and the Pacific Fur Company.

The Northwest Company came into the Inland Empire first. Its guiding spirit was David Thompson, a partner in the company. Thompson was a great surveyor and cartographer as well as a trader. His religious attitude would not allow him to trade liquor to the Indians. He supervised the building of Kullyspell House on Lake Pend Oreille in Idaho; Salish House near present day Thompson Falls, Montana; and Spokane House, ten miles northwest of Spokane, Washington. These posts were built in the late 1809-early 1810 period.

The second company to vie for the area fur trade was the Pacific Fur Company, which was headed by John Jacob Astor. This company was formed in New York in 1810. Its trade on the west coast began as a two party expedition. One party traveled overland from St. Louis and the other via ship around Cape Horn. Both parts of the operation eventually joined at Fort Astoria, at the mouth of the Columbia, the western headquarters of the company. The sea party built the post while the overland party plodded along and encountered great difficulties. Astoria was planned as headquarters for the western posts. This company, under one of its partners, David Stuart, soon built Fort Okanogan at the mouth of the Okanogan River where it empties into the Columbia River. Fort Okanogan, built in 1811, became the first American fur trading post in the present State of Washington. Stuart continued on into present British Columbia and built another post among the Shushwap Indians.

Another partner of the Pacific Fur Co., John Clarke, built Fort Spokan within a half mile of Spokane House. This post, completed about Christmas, 1812, was near the confluence of the Spokane and Little Spokane Rivers.

The Pacific Fur Company's posts were short-lived. Threats of the destruction of Astoria by a British Man-of-War during the War of 1812, brought about a forced sale of all the Astorian business operations in the Northwest. Final sale took place to the Northwest Company in May, 1814, after which time the latter company continued and expanded their operations using the Astorian facilities to do so.

The Hudson's Bay Company was the third fur trading concern with operations in the Inland Pacific Northwest. The HBC was given that name when it was chartered in 1670 by King Charles II of England. It controlled all the land drained by the rivers and streams flowing into the Hudson's Bay of Canada. Charles II gave the company certain Charter rights, including exclusive trading rights for this territory, which is approximately one-half of present Canada. The Northwest and Hudson's Bay Companies engaged in fierce competition for control of the fur trade in Canada. This self-destructive competition resulted in a merger of the two companies in 1821. From that point forward, the HBC was preeminant in the fur trade in Canada and the Pacific Northwest. The HBC is today still in business and could not have survived for more than 300 years if it had been built on deceit, dishonesty and mistrust.

The Northwest Company was a powerful organization and during the last years of its trading life a bloody conflict existed between them and the HBC. Eventually things got so bad that the two companies joined in the coalition of 1821. Most of the directors and partners of the Northwest Company transferred to the board and employ of the older company and directed its activities. At about ths time, Sir George Simpson was made Overseas Governor of the Northern Department and soon after became Governor of all of the Company's North American operations.

This will give you some brief background data on the companies that sought pelts in the Inland Empire. A description of the trade difficulties encountered by them follow and we shall use the procedures practiced by the HBC and later by the Americans, to show how the trade was conducted.

The Hudson's Bay Company had a set of written or oral instructions which were given to their men before they were allowed to venture into the field. The list contained values of other fur skins as compared to a prime beaver pelt, which was the standard of value in the trade. Still another list compared trade items with beaver pelts. Traders were instructed to use these lists religiously and as a rule committed them to memory.

A list of trade items used by men of the Hudson's Bay Company at Albany Fort, on the shores of Hudson's Bay for the year 1706, is the earliest that survives. Earlier lists have never been located. By 1706 the company had evolved a system of trade both fair to themselves and the natives with whom they traded.

To show a complete trade list would be too exhaustive, so the listed items are of common use. Note that the list shows the value of beaver compared to other pelts. In all cases we are talking about prime pelts, otherwise values decrease according to condition.

Two deer hides brought the same value in trade as one beaver pelt and so did foxes and otters. It took four martens to get as much in trade goods as one beaver would buy. Wildcat, bear cub and wolf pelts were equal to one beaver. A full grown black bear or a moose hide purchased what two beavers would. Castoreum, a scent made from the beaver's own glands and used to entice beaver into traps, was evaluated at one pound for one beaver pelt.

It took one beaver pelt for each of the following trade items: ¾ lbs. of beads; 1½ lbs. of gun powder; 5 lbs. of shot; 1 lb. of Brazilian tobacco and 1½ lbs. of Virginian tobacco; 1½ oz. of vermillion; 1 lb. of red lead; ½ lb. of black lead; ½ lb. of thread; and 1 yard of flannel cloth. You could get two each of combs, scissors, and caps for each beaver hide. Guns were traded according to length at 7 to 10 beaver. This is a far cry from the gun trade story.

Comparative lists have survived since that time, which show that the old Company's business ethics were always just and fair. At York Fort, on Hudson's Bay in 1776, the Company had a more complete breakdown of bead values. This list of values, for the wide varieties of beads traded, is the most complete list that I have seen anywhere else. This list may be found in the Fort Cumberland and Hudson's House Journals for 1775 to 1776 which were published in 1951 as part of the Hudson's Bay Record Society.

Trade goods were also used by the trading companies for services rendered by their non-Indian employees. These figures show that their own help was paid on the same basis as the Indians. In an account of the cost of provisions at Fort Alexander, a HBC fort in the Western Caldonia District which was built in 1821 on the Fraser River near the mouth of Quesnel river, we find that 1½ lbs. of common red beads cost one shilling seven pence and 1½ lbs. of rolled tobacco cost 1 shilling six pence. Over and above this was the cost of transportation to get the items there. The following items were paid for labor on a building in lieu of money: Two knives, one with a yew handle and another with a yellow wood handle cost ¾ pence each; ⅔ lbs. of tobacco at 8 pence; and 1/16 lb. of common round beads cost 1 pence.

Although much of the fur trade was handled in a very similar manner, there were marked differences between the American and English methods of doing business. The HBC hired salaried employees who signed contracts with them for a specific length of time, usually a period of five years. Following which period, they could sign another contract or become free traders and trap beaver on their own account. The HBC trade was generally conducted from their network of posts, the Indian and free traders coming to the posts to exchange furs for provisions and trade goods. In the Snake River country the HBC modified this approach by sending out large parties of employees to trap the rivers and trade with the Indians. These Snake Country Brigades were led by John Work and Peter Skene Ogden. Both left written accounts of these trading expeditions. This policy of sending out large parties was in response to American incursion and competition.

The American fur trader who worked from year to year, was of a breed of man unequaled anywhere else in the world. He was a rugged individual who thought more of his freedom than he did of his life. He put his life in jeopardy every day of his existence. His life was one continuous adventure. He was pitted against the elements, hostile natives, and injuries that could disable him on his often lonely pursuit of the beaver. The American Mountain Man faced death by bear, illness or murder. He did not have the security of a stockaded fort. His was a life of uncompromising harshness because even under ordinary circumstances his daily routine was very strenuous. Survival was always in question.

Partners in an American fur company had great responsibilities. Let us consider the difficulties (as well as the costs) sustained by trading companies in purchasing and eventually transporting trade goods to the Pacific Northwest of the United States. Perhaps then we may be able to comprehend why values skyrocketed the greater the distance they were brought from headquarters.

As an example, we will use beads as a species of trade. First, agents of the company had to contact and negotiate with the Doge (Chief Magistrate) of Venice in Italy to obtain an adequate supply of beads. This preliminary contact had to be

THE TRADER, by John Clymer, pictures a trader and helper leading a string of pack animals into a Sioux winter camp. Here making the sign for "trade."

done because the Doge controlled the bead factories which were on the nearby island of Morino. It was here that huge kilns belched forth beads of all types and sizes.

Venician beads were of excellent quality and texture and were much in demand by natives of North America. Beads were also sold to aborigines in many other parts of the world and because of this the fur trading companies had to pay a good price for them. Blue beads were particularly popular among the native women of North America. What pleased them usually met with the approval of their men. The men used much of the finery that was decorated with the beads, such as beaded clothing and possible bags.

After the beads were manufactured and purchased, they were loaded aboard ships in kegs and brought to London, New York or other trading centers. Here they were repackaged into smaller lots of a given weight that would be easily handled for shipment overseas or inland. For the HBC these beads would be sent, along with other purchased trade items, to York Factory on Hudson's Bay from London. There the beads and trade goods were assembled into "outfits." These outfits were trade goods that were required for a given trade region. From York Factory the various outfits were sent by batteaux or canoes to posts further inland. For the Americans, St. Louis was generally the point where these outfits were prepared.

Rivers were the highways of travel at that time and a batteaux or canoe trip via a chain of rivers and lakes was a long involved process. Obstructions in the streams such as falls, huge boulders, white rapids, and strong currents made travel difficult. If the current was flowing too strongly against them, the boatmen (also called voyageurs) would take out a long rope and cordel, or pull, the boat until they reached an area where they were able to row or pole up the river. If a large boulder strewn area blocked stream progress, or the rapids were too steep, the supplies and trade goods were taken out of the boat and carried on the backs of the men around that part of the stream until a free flowing section of the river was reached. When the outfits were put together, packages of 90 lbs. each were made in anticipation of such portages. It was not unusual for a man to carry two of these packages over the portage trail. At the point where boat travel could be resumed, the boat (which had to be carried or pulled around the obstruction) was reloaded and the voyage was continued. Sometimes, a batteaux upset and its contents were lost in whole or in part, thus adding to the cost of operations.

For the Americans operating out of St. Louis, a keelboat, or some other type of water conveyance, had to be bought or built with which to transport the goods and men up the Missouri River and eventually to the Rocky Mountains. These keelboats would move up river until a place was reached where it would be more feasible to haul the trade goods via pack train. From this point a long and arduous overland trip was made to the pre-arranged rendezvous site with the mountain trappers. For the American Fur Company operating out of posts on the Missouri River, these keelboats continued further up the river. In later days steam powered paddleboats were used to transport goods as far up river as Fort Benton.

A keelboat trip, bucking against the Missouri River current, was no childs play. Sometimes a sail could be used when the wind was right. Usually oars, or long poles, aided by back breaking cordelling, made each mile a well earned one. Cordelling the craft was perhaps the most difficult part of river operations. This was done by attaching long stout ropes to the main sail mast and putting a crew of men on shore at the other end of the rope. This crew would tug and pull against the current and move forward perhaps a mile an hour, if that fast. Men cordelling would wade in sand, mud, through reeds, over rocks and fallen trees. The men had to overcome all the shore line offered in the way of obstacles.

A salary had to be paid for every man on the crew even though nothing was derived from their services until an actual trade was made. These salaries, plus river losses as described above, as well as losses through theft, had to be added to the cost of trade operations.

When the expedition reached its headquarters destination, larger packs of goods were broken up into smaller packages and put into trading outfits that was scheduled to go into a given area, such as the Snake River Country. For the HBC trade operations in the Pacific Northwest the above described transportation process was drastically reduced. Goods were shipped from England to Fort Vancouver on the Columbia River. From there the outfits were made up and transported up the Columbia to the various inland posts. Because of the proximity of Fort Vancouver to the trapping grounds, transportation costs were reduced.

Prior to 1818, Spokane House was the headquarters for the Snake River Brigades. It was here at Spokane House that the trade parties were prepared and organized for this vast trading area. After the trade caravan reached the general area to be serviced by the brigade, smaller parties with trade goods were dispatched into remote areas. It was only after thousands of miles and months of travel that the beads and other trade goods were brought into a location where they could derive some income. Business was lucrative but it was also dangerous. Many men lost their lives through accidents and Indian attacks. Natural causes also levied their toll of lives.

When a village of friendly Indians was located trade would begin. The natives would exchange their furs, pemmican and other dried meats and fish. The furs and other items would be evaluated as to condition and worth. Trade goods would be measured out according to their value and the company's standard of trade. Bartering would continue item for item until the tradeables of either party were exhausted. If the fur trader still had goods for barter he would continue on his way to another village where the cycle would continue.

In the American fur trade the unique feature was the mountain man rendezvous. As described earlier, the trade goods were prepared in St. Louis and transported to the mountain rendezvous site. When the trade caravan reached this site, the trading began. In this system the company trappers, various parties of free trappers and friendly Indians gathered in one place. Many of the rendezvous sites were in the Green River area of Wyoming. As all parties gathered for the annual trade fair, they formed a colorful panoramic picture of teepees, piles of trade goods, furs, and humanity.

Animated trade took place. The company would receive various types of pelts in exchange for knives, guns, ammunition, beads, stroud cloth, blankets, kettles, needles, tobacco, and trade trinkets and baubles. The Indian and trapper would exchange their year's work for the next year's outfit. Each would talk over trade values and would congratulate themselves on surviving another year. They would wonder how good the year's trade would be and whether they would be able to pay off debts to the company. Many of the company trappers would hope to become unincumbered by debt and be free trappers, trapping and working on their own account. The company partners, who had come out from St. Louis with the trade goods, also wondered how good the trade would be and hoped they, too, would be able to pay off their creditors.

Visitors new to these mountain trade fairs were amazed and sometimes shocked at the licentiousness displayed before their eyes. People of religious inclination found this to be singularly obnoxious. Marriages were entered into, "in the manner of the country" as it was called. Exchanging trade goods for companionship. Murders and shootings, although not common, did take place.

In this John Clymer painting, TRADER AT PIERRE'S HOLE RENDEZVOUS, a trader displays his trade goods to attract the Indian trade.

The story of liquor and its effects on the natives should be told here. It was used in trade, many times to the detriment and sorrow of the natives, who had a natural craving for the liquid. Although the use of liquor as a trade item with the Indians was outlawed by the United States, it was generally much in evidence at the annual rendezvous. During the early days of the fur trade it played a prominent role in trade with the Indians.

Perhaps you may wonder how liquor was obtained despite it being forbidden by the government. In order to get an ample supply of liquor, traders found it expedient to build stills on the Missouri River where the fiery liquid was distilled and bootlegged. It was also illegally transported into the Indian country by the overland caravan, hidden among the other trade goods.

During the early days in the Pacific Northwest, the HBC representatives had a policy of not introducing liquor as a trade item. This was a laudatory move. They had learned the hard lessons during the days of intense competition with the Northwest Company, east of the Rocky Mountains. It was here that liquor was used generously. An excellent source on the abuses created by liquor in the eastern fur trade may be found in the journals of Alexander Henry, the Younger. His valuable account of the early fur trade was published in 1897 as a three volume set of books entitled, "New Light On The Early History Of The Greater Northwest. The Alexander Henry - David Thompson Journals."

Henry told that he traded liquor to the Indians until they became sodden, quarrelsome or vicious. When this happened he would escape into the darkness outside the Indian camp, where he would watch what transpired. Many times murders were committed as a result of the debaucheries. Suicides were also prevalent during the sobering process that followed. The abuse of liquor as a trade item is an ugly blot on the pages of history of the fur trade. The HBC policy excluding liquor as

In WHISKY, WHISKY, John Clymer shows a small group of trappers coming into rendezvous lured by whisky and celebrating with old friends.

a trade item west of the Rocky Mountains was a result of their experiences and seeing the horrors of the liquor trade. By limiting the introduction of liquor, they rid themselves of drunken and troublesome natives. All of which interfered with the business of trade.

American fur traders also had tragic results from liquor. During a drunken frolic at one mountain rendezvous, a fur trader was saturated with trade whiskey, rolled in a nearby fire and died as a result of the burns. Life as a fur trapper was sometimes cruel. It happened that an Indian feeling morose because of a debauch would committ suicide or kill his wife as a direct result of too much trade whiskey.

Getting back to the business of trading. The fur company had to, after the trade was completed, next get the skins back to headquarters. With the results of the year's trade with the natives and free trappers, plus the furs taken by the company's employees, the skins were loaded and transported back down river. This return trip was not without danger or incident itself. After the fur caravans reached headquarters, the furs were graded and baled to await shipment. Various shipping points were used, depending on which company was involved. If it was a Hudson's Bay Co. expedition, the furs would be shipped to London from either York Factory on Hudson's Bay or from Fort Vancouver on the Columbia. Headquarters for the Northwest Company was Fort William, on the western shore of Lake Superior, with the furs being transported from there to Montreal. From Montreal the furs would be shipped to markets in Europe. For the Americans, New York and St. Louis were used.

Many of the furs taken in the Pacific Northwest found their way to Asia. The British East India Company controlled much of the oriental trade. This company had exclusive trade rights, granted from the British crown, just as the HBC had exclusive British North America trade rights. The HBC had to work through the East India Company to market its furs in Asia. The Americans did not have to. This gave rise to the Boston sailing merchants purchasing furs on the west coast, sailing to Asia and exchanging the furs. The furs obtained in America were exchanged for silks, tea, cloisonne, gold and silver filigree work, exquisite porcelains and rugs. These Asian products found a ready market in Europe and the cities of New York and Boston. Pacific sea otter furs were especially in great demand in the Orient which led to its near extinction.

The furs shipped to London were made into fur coats and beaver hats. The great North American fur trade evolved around the fashion of wearing beaver hats, which were much in vogue at that time. The fur trade declined drastically after the beaver hats fell out of favor and were replaced by the silk hat. While this type of finery was in its heyday, the fur trade wheel kept turning. As long as the demand for beaver hats continued, the fur trade thrived. Trade goods were manufactured and sold in Europe, exchanged for North American furs, and in turn made into beaver hats. The fur trade in the United States seems to have declined about 1840, and by 1845 nearly ceased. After this time, some companies did continue trading operations and some individual free trappers still roamed the Rockies for years thereafter. After 1845 much of the fur trade shifted from the mountains to the Missouri River and from beaver pelts to buffalo robes.

As I mentioned previously, many modern Indians seem to think that their people did not use good judgment while trading during those early days. Let us evaluate some other aspects to find out if this was true.

First of all, in order to make a simple gorget or a bead made from bone or stone, to hang as a necklace, an Indian woman had to find the materials. It may be an agate, some other pretty flat stone, or a piece of bone. Now, after she had the raw material, her work began. She had to use a pointed awl of stone plus an abrasive like sand to help cut through this hard surface. After many turnings and many applications of sand, a hole would appear as the awl cut through. If it did not crack under pressure, she could thread a thong of buckskin through the hole and wear the ornament, much to her pleasure and satisfaction.

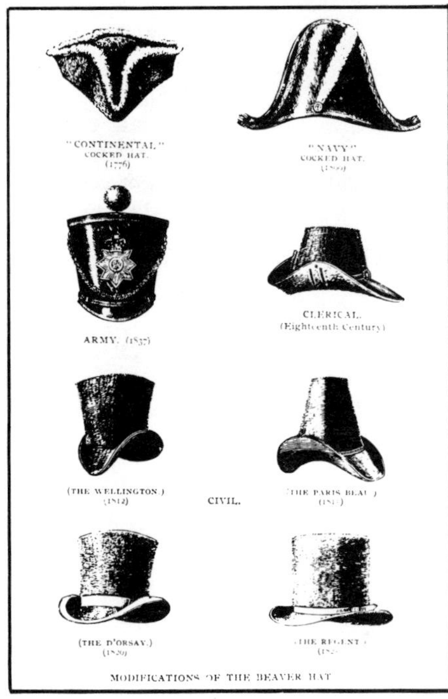

Courtesy Hudson's Bay Company

Modifications of the Beaver Hat. Taken from Horace T. Martin, *Castorologia* (London 1892).

Was it not much more sensible for her man to trade beaver pelts, common to the area and easily procured, for a handful of colorful beads? It made good sense economically and psychologically for the native to deck his women, his children and himself in finery that cost him so little time and effort. Indians try to evaluate real property deals of that period against value today. This is wrong because what may have been a perfectly reasonable trade at the time now seems outrageous.

A more sensible approach would be for the present generation to steep themselves in the history of that era. Then they can come to conclusions which I am sure will be different than are accepted today. Living the life and thinking about it are two different things.

Now, let us bring down to the present-day some of the trade items we have been discussing. There are many people who will pay a substantial price for either the native items or the bead necklace she got through trade. Thus we have come the full circle, because the item is as valuable today, comparatively, as it was at that time. Who made a poor trade? Not the Indian, obviously!

Corn-husk bags and buckskin dresses, as well as the trade cloth that replaced them, have a high sales price tag on the present day antiquarian and nostalgic market. Woven baskets, as well as the brass and copper trade kettles of the fur trade era, are collector items also. Turquoise rings, bracelets and necklaces, as well as Navajo rugs and blankets, are particularly expensive these days and native workers have a ready market for their artistic output. They sell these craft items at good prices. The coin has turned and the Indian is returning the compliments to his white brethren. Excellent results bring forth huge prizes in art festivals for those native artisans who excell. Items that win prizes sell for very high prices, some well up in the thousands of dollars.

Just as in the fur trade days, some shoddy items are sold at first class prices. Low class turquoise is doctored up with plastics until it looks like top grade material. Just as in the time of the fur trade, let the buyer beware.

Once again the Indian is trading a common commodity for items he needs. He is mining and manufacturing in ever increasing quantities to produce products. Blankets made of sheep's wool (also a common commodity) are being made as quickly as possible into rugs and are being sold just as soon as they are brought to market. The natives have learned to use reservation properties to their advantage, both as to mineral rights as well as recreational usage. As a result, they are obtaining much needed money for their products and facilities. Beadwork is sold extensively today, at all the market will bear. The better the beadwork, the higher its price.

Things haven't changed so much after all. Human nature is the same as it has always been. There is larceny in all of us, or at least the desire to get something for little. We all fall for some sort of bargain or gimmick. Whether it be in the market place, Wall Street, or on the reservation. The fur trade was not much different. But on the balance the fur trade was beneficial and equitable for all parties involved, the large companies, free traders and Indians alike.

Timberlodge

by ARDEN JACKLIN

Timberlodge is the name of my cabin high up on the mountainside on the west side of Garfield Bay, Pend Oreille Lake in northern Idaho. The story of its acquisition and development, and surrounding acreage is intriguing and complicated.

Pend Oreille Lake is a large, cold, deep lake averaging over 1,000 feet in depth, with its deepest spot 1,158 feet deep. From the Naval Base at Bayview on the south end of the lake, it is used for deep water research. Its summer elevation is 2,062.5 feet and in winter is 2,048 feet.

The name Pend Oreille is derived from an Indian tribe of that name who were also called "Earbob" Indians by the early French trappers because they wore pendant ornaments in their ear lobes. The tribe name of Pend Oreille probably derived from the ear-like shape of this lake where they lived.

The name of Idaho is a contraction of the Shoshone Indian word "Ea-dah-how" which figuratively or poetically translated means "gem of the mountains."

ARDEN JACKLIN has long been associated with Spokane Valley. His family, in 1936, started the Jacklin Seed Company in the Spokane Valley. He today remains a consultant to that firm.

The

PACIFIC NORTHWESTERNER

WESTERNERS, SPOKANE CORRAL

Vol. 34   No. 3   1990

Isaac Stevens' Greatest Mistake:
The Second Treaty Council
at Walla Walla, 1856

by JEROME PELTIER

A LTHOUGH REAMS of copy have been written about the treaty at Walla
Walla, Washington Territory, in May, 1855, as well as the many problems it
created, it is not generally known why the Walla Walla valley was chosen for this
important meeting between representatives of the federal government and the chiefs
and headmen of various allied tribes of eastern Washington and northern Idaho.
Hazard Stevens, son of the governor of Washington Territory, explained this little
known historical fact, when he wrote that Kamiaken, spokesman for the allied
tribesman, suggested where the meeting should be held. Kamiaken gave a logical
explanation for selecting this beautiful valley as a meeting place. He said, "There
is a place where in ancient times, we held our councils with the neighboring tribes,
and we will hold it there now."[1]

No doubt he felt his people would be dealing with a difficult problem and
it would be well to do so in familiar surroundings. He must have realized the Walla
Walla Valley was the crux of many of the problems to be solved in council and
would enter into the negotiations that were to follow because of events that had
occurred there and which must be solved there.

It was not accidental that the first council was held there, but Lieutenant
Lawrence Kip became a member of the treaty party by being in the right place
at the right time. He was at Fort Dalles when Governor Stevens was enroute to
the Walla Walla meeting and showed an interest in what was to transpire.

JEROME PELTIER is a valuable resource for information on Northwest history. A founder
and the first Sheriff of the Spokane Corral, Jerry is a frequent presenter of papers to
Westerners. Formerly a used book dealer, he has devoted his retirement time to civic
and community volunteer organizations. He is also a distinguished author and is currently
finishing work on his bibliography of the best books on Inland Northwest history (being
readied for publication by Ye Galleon Press). In this paper Jerry has utilized an Andrew
Pambrun manuscript from his personal collection.

Vol. 34   No. 3   1990

Published quarterly by the Spokane Corral of The Westerners, P.O. Box 1717, Spokane, WA 99210. Subscription $10.00 per calendar year. Back issues available, $2.50 ea. Articles appearing in this journal are abstracted and indexed in HISTORICAL ABSTRACTS: and/or AMERICA HISTORY AND LIFE.

ISSN: 0030 - 882 X

Kip was invited to accompany the party and it is fortunate that he was. He wrote a very complete account of what occurred at the treaty grounds in a pamphlet entitled **The Indian Council At Walla Walla, May and June, 1855,** San Francisco, 1855. It is one of the source documents of the council.

Kip mentioned one reason why the council had been called with the allied tribes. He wrote: "For some time they (the natives) had been restless, numerous murders of emigrants crossing the plains have occurred, and it is deemed necessary by the Government to remove some of the tribes to reservations which have been selected for them."[2]

In order to have an understanding of the second council at Walla Walla, we must know something about the 1855 treaty negotiations and the bad feeling they engendered. The 1855 council was more ably reported than the second meeting and as a result gives us a fine picture of one and a suggestion of the color and drama of the other.

IT WOULD depend on your personal viewpoint whether you thought the treaties were famous or infamous. It is a fact that many Indians, past and present, place them in the latter category.

It is true that a treaty was badly needed because many white settlers were moving or had moved into the Walla Walla valley as a result of the Donation Land Law. As a means of protecting the rights of older settlers, the Donation Land Law was devised. Any man who was a citizen of the United States prior to December, 1850, or declared his intention to become one prior to that date, was assured 320 acres of land. If he was married, he could have 640 acres. It is also a fact that this movement was made despite the fact that the native rights of the area Indians had not been extinguished by agreement between the chiefs, their tribesmen, and the United States Government.

The projected treaty was designed to lay out by certain metes and bounds, areas within which settlers could homestead, as well as laying aside other land masses which were to be maintained as reservations for the natives. Both were to be protected by federal edict and military might.

If either race overstepped the boundaries that had been agreeable to both, trouble was bound to start between the two dissimilar cultures and when that happened the government would have to step into the breach in order to settle such disputes.

It is not surprising under the circumstances that difficult problems did arise despite the fact that measures were taken to forestall just such confrontations.

BUT FIRST, let us describe some of the more picturesque elements of the council before we move on to the sober deliberations of the council members and the results of the meeting.

Kip described what he saw when he arrived at the council grounds in what is now the present city limits of Walla Walla.

"Wednesday, May 23rd. At two o'clock P.M. we arrived at the ground selected for the council, having made the march in six days. It was in one of the most beautiful spots of the Walla Walla valley, well wooded and with plenty of water. Ten miles distant, is seen the range of the Blue Mountains, forming the southeast boundary of the great plains along the Columbia, whose waters it divides from those of the **Lewis** river (present Snake River, ed.). It stretches away along the horizon until it is lost in the dim distance where the chain unites with the Snake River Mountains.

Here we found General Palmer, the Superintendent of Indian Affairs for Oregon, and Governor Stevens, with their party, who had already pitched their tents. With the latter we dined. As was proper for the highest dignitary on the ground, he had a dining room separate from his tent. An arbor had been erected near it, in which was placed a table hastily constructed from split pine logs, smoothed off, but not very smooth."

The next day Thursday, May 24, 1855, Kip described the panoply of colorful costumes worn by the Nez Perce when they came to the council grounds. Kip wrote: "This has been an exceedingly interesting day, as about 2,500 of the Nez Perce tribe have arrived. It was our first specimen of this Prairie chivalry, and it certainly realized all our conceptions of these wild warriors of the plains. Their coming was announced about ten o'clock, and going out on the plain to where a flag staff had been erected, we saw them approaching on horseback in one long line. They were almost entirely naked, gaudily painted and decorated with their wild trappings. Their plumes fluttered about them, while below, skins and trinkets of all kinds of fantastic embellishments flaunted in the sunshine. Trained from early childhood almost to live upon horseback, they sat upon their fine animals as if they were centaurs. Their horses, too, were arrayed in the most glaring finery. They were painted with such colors as formed the greatest contrast; the white being smeared with crimson in fantastic figures, and the dark colored streaked with white clay. Beads and fringes of gaudy colors were hanging from the bridles, while the plumes of eagle feathers interwoven with the mane and tail, fluttered as the breeze swept over them, and completed their wild and fantastic appearance."

NO DOUBT THE Indians came to the council because they anticipated that there would be many fine gifts and much money given out by the commissioners as an incentive for them to sign treaties.

Captain T.J. Cram in his Topographical Memoir of the Department of the Pacific wrote (pp 81) "That about eight tribes with 5,000 members represented on May 29, 1855 — at the sittings of the council, however, there were present about 1,000."

Cram, too, described the Indians as follows, "The tout ensemble of each tribe, on this occasion, was magnificence in the extreme; while that of the whites, on the contrary, was meagre and insignificant. It was humiliating to witness the contrast, so unfavorable to the success so earnestly hoped for." — Cram described the beauty of Indian garments and their equipage. Following this he continued: "Not so with the whites; the retinue of the commissioners was shabby, diminutive, and mean in appointments generally, and deficient in all those points of show, in particular, that are so well calculated to strike the fancy or command the respect of an Indian."

He also reported — "The pitiful escort of the commissioners of only thirty or forty United States Infantry soldiers, mounted on lame, gaunt horses and mules, literally fed on nothing, — contrasted most unfortunately with the array presented by 1,200 Nez Perce horsemen. By allowing themselves to go into council under such circumstances, the commissioners, at the outset, jeopardized the very object of the negotiations. Even the Cayuses, the smallest in numbers, manifested utter contempt for the military escort, —."[3]

It would appear the treaty of 1855 was ill conceived and poorly executed because of the seeming ignorance of Indian culture shown by Washington's first territorial governor, Isaac I. Stevens.

Stevens, nonetheless, was the proper man to head treaty negotiations because although he was the Governor, he was also Indian Commissioner for the newly created territory. He was a brilliant man having graduated first in his class at West Point. He was also an experienced soldier and one who could make quick and accurate decisions. He had served as leader of the Northern Railroad route survey just two years previously, and had completed it expeditiously and completely. He had recently organized a territorial government. He knew much more about the natives than he implied when he had the colossal effrontery to suggest to the assembled Indians that they should all move onto one gigantic reservation.

It is easy to see how unfeasible his plan was, when one considers that all tribes East of the Cascade mountain chain in Washington Territory were urged to live together.

He must have observed while he was speaking to them, that several interpreters were on hand translating his remarks into several linguistic-patterns and he should have realized that the language barrier alone would make his plan unfeasible.

SOME OF THE TRIBES at the council were unfriendly with others and as a result would find it impossible to live in peaceful co-existence with them because of age old enmities.

It may well be that he was craftily creating a psychological advantage for himself by suggesting such a ridiculous proposition. This approach would make more sense because he could then offer an alternative plan that would be more readily accepted. Perhaps this explains what happened.

It was during this part of the talks that many of the chiefs got up and spoke out strongly against selling their mother earth. They used allegorical terms but were very clear in their complaints. As an example of the feelings of the Indians about the negotiations that were taking place we shall have Lawrence Kip tell what happened to him.

"There is evidently a more hostile feeling towards the whites getting up among some of the tribes, of which we had tonight a very unmistakable proof. The Cayuse, we have known, have never been friendly, but hitherto they have disguised their feelings. Tonight, as Lieutenant Gracie and I attempted, as usual to enter their camp, they showed a decided opposition; we were motioned back, and the young warriors threw themselves in our way to obstruct our advance. To yield to this, however, or show any signs of being intimidated, would have been ruinous with the Indians, so were obliged to carry out our original intentions. We placed our horses abreast, riding round the Indians, where it was possible, and at other times forcing our way through, believing that they would not dare to resort to actual violence. If, however, this hostile feeling at the Council increases, how long will it be before we have an actual outbreak?"[4]

ISAAC STEVENS and Joel Palmer, Indian Commissioner for Oregon Territory, persevered, cajoled, and threatened until they eventually worked their way through the negotiations. Eventually agreements were signed with the three major tribes represented, placing them on separate reservations. There were lands allotted to the Nez Perce, the Yakima, and the Umatilla.

The northern tribes had little or no representation at Walla Walla that year with the result that they were virtually disregarded during this council. Governor Stevens let them know that he would treat with them later.

No one seemed to be happy with the results of the treaty meeting, except the peace party. During the next three months disillusionment and anger grew in the hearts of many of the chiefs who soon realized that they had received a poor deal. Inter-tribal discussions fanned into flaming action what had been only individual thoughts of war. Ill feelings extended among the river tribes until tribal anger culminated into a full fledged war, which lasted through the latter months of 1855 and the early part of 1856. Most of the tribes involved in the treaty except the Nez Perce were at war, along with some of the coast tribes.

The single most important cause of the outbreak was the murder at Wahk-Shum Springs near Goldendale, Washington, of Sub-Agent Andrew J. Bolen who had hurried to the Yakima valley from the Spokane country to ascertain the truth of rumors that area Indians had slain eight white miners who had been enroute to the Pend Oreille mines.

Bolen had been placed in charge of handling trade goods, gifts, and foods which were to be used by Governor Stevens and the Peace Commission during a projected council with the Indians of the upper country vis., The Spokane, Coeur d'Alene, and Colville.

Antoine Plantes' place on the Spokane River had been chosen as the council site and it was then that Bolen had been told about the deaths of the miners by Chief Spokane Garry. He rushed to the Yakima valley to his death. This tragedy ignited the torch of war!

A few victories and several defeats inflicted on them by a superior armed and trained enemy forced the natives to sue for peace in the spring of 1856. It was, at best, an uneasy truce because the Indians were bitter and apprehensive about what ulterior plans these powerful interlopers were working out for their eventual destruction.

Realizing that something was radically wrong, Stevens attempted to rectify the problem by calling the tribesmen back for another meeting. It is evident that Governor Stevens intended to treat with the northern tribes who had not participated in the hostilities because he asked all of the friendly Indians as well as those that had lately been hostile to attend a meeting.

It was anticipated that the 1856 council would command a larger audience and would salve some of the wounds caused by the treaty of 1855 and the late war. It is evident that the Governor recognized the fact that a council was badly needed in order to avert still another war. As proof of this, Hazard Stevens, the governor's son, had this to say about it in his book entitled "Isaac I. Stevens":

"The Governor therefore decided to proceed in person to Walla Walla and there hold a council with the Indians, in order to confirm the friendship of the Nez Perces and restrain the doubtful and wavering from active hostility."

Hazard also noted that the Governor directed William Craig (early mountain man settler in the Craig's Mountain area of Idaho near present Lapwai, Idaho), and Colonel B.F. Shaw (of the United States Army) "to summon the hitherto friendly Indians, the Nez Perces, Spokanes, Coeur d'Alenes and friendly Cayuses, to the Council."

Stevens requested through Craig and Shaw, that the hostiles attend, "under the sole condition of submission to the government, requiring them to come unarmed and assuring them of safe conduct to, at, and from the council."[5] His terms were unbelievably harsh when one realizes he was attempting to mend fences. Despite the brusqueness of the invitations the Indians came from near and far to hear what his plans were.

ONE ORIGINAL SOURCE of valuable data concerning the treaty, shed much light on the negotiations that took place. Andrew Dominique Pambrun (a son of Pierre Christologue Pambrun, early day Hudson's Bay Company fur trader at Fort Walla Walla) wrote an unpublished narrative in which he recalled many phases of his interesting life. A part of it covered the second treaty at Walla Walla.

Pambrun had attended the first council meeting in 1855, and was an active participant in it. He had this to say about it. "In the meantime Governor Stevens and General Palmer, acting Indian Commissioners, with a large retinue of teams and packers, and escorted by a company of soldiers came to hold treaties with the several tribes of the Columbia Basin. Several days were occupied in feasting and talking, but apparently making no progress in the aim of the meeting, finally the Governor recapitulated all that had been said and offered and concluded by saying, "If you do not accept the terms offered and sign this paper (holding up the paper) you will walk in blood lance deep."[6]

Pambrun who was one of the several interpreters employed, mentioned that the priest (Father Prando?) felt the threat made by Stevens was a grave tactical error.

Eventually, all of the chiefs and headmen signed the treaties but their feelings were hurt and they were resentful. Pambrun's description of the Yakima chief, Kamiaken as he signed the treaty, shows (as an example) what admirable restraint the chiefs used to disguise their anger and frustration at this dismaying turn of events.

Pambrun wrote: "All the chiefs signed, Kamiaken was the last, and as he turned to take his seat, the priest punched me and whispered, "look at Kamiaken, we will all get killed, he was in such a rage that he bit his lips (so) that they bled profusely."[7]

Looking Glass, one of the major chiefs of the Nez Perce tribe, made a dramatic appearance late in the proceedings and was very angry with his tribesmen for signing the treaty during his absence. He railed against Lawyer but was convinced finally that he should sign the treaty, too. He did so with seeming reluctance.

For awhile it looked as though hostilities might begin — but eventually cooler heads prevailed and an uneasy peace prevailed.

Pambrun observed this and wrote the following: "After the distribution of beef, flour, sugar, and coffee everything appeared to be tranquil but only apparently so. I expected an immediate outbreak but from one cause or another (it) did not occur till autumn, but their plans were not then matured."[8]

It did not take long for their "plans to mature," because by autumn Kamiaken had organized his people and their allies into a united fighting unit and a full fledged war began, following the murder of Sub-Agent Andrew J. Bolen near the present community of Goldendale, Washington.

Hostilities were in progress at the time Stevens was talking about a peace treaty with the Coeur d'Alene and Spokane Indians at Antoine Plante's ferry site on the Spokane River. After a heated discussion with the Coeur d'Alene and Spokane tribesmen he headed toward Olympia via the Nez Perce country, a round-about route back to his headquarters.

Meanwhile, Andrew Pambrun was having a trying time in the Walla Walla valley. His problems were vexatious! Angry natives were killing any individuals or small parties they could find and Pambrun was evacuated, by the military, from his home along with other settlers to Fort Henrietta, where they remained for awhile. A short time later these people were moved to an unidentified place which proved to be indefensible so they were brought to the Catholic mission (which I would judge was St. Rose Mission) where Pambrun planted some seed wheat. This crop was not allowed to mature because it was destroyed by the natives before it was ripe.

Next Pambrun moved out of the Walla Walla valley to Eight Mile Creek near The Dalles, Oregon where he felt so secure that he planted another garden and sent for his family. As a word of explanation, he had sent them to Fort Vancouver for safekeeping as soon as the war broke out. Now, he felt that they would be relatively safe with him at The Dalles.

Meanwhile hostilities had ceased and an uneasy peace prevailed. His family had scarcely settled down in their new surroundings, near The Dalles, when he received a message from Governor Isaac I. Stevens, asking him to be his interpreter, secretary and guide just as he had been at the first Walla Walla council. His salary was to be $5.00 per day, paid in gold coin.

Pambrun accepted the offer, and a short while later the Governor, his expressman W.H. Pearson, and Andrew left The Dalles with two pack animals loaded with supplies. Hazard Stevens, the Governor's son, reported that they left The Dalles on August 19, 1856.

THE GOVERNOR tried valiantly to keep up with the rapid pace set by Pearson and Pambrun but was unable to do so, because his double hernia was bothering him. The journey was resumed as soon as Stevens was able to make himself comfortable enough to ride! Andrew Pambrun noted that Stevens was always cheerful despite his painful condition. When their small party arrived at the meeting site in the Walla Walla valley, they found the entire treaty party assembled including the slow moving ox train of forty wagons of supplies that had preceded them.

There is a discrepancy between the Pambrun and Hazard Stevens accounts because Hazard wrote that his father left The Dalles, in advance of Steptoe's military column, with a train of thirty wagons drawn by eighty oxen and two hundred loose animals. He had no escort except for the employees, and reached Colonel B.F. Shaw's camp in the Walla Walla valley on the 23rd. Here he found, according to Pambrun, that Colonel B.F. Shaw, who had been pursuing Indians in the Grande Ronde country with impunity, had recently sustained a humiliating defeat during a retaliatory attack near Milton, Oregon, while on his way to the council. Ten Walla Walla and two Cayuse had attacked his military party about sundown and forced them to abandon their pack train and riding animals. They made their escape under cover of darkness!

The disorganized group reached Stevens' camp and reported the story of their defeat and escape to him. Stevens was very angry and rebuked those in charge of the operation. The next morning the Volunteers overtook the gleeful Indians and attacked them. Three unsuccessful attempts were made to recapture the pack train but to no avail.[9]

What was really humiliating about the entire episode was the fact that when the council convened, several grinning Indians came into camp riding some of the purloined mules and wearing some of the clothing that had been in the pack train supplies. The garments were to have been given to the Volunteers to cover their nearly naked bodies — and now, these men wearing threadbare outfits were confronted by natives who flaunted the clothing intended for them at a time when a confrontation about them would be inadvisable. What really climaxed the entire unsavory episode was the knowledge that the entire treaty party had to smile during the proceedings despite their bitter feelings to the contrary.[10]

Hazard Stevens noted that William Craig, early day fur trader and the man who named Idaho, as well as Dr. Lansdale, who was the agent for the Flathead Indians in the Bitterroot Valley, rode into camp on August 30th. They were accompanied by some Nez Perce chiefs.

Nicholas Montour and Antoine Plante arrived the next day. They were asked to represent the Spokane. They brought a message to Stevens from the Spokane that although they "professed a friendly disposition" would not attend the council.[11]

Stevens appeared to be confident that this council would succeed where the first one had failed. In a letter from the Walla Walla valley dated August 31, 1856 he wrote, in part:

"I find things in the upper country in as good a condition as I expected. The

Nez Perce are very friendly. The advance of them reached my camp yesterday, and the whole nation will be here on Wednesday. My expresses have been among the tribes on and in the neighborhood of the Spokane the last five days, and Father Ravalli, the superior of the Coeur d'Alene Mission, and a gentleman of great worth and intelligence, is of the opinion that they and the hostiles in that quarter, will come to the council. In about five days I shall have definite information in relation to the parties who will be present at the council!

"The object of the council is primarily to strengthen the friendship of the tribes that have not joined the hostiles, and secondly, to give an opportunity to come in such hostiles as are willing to submit to the justice and mercy of the government.

"It is not to be disguised, however, that there is much uneasiness in the interior, and that, excepting the Nez Perce, a little thing may precipitate all the remaining tribes into war. I have letters written within the last thirty-three days, from every chief of the friendly tribes to the northward, and between the main Columbia and the Bitterroot mountains, which show this to be the case. I have letters from Owhi and his son, the terms of which are utterly inadmissible. These letters are unquestionably the true dictations of the Indians, as they are written by Father Ravalli, in whose word I can place implicit confidence."[12]

R EALIZING THAT a meeting with so many hostiles might prove dangerous, Stevens requested military aid from Major General Wool but because he did not receive a straight answer decided to use volunteers.

In a letter to Lieutenant Colonel E.J. Steptoe dated Walla Walla, August 25th, 1856, he wrote, in part: "The term of service of the volunteers will expire on the 8th of September, and that of one company on the 30th of this month. They number one hundred and fifty-six officers and men. I have asked them to remain till the council was concluded, and the valley was occupied by regular troops, to which they very willingly assented.

"From present appearances, I do not think the council can be opened till next week and perhaps not till the middle of the week. I particularly desire your presence, and that of at least a portion of your command during the council! I will ask, however, that you place your troops somewhere in the general vicinity of the council ground, till the council is through. My object is to show the Indians the strength of our people and the unity of our councils."[13]

A few more communications between the two men took place and finally Steptoe wrote from his camp on Mill Creek in the Walla Walla valley on September 10, 1856: "If you had informed me this morning that you desired the presence of my command, I would have encamped near you tonight; as it is, I am now some seven or eight miles beyond you!

"It is necessary for my train to start back to The Dalles in the morning, and I have occupation very constantly for the dragoons in one way or another — all which leaves me but a small force to prepare and guard my winter camp!

"My advice (if you will permit the liberty) is that the council business be adjourned, so far as possible, to some more convenient time. It is plain that I shall not have the force you desire to despatch to the council ground, nor any force to remain there long. And permit me to say that my instructions from General Wool do not authorize me to make any arrangement, whatever, of the kind you wish. Pardon me for writing so much, but the fact is, my position is one which seems to compel a lengthy explanation. In short, if I thought you were in the least danger, I would not hesitate to move down at once the whole of my force; as it is, I can not accede to your request."[14]

The above letter shows clearly how strained relations were between General Wool and Governor Stevens. Both were strong, opinionated men who had different ideas on how to handle the war and the Indian problem, and both presented in print their ideas to the public and to government authorities.

As this account progresses it will be evident why it was necessary to interject the data just read into this narrative.

Pambrun wrote that the Nez Perce rode into the treaty area and were saluted by three discharges from a small cannon. The third shot caused the barrel of the cannon to blow up into many pieces and despite the fact that there were many people gathered around it, no one was hurt!

Homlie, chief of the Walla Walla, upon being told why the meeting was taking place, said that he was not whipped but had ceased fighting because of his pity for the old and infirm of his tribe. He told Governor Stevens: "I am glad I have come, my friend, and I promise never more to hurt a white man, but be his true friend." Homlie then agreed to make peace, and Pambrun who wrote the above quote, added: "He kept his word."[15]

THAT NIGHT the Nez Perce performed a dance in anticipation of a peaceful co-existent future. Several members of the Stevens' party watched them dance. Pambrun was not present because he was busily at work writing his report of the day's occurrence. Stevens interrupted him and asked him to gather the commission party together so they could officially greet the Cayuse who were coming to the treaty grounds.

While doing his bidding, Andrew had a problem getting Doctor Burns out of the Indian camp because the Doctor insisted on continuing to eat and visit with his Indian chief friend Staketla, in spite of being surrounded by unfriendly natives. Pambrun had to threaten a Cayuse named Ta-kin with his pistol before the angry natives would let him and the Doctor through their lines.[16]

In camp, a short time later, he was amazed to find that Doctor Burns and Staketla were in the former's tent drinking from a can of alcohol. Pambrun soon confiscated the liquor because he did not want the chief to get drunk and cause trouble.[17]

By the time all of the tribesmen arrived for the council there were about 4,000 natives present, principally, Nez Perce, Cayuse, Walla Walla, and Yakima. There was a sprinkling of others, too.

As events transpired during the talks, feelings became tense between the Indians and the commissioners. No doubt the Indian leaders realized how divided the white forces were because of statements that Steptoe made. There is little doubt that Steptoe was only echoing the orders he had received from General Wool.

Because things were not turning out as had been anticipated, a plan of action was discussed, at which time it was decided to move camp to a more defensible position. The present camp was situated among some brush which could be used to the advantage of the native should they decide to attack so they moved "some distance above on Mill Creek"[18] closer to the military camp of Lieutenant Colonel Edward J. Steptoe.

IN A LETTER from Fort Vancouver dated September 20th, 1856, Colonel George Wright wrote in part: "The Colonel has selected a position on Mill Creek for the military post. It is five miles below Whitman's old mill site and is directly on the trails from the Nez Perces, Spokane, and Palouse country and controls the entire valley."

This would verify Pambrun's statement about their camp location. Things were not progressing as smoothly as Pambrun's notes implied. Steptoe had received direct orders from General John Wool (his superior) not to aid Stevens or the council commission, but to remain nearby to serve as a peaceful agent between the Army and the natives.

Stevens asked Steptoe to camp close by his party, but the latter ignored his request and moved his camp seven miles away from Stevens' campsite. Steptoe went so far as to tell a number of Indians while in a conference that "My mission is pacific. I have come not to fight you, but to live among you. Come into my camp whenever you please. I trust we shall live together as friends." When he made this statement he showed the hostile natives present at the meeting just how divided the Army and the Commission were. As a result he did immeasureable harm to the peace party and its objectives.

It was not until hostile Indians burned the grass around Stevens' camp that he allowed Stevens and his people to move closer to his camp. Another reason he changed his mind was because the hostile chiefs did not come to meet with him as they had promised. Steptoe also found it expedient to make use of Stevens' wagons in order to move his supplies to the Umatilla country where his horses could find forage.[19]

Stevens agreed to the proposition and the move began. This gave the entire party united strength. It is fortunate for both parties that they did join forces as will be seen later. Two documents illuminate what happened. One of them was confidential in character. Both follow:

Confidential
Council Grounds, Walla Walla Valley, Washington Territory
September 13th, 1856

Lieutenant Colonel E.J. Steptoe:
My Dear Sir:
The council did not adjourn yesterday till near sundown, too late for me to visit your camp. I understood the feelings of the Indians from what was developed yesterday.

The want of a military force on the ground seriously embarrassed me, (I have retained for a day some fifty of Goff's company), but having called the council in good faith as the Indian superintendent and also, as the Commissioner to treat with the Indian tribes by the appointment of the President. I shall go through the duty I have undertaken. One half of the Nez Perces and all of the other tribes, except a very few persons are unmistakably hostile in feeling. The Cayuses, the Walla Wallas and the other hostiles were so when they came in. Hence the requisition I made upon you for troops.

103

I particularly desire you to be present today, if your duties will permit, and I will also state that I think a company of your troops is essential to the security of my camp.

I shall as I said go through with this business whatever be the consequences as regards my own personal safety, but I regard it to be my duty to the public, to the Indians, and to my own character.

This communication is marked "Confidential" but it is intended as an official communication, and will go on my files as such, only I do not think it prudent, that my judgment as to the aspect of affairs, should at this time be disclosed to any other person than yourself.
I have the honor to be,
Very Respectively,
Your most obedient servant
Isaac I. Stevens
Governor and Superintendent

Steptoe's letter written the same day was not hopeful.

Camp on Mill Creek, Washington Terr.
September 13th, 1856

Governor:

I have received your communication of today, and regret extremely that you think a company of my troops to be "essential to the safety" of your camp.

In a previous communication I suggested that if you distrusted the safety of your position, the council might be adjourned to a more convenient time and place.

As you know, my camp for the winter is in preparation; the train has been unloaded and sent back to The Dalles, and much valuable property, which cannot now be removed, lies on my camp ground. If the Indians are, therefore, really meditating an attack, it will be difficult for me to provide for the defense of my own camp — **impossible** to defend **both** camps. Under these circumstances, if you are resolved to go on with your council, does it not seem more reasonable that you should move your camp to the vicinity of mine?

I send down the company of dragoons to bring you up to this place if you desire to come.

Allow me to say that your request for troops embarrasses me fully as much as you can be by their absence from your council ground. My force is so small, that, to be efficient against the large number of savages in the neighborhood, it must be concentrated, nor can I detach any portion of it, in execution of certain instructions from General Wool, while the Indian host remains so near to me.

Very respectfully, Your obedient servant,
E.J. Steptoe
Brevet Lieut. Col. U.S.A.

S TEPTOE WAS HEWING close to the line but he was soon to learn that his own plans were going awry and he would need help himself. It is evident what happened to change his mind so quickly when you read his next letter.

Camp, Sept. 19, 1856

Gov. Stevens, etc.

Council Ground:

Governor:

I have just received the note asking that the dragoons be sent to your aid.

Now, the Cayuses have burned all the grass near me. I shall have to send my animals quite a distance for grass, and if I send the dragoons to you I shall be unable to herd them. Besides that the company could not return to me for some time, and the Indians would probably turn all their attention to the few men left with me. I have no block houses, and shall expect to be annoyed much.

Under these circumstances, do you not think I had better use your train and move with you to the Umatilla, or some point beyond, where **you** would be safe from molestation, and **I** could find grass abundant? If I had my train I would not hesitate a moment, but would join you in the morning with my whole command rather than part with the only mounted men I have. What do you think of **returning to this camp tonight or in the morning,** taking my luggage up in your wagons, and our moving off together? Let me hear from you by Richard. I cannot help thinking that if you abandon (burn up?) your old wagons, you can easily get through with your pack animals; but what think you of my plan of going together?

Yours in haste;
e.j. Steptoe

I could probably send you Fletcher's company, with most ease, but I think it best for both of us that you loose a day and take up our baggage.

Lt. Col. E.J. Steptoe

After Stevens received this letter he joined Steptoe and his troops. He realized that the two parties would give material aid to each other.

While the volunteers and the teams with supplies went by way of the main road, a small party comprised of the governor, William Craig, Lawyer (the Nez Perce chief) and Andrew Pumbrun took another trail so they could observe the conduct of the Indians as they filed by.

They had proceeded a short ways when they were confronted by the Yakima chief, Kamiaken, and many of his warriors bedecked in beautiful finery. The natives rode abreast of each other and their line extended about three hundred yards long, according to Pambrun.

T HE GOVERNOR'S PARTY immediately formed into a defensive unit. The wily Kamiaken saw this maneuver and offered to shake hands. He was

105

told that such amenities would be forgotten until the entire commission party was safely near Steptoe's camp. This was good thinking because Stevens' party was outnumbered five to one.

Lawyer, the Nez Perce chief, later agreed with Pambrun, Stevens and William Craig that Stevens had been wise to refuse the proferred handshakes, at that time, because all of the Yakimas would have clustered around the smaller party in a seemingly friendly manner and taken them captive as they did so. Or perhaps there would have been a bloody hand to hand battle.

At any rate the party continued its march until it reached the new campsite which proved to be as poor as the old one. It was so situated that an enemy could have assumed control of the brush and water supply nearby. Fortunately, Lawyer, Homlie and Stakotla had assured the commission party that they would remain peaceful. This divisiveness among the Indians averted any attack that might have been planned by the hostile element of the confederated tribes.

One Indian took a daily walk in front of the leafy arbor that Governor Stevens called his office. He was evidently seeking an opportunity to slay the Governor. Pambrun accused him of this. The native denied the charge but was seen no more.

Several days were spent in vain trying to negotiate peace treaties. Seeing that natives were in no mood to do so, the Governor and his commission decided to return to The Dalles. Some gifts had been distributed during the negotiations but the rest of the supplies and gifts were repaced and soon the party was on its journey homeward. Its mission was a dismal failure.[20]

The entourage had gone only a few miles when Pambrun was told by George, an old Nez Perce, that the hostiles were massing for an attack. Looking where the friendly Indian was pointing, the assembled party saw (as Andrew described it) "squads of from thirty to fifty coming down the hills, their horses as well as themselves painted and dressed in all the varied colors of the rainbow. The scene was picturesque in the highest degree, and the effect in some of our party, was as varied, some gaze with defiance at the approaching conflict, others turned pale with excitement and perhaps fear, while two or three others were weeping for their families whom they never expected to see in this world."[21]

Andrew, according to his narrative, rode to the head of the column to warn the Governor of impending hostilities.

After a momentary halt, the column continued toward a small spring-fed stream where a defense and counter-attack could be mounted. Here, a corral was made of the wagons. Men and animals crowded into it for protection.

A GENERAL ATTACK began which was ineffective because it was fought at long range.

About seventy-five yards from the wagons there was a thicket of willow and rose bushes which could serve as a good cover for sharpshooters if it fell into the hands of the natives. In order to control this vantage point, Pambrun and seven others were sent to hold it.

An attempt was made to dislodge this party but the attack was aborted because a Nez Perce scout yelled a warning that a charge was being made. Knowing that their target had been alerted the natives made no further move in that direction.

A couple of men in the party who exposed themselves unnecessarily, were shot and both died as a result of their wounds.

Colonel B.F. Shaw saw a large party of Indians clustered together. He and thirty volunteers charged them. He didn't realize that he was being lured into a trap where about three hundred warriors lay in wait for him and his men.

One old Indian seeing his friends fleeing from such a small party, called them cowards and ordered them to turn back and fight the soldiers. Strange to say they obeyed his command. Realizing that their projected plan was ruined the large party rushed out of the ravine, where they had hidden, and attempted to kill Shaw and his men.

When the Stevens commission party saw what was happening, they made a counter charge that extricated Colonel Shaw and his men from their dangerous position. It was impossible to tell allies from enemies as the spirited battle took place. Between one and two o'clock the regular army under Lieutenant Colonel Edward J. Steptoe came to help and soon thereafter fighting ceased.

Ox teams were hitched and horses were saddled for the move to Steptoe's camp. Hostile Indians rode parallel to the moving column firing their guns but made no impression except to frighten some of the men. Teams were halted near a small branch of Mill Creek, while soldiers moved ahead scouring the timber for skulking Indians. The moon came out and exposed the waiting teamsters to shellfire from a neighboring hill. Despite this desultory shellfire from the natives, no one was hurt. As soon as the soldiers returned, the interrupted march was resumed until the combined party reached Steptoe's campground.

THE NEXT DAY, Andrew and seven soldiers got into a sharp exchange of rifle fire with some of the Columbia tribe of Indians during which Andrew claimed that he shot a brother of Moses through the thighs with a minie ball from which he later died at Rock Island. This is the first mention of the use of a minie ball shooting rifle in action in the Pacific Northwest. Andrew Pambrun described it as follows in his narrative:

"The Minnie Rifle then used by the Army, was a fine arm, shooting with accuracy at long range, and with such tremendous force."

This statement causes me to doubt Pambruns' account in this case because if Steptoe's men were armed with these superior weapons in 1856, why didn't they use these excellent arms in May 1858, at Rosalia, Washington, where they were defeated by the confederated tribes? The muskets used in the battle which took place May 17, 1858, had such poor firepower that they were largely responsible for that defeat.

Rifles firing minie balls were used by Colonel George Wright in the autumn of the same year and this new, powerful weapon was lauded as a super arm. Perhaps Pambrun's recollections were clouded because of the passage of time when he wrote his narrative. Or there could have been a few guns sent west which were used as experimental weapons prior to 1858.

Following this skirmish, during which several Indians lost their lives, the Indians withdrew. According to Pambrun's account, this ended hostilities.

Dunnage was packed and the disappointed peace party made its wary way in safety to Fort Dalles where Andrew reported that he "had to work day and night" to prepare reports of the abortive peace party negotiations while "the Governor (was) awaiting impatiently for the documents."

Andrew reported: "His Secretary here met us but was unable to assist me from mental incapability." I think Pambrun was very observant because it is claimed that James Doty took his own life a short time later. Perhaps he was showing signs of mental problems at this time.

The second Walla Walla treaty expedition which was born in optimism was like a tree that died without bearing the fruit of peace which Governor Stevens hopefully expected of it. It did bear bitter fruit that was harvested two years later in the Steptoe and Wright campaigns of 1858. The crop is still being harvested periodically when descendants of these people let it be known that they still nourish enmities that are the direct result of the Walla Walla treaties of 1855 and the Indian campaigns of 1855 and of 1858.

NOTES

1. Stevens, Hazard. **The Life of Isaac Ingalls Stevens.** 2 vols. Boston, Houghton, Miflin and Company, 1901. Vol. II, page 27
2. Kip, Lawrence. **The Indian Council in the Valley of The Walla Walla.** San Francisco, 1855 reprinted Eugene, Oregon, 1897.
3. Cram, Thomas J. **Topographical Memoir . . . Relative to the Territories of Oregon and Washington.** Wash., 1859. House Doc. 114.
4. Kip, op. cit.
5. Stevens, op. cit., II pg 203
6. Pambrun, Andrew. Mss in the personal collection of the author. Pg 124-125.
7. Ibid., pg 125
8. Ibid., pg 125
9. Ibid., pg 135
10. Ibid., pg 135-136
11. Stevens, H. op. cit., II pg 210
12. Stevens, Isaac I. **Message of the Governor of Washington Territory, also the Correspondence with the Secretary of War.** Olympia, 1857. Pg 122-123.
13. Ibid., pg 172
14. Ibid., pg 177
15. Pambrun, op. cit., pg 136
16. Ibid., pg 136-137
17. Ibid., pg 137
18. Ibid., pg 138
19. Stevens, H. op. cit., II 220-233
20. Pambrun, cop. cit., pg 138-140
21. Ibid., pg 140

The PACIFIC NORTHWESTERNER

WESTERNERS, SPOKANE CORRAL

Vol. 36   No. 4   1992

Christmas in the
Pacific Northwest

by Jerome Peltier

The celebration of Christmas in the Pacific Northwest has a short history. Christians did not penetrate inland beyond the Pacific coastline until the late 17th century and exploration and trading did did not begin until the early 1800s. But the Yuletide season which surrounds Christmas and New Year's Day saw many noteworthy events which should be recalled. This paper will comprise stories of Christmases past in the Northwest, separated in time, but united in their sharing of the season.

During the early days of the fur trade, one particular Christmas made a lasting impression, in a historical sense, upon the Spokane area. It was celebrated at a distant point geographically from the falls on the Spokane River and although what occurred had no immediate result, seemingly, it did have a powerful delayed impact. Negotiations took place at Fort Astoria on Christmas Day 1813 which were to spell doom to the Astorian fur trade enterprise in the Pacific Northwest and, as a result, Fort Spokane was abandoned. As a word of explanation, Fort Spokane was a neighbor to Spokane House at the confluence of the Spokane and the Little Spokane rivers just ten miles northwest from downtown Spokane.

Jerome Peltier is the author of numerous books and articles dealing with Western American history. His interest in original documents and accounts from the fur trade era and concerning the Pacific Northwest was a natural result of his many years in the antiquarian book trade in Spokane. Jerry was a founder and first sheriff of the Spokane Westerners.

Vol. 36   No. 4   1992

Published quarterly by the Spokane Corral of the Westerners, P.O. Box 1717, Spokane, WA 99210. Subscription $10.00 per calendar year. Back issues available, $2.50 ea. Articles appearing in this journal are abstracted and indexed in *Historical Abstracts:* and/or *America History and Life.*   ISSN: 0030-882 X

Articles dealing with the history and development of the American and Canadian West are welcomed for consideration. Submissions should be directed to the editor, Robert A. Clark, at the above address. All submissions should be accompanied by a self-addressed stamped envelope for return.

The people at Fort Spokane celebrated the holidays as usual with drinking, smoking, jokes, laughter and the presentation of gifts. No one there knew that on the same day, five hundred miles away at Fort Astoria, events were transpiring that would seal the doom of their business operations in the Spokane country as well as in the entire Oregon country.

One year earlier the Astorians had confidently moved into their newly constructed quarters at Fort Spokane, close to their major competitor, and thanked the Lord for their warm home and good food. They had celebrated its beginnings as well as the birth of the Christ-child at that time.

Alexander Henry, one of the best writers among the "scribbling clerks" of the fur trade era in the Pacific Northwest, kept a fine narrative journal of his experiences and it is to him that we owe a debt of gratitude for preserving this moment in history.

He reached Astoria on November 15, 1813, after a wearisome overland trek from the East. He had become somewhat acquainted with the customs of our west coast Indians by the time the Christmas season came around and his entries of December 24-25 are of great interest because he tells us much about life at this isolated trading post, including how Christmas day was spent at Astoria. The two entries follow:

Friday - 24 - Rain and foggy weather but calm, these incessant rains are truly unpleasant, and fere [fear] very much will have some bad effect upon our common men, who are now employed building a house for themselves, and of course are daily exposed to the inclemency of the weather, and wet to the very skin, and trampling through mud and water all day long and at night have no other shelter than bars covered with matts which must be very damp and moist owing to the state of the weather, and the moisture on the ground. Even in the garret of our store house, which is perfectly tight and staunch, things become damp and mouldy and will rot, I fear ere the Rainy season is over. There is no moving out of doors, but you must be walking through the mud and water. If you tread upon a stone, root or billet of wood, it is ten chances to one if you do not measure your length on the ground, everything is as slippery as glass; and covered with Green Moss, and even the Stokades and buildings are becoming very fast encrusted. It is even dangerous to walk on our platform of boards which are covered with Moss although exposed to the South. Messrs S. [Seton?] and K. [?] finished packing up the goods intended to be sent in the interior about the beginning of January, this afternoon our Clatsop hunter brought us the flesh of a Biche, [a female deer over 3 years old] for which he received immediate payment which is always customary, for everything they bring. At 10 o'clock P.M. we had a very loud peal to Thunder extending from North to South and the rain continued to pour in torrents accompanied by a strong Gale of Wind, from the SouthWest, which altogether presented us a most gloomy night. Cartuis House was finished and Mr. Halsay and Franchere took up their lodgings with him.

J.C. Halsey and Gabriel Franchere (who had both come to the west coast on board the ship *Tonquin*) wrote accounts of their experiences with the Astorian enterprise. It would seem reasonable to assume that Cartius, Halsey and Franchere spent a delightful Christmas eve under their new roof even if Alexander Henry said that the night would be gloomy. Imagine their collective relief to be warm and dry after being under a mat shelter for such a great length of time.

Alexander Henry continues with his journal entry:

Saturday - 25 - Christmas - fine clear and calm weather on the land, but as usual a thick fog at sea, and towards the Cape which is totally enveloped in mist. At 11 o'clock Bellaire and Thomas McKay arrived from the Willamette River, with one man, they bring letters from Mr. W. [?] Henry of the 19 inst/intelligence from that quarter is Beavers are numerous, but the Natives who are also very numerous

An aerial view of the site of Spokane House at the confluence of the Litle Spokane and Spokane rivers. Foundation remnants and impressions can be seen at the point where the road curves. *Courtesy Eastern Washington Historical Society.*

will not hunt them, their only sole employment is digging Roots, Commass, Waptoes etc. and stealing the Beavers that are caught in traps when an opportunity offers! Deer are also very numerous, but a very small kind, Biche there are a few, our people there could collect a reasonable quantity of meat, were not the Indians so numerous and so much given [to] thieving, when our people kill a Deer if they do not carry it home instantly, nine chance to one, if it is not stolen by the Indians, who are always going about like Wolves, and are attracted by the report of the Guns to the Spot, they are exceeding fond of meat, and will barter everything they have for it, they prefer it to any of our goods.

This afternoon an Indian brought in some Salmon which is now so very bad as to be unfit for use, even our men refuse to eat them. Mr. McDougal [Duncan M'Dougall who also came to Astoria via the brig *Tonquin*] accepted the terms offered him by the North West Company. We had an excellent dinner with Wine, Spirits, Porter, Ice (etc) - 13 at table - Bill Fare - Joseph Bouiller - Salt Beef, Potatoes, Pie, Rice Pudding, C. Tart (cherry?), cheese, biscuits etc. This evening it rained very hard and strong South West Wind.

It seems ironic that McDougall would choose Christmas day on which to complete negotiations that would ruin John Jacob Astor's enterprise in the present-day Northwest. Henry's entry that "McDougall had accepted the terms offered him by the North West Company" meant that McDougall had sold out the company's interest in the trading posts of Astoria, Okanogan, Shushwaps, Spokane and other lesser known posts owned by Astor and his partners.

Some background data is necessary at this point for a proper understanding of what occurred. Great Britain and the United States were embroiled in the war of 1812 at this time. McDougall had received threats through his competitors that a British Man of War was nearby and that when it sailed up the Columbia River it would blow Fort Astoria off of the face of the earth!

McDougall was fearful that these threats would be fulfilled, so without consulting his partners or weighing the fact that most of the company posts were inland, proceeded with the sale of his company's posts and its possessions to the Northwest Company.

No doubt, other men at Fort Astoria knew what had occurred and instead of cheerfully celebrating Christmas with a fine meal, some of them must have felt deeply the perfidy perpetrated by McDougall that day. It might be well (in extenuation) to point out that McDougall had formerly been a member of the Northwest Co. and had always had definite leanings toward them, even though he had reluctantly hired out to John Jacob Astor as one of his partners.

It is plain to see that this day changed the course of history in the greater Northwest and as a result it is engraved indelibly in the book of important Inland Empire Christmases.

1812-1814

Ross Cox, a young Irishman who had come to the Northwest coast with the Astor expedition, spent a couple of Christmases in our area that are worth recording. He came to the Northwest coast aboard the second ship sent westward by Astor, *The Beaver.* It landed at Astoria and very soon thereafter trading parties were assembled from its personnel and sent into the interior to trade with the Indians for furs. Ultimately trading posts were built in likely spots and business began to assume a definite pattern.

It was while enroute between Montana and Spokane that Cox

spent some very trying days during the Christmas season of 1812-1813.

He had helped build a trading post, possibly near Noxon, Montana, and during the building of the main house many Flathead Indians had come to trade. A part of the village also visited the N.W. Co. post nearby. Although the natives had recently been defeated by their traditional enemies, the Blackfeet, while hunting buffalo, they still had a few beaver pelts left to trade. The Astorians traded tobacco for the pelts.

When the main building was finished, Cox set out on Dec. 18th for Spokane in a cedar bark canoe, travelling down the Flathead (the present Clark's Fork River). He was accompanied by six companions.

Progress was slow because of dangerous rapids and obstructions in the river. For three nights the party had to sleep practically standing up on the steep bank. According to Cox on Christmas Day they arrived at a place where the river divided into several small channels. Choosing the central channel, they pursued their course. Soon their water route was full of sharp snags and they were forced to land on a marshy island because the sawyers had pierced their canoe and broken several ribs, making it unsteerable.

The island was dotted with small willows. There was no dry material with which to make a fire so Cox and his men spent the remainder of Christmas day and night perched on fallen trees, their heads covered with their blankets and their feet hanging ankle deep in the water. To add to their misery it began to snow about midnight and continued until morning.

The next morning amid the new-fallen snow they succeeded in patching their canoe well enough so they could paddle it to shore. They completed the job of repair the next day and resumed their journey, eventually reaching Fort Spokane in time to participate in New Year's festivities. This day was particularly joyous that year because a large well-built fort had been completed just a few days previously.

It was at this time that Cox described the number of buildings in the new post. He also listed a number of edibles that were available in the area (these included horse meat and carp). He gave his impressions of the natives and the crafty methods his company used against the opposition fur traders in order to take the trade from them. He also gave a general idea of the layout of the Indian village and cemetery that lay close-by the fort.

Here Cox remained for some time in comparative comfort, before once again taking up his difficult trade. During this period of dealing and double dealing, fur trading sometimes became a struggle for survival.

Christmas 1814 was a case in point. On the 5th of August that year, Cox left Fort George for the interior. He and other traders traded for furs that were gathered together at Fort Okanogan, located at the confluence of the Okanogan and Columbia rivers. This accumulation of furs was brought from Okanogan on the 8th of November to headquarters at Fort George, formerly Fort Astoria.

The journey back became a virtual nightmare for the Spokane brigade after it left Okanogan on December 13th during its final lap to Fort Spokane.

The party consisted of Alexander Stewart, one of the McTavish's, James McMillan, Nicholas Montour, Ross Cox, twenty-one Canadians and four Hawaiians. Their pack train comprised of twenty-six horses loaded with ordinary provisions plus the butchered carcasses of forty dogs which the party had purchased for food from the natives at Fort Okanogan.

Snow lay a foot deep on the ground and it was bitter cold. It began to snow heavily and incessantly. Soon a gap appeared in the line of march and the front and rear divisions were miles apart.

Cox and McTavish were in charge of eight loaded horses and were aided by four Canadians and two Sandwich Islanders. They had fallen far to the rear when a heavy storm blew up which continued until nightfall. When it subsided and a freezing cold settled upon them, they realized that they were lost. They dug a large hole in the snow so that they would have some buffer against the cold and settled down for the night in it. A freezing dawn found the party with two badly frost bitten Sandwich Islanders and one dead pack horse.

After they had struggled three miles through the snow, Cox noticed that his gun was missing so he returned to the previous night's camp ground and was chagrined when he reached it to find that he had been carrying the gun in his numb arms instead of on his shoulder as had been his habit.

Shortly after he rejoined his companions, they saw a heavy smoke amid a cluster of trees and here they found and rejoined the remainder of the brigade who were seated around the cheery fire eating breakfast. Cox's party joined them and quickly wolfed down part of a hindquarter and some ribs of roasted dog.

The remainder of the trip was filled with misery of a like nature and by the time the party reached Fort Spokane on Christmas eve they had lost five horses out of the pack string and many of the men were frost bitten.

No doubt all members of this party must have been very grateful for the wonderful conveniences at Spokane House that Christmas day 1814 after such a providential escape from nature's wintry grip!

DeSmet

During the year 1843 the Rev. Peter J. DeSmet was busy trying to obtain personnel for his Oregon missions. He spent a great deal of the year in Europe getting help for them. His time was not wasted because he eventually returned to the northwest with a priest and a brother from Belgium, three Italian fathers, and six nuns of Notre Dame de Namur. He and his religious contingent reached Astoria, Oregon, on July 31, 1844. By late fall he was among the Coeur d'Alene Indians. In November he attempted to go to St. Mary's mission in the Bitterroot Valley, but was stopped by bad weather. On December 4th he attempted to reach the Flathead country via the Clark's Fork River and was once again foiled in his efforts by inclement weather conditions. Taking advantage of the fact that he was temporarily among the Kalispells, he began to teach them Christianity. They responded so well to his teaching that he was pleased to write about the great day as follows:

> The great festival of Christmas, the day on which the little band (124 people) was to be added to the number of the true children of God, will never be effaced from the memory of our good Indians. The manner in which we celebrated midnight mass may give you an idea of our festival. The signal for rising, which was to be given a few minutes before midnight, was the firing of a pistol, announcing to the Indians that the house of prayer would soon be open. This was followed by a general discharge of guns in honor of the birth of the Infant Savior, and 300 voices rose spontaneously from the midst of the forest, and intoned in the language of the Pend d'Oreilles the beautiful canticle "Du Dieu puissant tout annonce la gloire," "The Almighty's glory all things proclaim." In a moment a multitude of adorers were seen wending their way to the humble temple of the Lord—resembling indeed the manger in which the Messiah was born. On that night, which all at once became bright as day, they experienced I know not what, that which made them exclaim aloud, "O God! I give thee my heart," Oh! I trust that the happy impression which this unwonted spectacle made upon their hearts will never be effaced.

> Of what was one little church of the wilderness constructed? I have already told you—of posts fresh cut in the woods, covered over with mats and bark; these were its only materials. On the eve, the church was embellished with garlands and wreaths of green boughs;

forming, as it were, a frame for the images which represent the affecting mysteries of Christmas night. The interior was ornamented with pine branches. The altar was neatly decorated, bespangled with stars of various brightness and covered with a profusion of ribbons— things exceedingly attractive to the eye of the Indian. At midnight I celebrated a solemn mass and the Indians sang several canticles suitable to the occasion. That peace announced in the first verse of the angelic hymn—the "Gloria"—"Peace on earth to men of good will," was, I venture to say, literally fulfilled to the Indians of the forest. A grand banquet, according to Indian custom, followed the first mass. Some choice pieces of the animals slain in the chase had been set apart for the occasion. I ordered half a sack of flour and a large boiler of sweetened coffee to be added. The union, the contentment, the joy and charity which prevaded the whole assembly might well be compared to the agap'e of the primitive Christians.

This was the first Christmas celebrated among the Kalispells. It took place just across the Clark's Fork River from the present town of Usk, Washington.

Of further interest to us is the Christmas of 1859 that DeSmet spent among the Coeur d'Alene Indians. That Yuletide season might well be compared with that period spent by the prodigal son of biblical fame shortly after he returned to his father.

There is an analogy to be drawn between the prodigal son and the returning Coeur d'Alene families that had been shepherded back to their people by the good Father DeSmet after they had spent nearly a year as hostages at Fort Walla Walla where they had been sent as a result of the Indian war of 1858.

Father DeSmet, who was General Harney's chaplain, had worked a small miracle by talking the military leaders at Fort Walla Walla into releasing their prisoners to him long before they were supposed to be freed. The Coeur d'Alene Indians as well as some Spokanes, because of their exemplary behavior, had earned the respect of the officers at the fort and as a result were allowed to go home for the winter. They reached home about a month before but it is easy to imagine what a Christmas celebration followed! No doubt the hostages were feted and regaled by their people in partial repayment for the long lonely year they had spent away from their relatives and friends in expiation for tribal punishment.

James Milo Nosler

J.M. Nosler was a person who saw much of our western country as he traveled in search of that elusive element called success. In his humble way he achieved it because he was intelligent enough to keep a daily diary which recorded what he did.

He was born in Indiana on April 30, 1843. He moved to Iowa in 1850 and to Illinois in 1853. His mother died on the trip and because of her loss the family broke up.

James Nosler joined the 2nd Iowa Cavalry at age 18. His enlistment took place in Des Moines.

After the war of the rebellion ended he moved westward and while in Nebraska he met the famous scout and fur trader, Jim Bridger. It was here, too, that he married Sally on May 5, 1866. They went by wagon train to Colorado and eventually moved to California. During the interim they had two children.

In August 1871 he left the Oakland area of California and headed northward for the far famed Willamette River Valley of Oregon. Enroute he left the rest of the train and went cross country from Eugene to the Deschutes River country. While camped on Crooked River he decided to go to the Palouse country. By Tuesday, September 5, 1871, he camped on the Touchet River near Waitsburg and by the 3rd he reached the Snake River. Two days later he nooned on Alkili Flat and spent the night with a man named Rhineheart on Union Flat. On the 6th he got to the forks of the Palouse. Here he decided to "look around a little." A Mr. Walling who lived there suggested that Nosler should jump a claim up creek. His diary reads

> Sun. 8th move up near Mr. White and camp. I go up to my claim, then over to the mouth of Silver Creek. See a claim here that I like. Conclude to move on it tomorrow. Going home meet Jno. Mathews. He offers me his claim very cheap which is on the creek three miles above the forks....
>
> Mon. 9th work at his claim. See there is a bargain and buy it for $43, payable in four months. Move on it and camp.

October 11, 1871, he was hard at work hauling logs for a house. Its dimensions were 14 by 16 feet.

Saturday, November 4th he was putting the finishing touches on his house. A few days later he had completed some furniture and made the place livable for his family. On the 24th it rained and snowed all day and by the 26th there was 4 inches of snow on the ground. He went for supplies to Waitsburg at which time he more than likely bought Christmas presents. After loading his wagon with them he went to a friend named Than who gave him two pigs and eight chickens. After a most difficult trip he reached home on Dec. 2, 1871. During the interval between that date and Christmas he aided his neighbor Walling. He also cut rails and built a shed for his horses.

His entry for Christmas day reads: "Monday 25th Christmas.

Old Santa Claus brought Flora a pictorial primer and some candy. He brought Edie a little sled and candy. Snow a foot deep. Haul two loads of feed. Invited to a roast, but too cold to go with the family."

The diary sounds prosaic but the actual scene must have been very warm and fulfilling to this man who had worked so hard to make a shelter for his family under difficult conditions.

The following year showed improvements in the Nosler household as a stove had been received the previous spring. By mid-December the Northwest winter was beginning to settle in.

Sun 22nd snows all day. Evening snow about 16 inches deep and still snows. Have the neuralgia a little in my teeth. Mon 23rd snow about 18 inches deep. The dance, [planned for] Christmas has about fell through with. I forgot to say that we had two shocks of earthquake Saturday night—16th inst. We had retired and did not get up. The shock had a rolling, gyrating motion and shook things till they fairly rattled, scaring the women and children, shaking the chickens off the roost.

Tues. 24th not much stir.

Christmas 1872.

This evening a lot of people came in to dance. 11 couples. Give them our new room and get up supper. Commences raining in the night—up all night! Thurs 26th a good many here all day. Rainy.

Fri 27th the last of the dancers leave. Cleared about $40 since Wednesday morning.

Sat 28th still warm and thawing, Everything a perfect slush.

Sat 29th [note date discrepancy, actually Sunday] froze a little last night. Dull today. Another dance talked of. I am to get up the supper for $2 a no.

Mon. 30th Fixing for the dance

Tues 31st Getting up the supper. Have (three) men cooking.

Wednesday, 1st. Jan. 1873

Sallie took sick about midnight—a little before daylight; I got Mrs. Wolford, Mrs. Belcher, and Dr. Eagen about nine A.M. We were presented with a little girl less than either one of the other children were. About 25 persons took breakfast here and the cooks went ahead as though nothing was wrong. We closed the Bar room all day. Tonight have a big supper and they dance in the store.

What a busy and varied Christmas season!—snow, earthquake, entertainments, and a New Years baby to round out the festivities! Who could ask for more variety!

Nosler soon sold his Colfax holdings and moved to Oregon, and then Colorado. The Christmas of 1876 found the family struggling with jackrabbit for dinner and hickory nuts for gifts. In early

1877 their daughter, Flora, died and they soon moved on to California. Finding things not to his liking, Nosler moved northward to be among his old friends in Colfax.

He opened an office in the Court House and sold real estate. His wife Sally opened and operated a boarding house. With a borrowed cook stove and through hard work and good business sense she built it into the Colfax Restaurant. During the summer of 1878 they sold the restaurant, then bought it back again. Perhaps the buyer defaulted on payments. About the middle of September Nosler got a hack and took his family to Spokane Falls for a two day stay. At the same time he determined to close out his operations in Colfax and move to Spokane Falls.

The Noslers sold out their business and set out for Spokane Falls on October 25. They reached their new home the following day. Mr. James Glover was their host for two days after which Nosler and family moved in to a soldiers cabin he had fixed up. Moving quickly he opened an office over Cannon & Warners store and filed a soldiers Declaratory Statement on 169 acres of land near town. Ten days after he arrived he was appointed Justice of the

Spokane Falls in the 1870s, during the time of early settlement and the arrival of James Nosler. *From the author's collection.*

Peace and some time before January 21, 1879, he was appointed Commissioner of Deeds for Oregon.

Wednesday, December 24, 1879, he wrote, "Get the children a few presents this evening and tonight put them in their stockings. Eddie gets a rubber ball. Maggie and Murtie a ring each; all of them candy and nuts.

"Thurs 25th, Christmas. We have a roasted chicken and fine dinner. Very dull in town."

New Year's day seemed to be bigger family affair than Christmas. "Thurs. 1st. New Years day and Maggies' birthday. She has a dinner, has Mamie Cooper, Manda Park, and Goodners children. Eddie gave her an autograph album and her Ma gave her a set of vases, and Ada Renshaw sent her a lot of stationary [sic]. I go up the river and show a man a claim."

Nosler's Christmas 1880 diary entry reads: "Saturday 25th. We all go to the tree, Graham's Hall is full. Eddie gets a pair of skates from Clark and a lot of other trinkets, comb, etc. Maggie and Myrtle get a doll each, necklace, etc. Sade gets set of knives—cost $3.75 and I a silk handkerchief."

On New Year's day, Nosler wrote: "Busy in office. Have a New Year dinner at home. Kill a turkey. This is Maggie's birthday. She has Josie Clark and one of Cowley's little girls. Evening go sleigh riding. Snow tonight. Go over to Mr. Cowleys." This is doubtless the daughter of the Rev. Henry T. Cowley who came to Spokane Falls in 1874 and after whom Cowley Park is named.

The year 1881 was full of prosperity for Nosler and family. The railroad arrived in Spokane and the city boomed. He built a new

Henry T. Cowley, early Spokane settler and preacher. Cowley, with Henry Harmon Spalding, worked to build the Presbyterian congregation among the Spokane Indians. *Courtesy Eastern Washington Historical Society.*

These Spokanites await the arrival of the Northern Pacific Railroad at the formal celebration of the route's completion in September 1883. *From the author's collection.*

home. As the year wound down, he reported in his diary in late December:

> Saturday 24th:—About ten oclock they have a terrible collision on the R.R. 1 mile from here. An engine with 20 cars collides with one with caboose and tender, completely telescoping some of the cars and throwing some on top of others. Two men conductors and firemen are killed, and are in the Pallace Hotel opposite to my building. Have a good deal of business today. Tonight we have a Christmas tree at home.
>
> Dec. 25th We stay at home as it is too cold to take baby out for first time. [Boy baby born Nov. 26th.] Have a Christmas tree for the children. Eddie and I go to the wreck of [the] train. It is awful to behold.

The year 1883 was one of expansion for the rapidly growing community of Spokane Falls and Nosler was in the right business to derive a great deal of financial good from it through his lumber and real estate dealings. He wrote under date of "Sunday 9th of September Villard and the 'Golden Spike' party passed through. Among them Gen. Grant and many English and German nobles."

Nosler had written on August 31, 1883, that "The N.P.R.R. was connected [finished] the 22nd but the operation of formally driving the golden spike by [Henry] Villard will take place on the 8th of September." The golden spike was driven at Gold Creek in Montana.

Christmas during this important year as recorded by Nosler read as follows:

> I published an argument in favor of female suffrage a week or two ago. Said to be good. Last night we went to a Christmas Tree. Children got the usual round of presents. I got a pair of slippers and Sadie got $10 pair of bracelets. Had an average time. Snowed most of the day. Our snow a month ago all went off in a day or two. I borrowed $1000. last week. Intend fixing up some buildings in town to rent. Snows hard all day today, but is warm. We all stay at home.

Spokane in 1887. Looking north from South Hill above the current site of Lewis and Clark High School. Howard Street extends to the Spokane River. *From the author's collection.*

Have a nice dinner and general good time. Children playing with
toys. Eddie reading, snowballing the hired girl, etc.

It is plain to see from the few diary entries we have read that
J.M. Nosler was a "ball of fire" when it came to business deals.
Christmas day was business as usual with him!

Besides handling his real estate and other businesses, Nosler
became involved in the Spokane Transportation Co. which was
organized to "haul freight and passengers to the Coeur d'Alene
mines."

N.W. Cole's circus came to Spokane Falls July 29, 1884. There
were 700-800 people in Spokane at that time.

Christmas 1884 was evidently one of those bad days because
Nosler wrote "Snows most of day. All stay home and growl."

Thus, the last Christmas entry in his diary ends on a sour note.
Life is like that for all of us. Some days are happy, others are sad. We
all have highs and lows. Some of each come on Christmas day. His
were no different.

1884

Mrs. Lula Downen, a long-time pioneer of Pullman, Washington, wrote a booklet of her experiences in the above community. It is
a very informative little booklet and was published in 1937. An edition with photographic additions has been printed by Ye Galleon
Press at Fairfield, Washington.

Mrs. Downen adds her contribution to our Christmas essay as
follows:

> Christmas 1884, our school gave a Christmas cantata and King-
> man and Farris donated the use of their hall. J.F. Baymiller was the
> teacher and used this method to earn money to buy a large dictionary
> for the school. After all the work and expense we went to in giving
> this cantata, some one stole our precious dictionary out of the school
> house and we never got it back.

So, here once again we have a Christmas celebration activated
for the public good that turns sour because of human greed. It is
strange how the Christmas season has motivated *most* people to be
open-hearted but has created just the opposite instinct in a few others.

Vol. 39   No. 4   1995

RANDOM NOTES ON THE MISSOURI RIVER FUR TRADE PRIOR TO LEWIS AND CLARK

by Jerome Peltier

With the coming of the white man, the Missouri River became during the eighteenth and nineteenth centuries the natural route into the then unknown interior of the country. Its meandering waters cut through what might have otherwise been almost insurmountable geological formations, and opened the country on and near this great stream to any bold and courageous trader or explorer.

Stories of its early exploration were sketchy and inaccurate, but such records as are available reveal that the French and Spanish nations vied with each other for the trade with the Indians who lived along the Missouri River and its affluents, during those early years.

Father Jacques Marquette and Louis Jolliet discovered the mouth of the Missouri as they descended the Mississippi River dur-

Vol. 39   No. 4   1995

Published quarterly by the Spokane Corral of the Westerners, P.O. Box 1717, Spokane, WA 99210. Subscription $10.00 per calendar year. Back issues available, $2.50 ea. Articles appearing in this journal are abstracted and indexed in *Historical Abstracts:* and/or *America History and Life.*   ISSN: 0030-882 X

Articles dealing with the history and development of the American and Canadian West are welcomed for consideration. Submissions should be directed to the editor, Robert A. Clark, at the above address. All submissions should be accompanied by a self-addressed stamped envelope for return.

ing the month of May 1673. They were accompanied (and I quote them) by "five men who were quite determined to do anything and to suffer anything for such a glorious expedition—"

As they passed by, they recorded their observations in the following illuminating sentence:—"We heard the noise of a rapid; large trees entire with branches—real floating islands—came from the west so impetuously the water was very muddy." There is little doubt from their description that they saw the river at floodtide. They called it the "riviere Pekitanoui".

Nine years later Robert Cavalier, Sieur de La Salle, gave a further description of the mouth of the river in his writings. It was much more accurate than the hurried notes of the first party who saw it. One year later La Salle wrote, perhaps from hearsay, that two Frenchmen lived among the Missouri tribes. He did not mention whether or not they did business with the Indians, but it is very likely that they did.

Still other fragmentary accounts reported other trips upriver in which trading was a major consideration.

As years passed, more explorers ascended the river and accounts of some of the excursions are well documented. Among

Justice Goodsell in front of Marker at Spokane bridge post office.

Manito Park - 1944 - Pioneer Picnic

Front row, left to right - Sam Webb (decd. 6/10/69), Tum Morris (decd. 6/19/48), Seth Woodard (b. Kansas 10/14/1872-6/9/1960) W.W. Goff (decd. 7/29/45), J. Howard Stegner (b. 4/30/1888), Robert Butler (decd. 9/5/48), Zack Steward (decd. 6/5/48), H.D Kay (decd. 8/16/48). Back row, left to right - Madison A. Miller (decd. 9/12/63), Sam Glasgow (decd. 3/14/45), Grant Hunt (decd 4/3/53), A.A. Kelly (decd. 6/26/51), Charles T. Goodsell (b. 6/16/1880-3/8/1955), John Bruce Dodd (decd. 8/25/45), Ed Kohlhauf

Rev. Paul P. Sauer
Procurator for Oregon Province
Mt. St. Michael

The dedication of the Col. G. Wright memorial by the Spokane County Pioneer Society upon the site of the bloody slaughter of hundreds of Native American horses by the Wright command. Tum Morris dedicating, Mrs. Goodsell at right.

Howard Stegner and Seth Woodard.

Seth Woodard

The Stephen Etienne Liberty family.
See Alberta Murray, ''These my Children.'' pages 95-98.

Old Colville road near Plante Ferry used to carry mail to Fort Colville.
Photo courtesy of Henry Rust.

Spokane after 1889 fire.

1906 - Millwood area

Street scene at the corner of First and Post in 1884.

Spokane after 1889 fire.

them came stories of the discovery by natives of rich tin and lead mines. When stories of rich ore bodies reached the citizens of the settlements below there was an animated search for these mines. Soon they were located by whites and their production added materially to the economy of St. Louis and the neighboring area.

Father Gabriel Marest, a priest who was located at a mission among the Kaskaskia Indians, wrote to the famous explorer Pierre Lemoyne Iberville, on July 10, 1700, that the Missouri River was as long and as large as the Mississippi and that it was well populated with many Indians tribes. He mentioned also that he had seen Spanish horses among the Kansas Indians. This would lead one to believe that there was some sort of commerce between these natives and the Spanish because of the proximity of the Mexican-Spanish Southwest, to the lower Missouri tribesmen.

Pierre Le Seur, while searching for the mines mentioned previously and which he did locate, described the Missouri as well as the tin and lead mines. He said that the Missouri means "canoe" which he attributed to the tribesmen whom he called "peoples of the canoes." He further reported that war was being waged against the Pawnee Indians whom he called the Panis. His report was made in July 1700.

Old Cahokia (in the East St. Louis area) became a busy trading post shortly after the establishment of a Roman Catholic mission in 1699, with Father Marest as its missionary. Sixty five years later, the Chouteau family built a trading post opposite the old town and called it St. Louis. (There will be more about this later.)

The first known detailed report of a voyage of exploration of the Missouri River was made by Ettienne Veniard de Bourgmont, who had been placed in command of Fort Detroit in January 1706. He replaced Henri de Tonti in this then advanced frontier French post.

It was while de Bourgmont was defending this fort (Detroit) against attacking Fox tribesmen, that he met some Missouri Indians who had come to the aid of their French allies. (Here again we have a report that suggests knowledge of the Missouri River area from the East.)

He must have been strongly attracted to them, or very curious about these people because he made a special trip to visit them in their tribal lands during the year 1814. He became so entranced with their culture that he deserted his post at Detroit, married a Missouri woman, made his home with them and became a prime favorite of theirs. (It is not inconceivable that the magnet that drew him to them was the lady that he married. Who knows?)

It is claimed that he ascended the Missouri River beyond the mouth of the Osage River and gave a description of the natives who bore that name, and that furs obtained from them were of a superior quality. He described the Arikara villages and wrote as a note of warning to his countrymen that it was likely that commerce was being carried on with the Spaniards because they were not far away from the area. (Here we have, once again, mention of the Spanish influence among the Indians of the Missouri River basin.) De Bourgmont's account was valuable both in a geographical and commercial sense.

As years passed by, penetration of the upper Missouri became more complete, and contemporary maps reflected the knowledge obtained through these trading excursions.

In 1738 Sieur Pierre De la Verendre and his sons visited the Mandans, having come overland from Fort la Reine (present Portage La Prairie, Manitoba, Canada.) He made gifts of trade goods comprising Mandan villages in the name of the king of France, at the same time encouraging them to do all of their trading with the French. (It would be reasonable to assume that if he gave them powder and ball, that they must have been in possession of guns and must have had some previous trading experience with others which he was trying to discourage.) (If guns were traded, no doubt, beads, metal, tobacco and other items were bartered for fur s also.)

At the time La Verendre visited the Mandan villages, they were not on the Missouri River, as they were in later times when Lewis and Clark visited them. It is believed that they were located near the Mouse River at this time. David Thompson, in 1797, placed them on the Turtle River, as we shall read later.

Pierre La Verendre described a Mandan village and its fortifications and to quote him, it "was found that there were a hundred and thirty of them" (meaning houses). "Their fortifications are not Indian. . . This nation is mixed white and black. . . The women are fairly good-looking, especially the white, many with blond and fair hair." Much knowledge was derived from the report of this trip which was made on their return home while they re-outfitted for another trip.

Verendre's eldest son Pierre went back among the Mandans in the autumn of 1740 at the insistence of this father. Meanwhile the elder Pierre made a trip to Montreal and returned to Fort la Reine in October 1741, when he learned that his eldest son "had returned from the Mandans, not having gone farther for lack of a guide." "He gave me a cotton blanket after the workmanship of the whites which are on the sea." (Perhaps he is referring here to a blanket that was obtained through trade with the Spaniards.)

Chevalier de la Verendre and one of his brothers Louis Joseph and two companions, made another trip westward during which it is claimed that they reached the present Black Hills area. They were hoping to find the western sea on this trip.

They left Fort la Reine in April 1742 and returned July 2, 1743. During this trip they buried a lead tablet on a hill which overlooks the community of Fort Pierre, South Dakota, claiming the country thus explored in the name of the king of France. La verendre described it as follows: "I placed on an eminence near the fort a tablet of lead, with the arms and inscription of the King and a pyramid of stones for Monsieur le General; I said to the savages who did not know of the tablet of lead that I had placed in the earth, that I was placing these stones as a memorial of those, who had come to their country." (Note:-This lead plate was found by some school children who were playing atop the hill which overlooks the grade school in the community of Fort Pierre, across the Missouri from the state capital Pierre, South Dakota. The plate may be seen in the State Historical Society museum.)

Little mention of trading is to be found in the Chevalier's journal. He did, however, report that they visited Indians who spoke Spanish. An Arikara who spoke Spanish said that Spanish settlements were three weeks horseback ride away.

Abuses were common by this time in the fur trade with the Missouri tribes. Traders treated some of the natives with physical violence and cheated them outrageously. The Indians were becoming incensed with this treatment and threatened to make trouble. French officials evolved what they thought was a solution.

In 1744 an agreement was made between French officials and a Canadian named Deruisseau which gave him exclusive trading rights on the Missouri and its tributaries. Certain specified provisions were to be met in return for these favors.

Deruisseau, according to the agreement that he signed, was to build a fort, feed the soldiers that were to be garrisoned there, and pay for most of the presents that were to be given to the Indians during trading expeditions as well as when they came to the fort to trade. He was also expected to conduct his business honestly, and was to sell no liquor to the Indians.

His immediate superior, a man named Vaudreuil, wrote twenty articles which were guidelines for the construction of the fort, as well as containing suggestions for trading on the upper Missouri. Mention is made in official correspondence dated March 15, 1747, that proves that a fort was built. No signs of this early post remain.

Spain obtained the western half of the Mississippi from the

French, by treaty, at the close of the Seven Years War, but they did not take possession of it until six years later.

It is not known definitely whether Deruisseau's fort was Fort Cavagnolle or not. The latter post which was situated on the Missouri was commanded by Chevalier de Villiers, a cadet from Canada who had risen in rank to lieutenant by this time. With the establishment of Fort Cavagnolle, at the Kansas Indian village, it became necessary to negotiate a treaty with the Jumanos and Comanches in order to assure safe passage for their traders along the route to the southward.

Prior to this, the French had done very little trading with the Comanches, but following the treaty, thirty three Frenchmen were reported to have gone among the Comanches to trade in the year 1748. This advance group was followed by others who traveled via the Arkansas River eventually reaching Santa Fe which was Spanish headquarters in the Southwest. Others reached the same place by following the Missouri and branching to the southward. One such party seemed to go with the blessings of the authorities in Louisiana. Still further agreements were made between the Comanches and the Jumanos, as well as the Comanches and the Pawnees.

Jean Chapuis obtained a license to open a trade route to New Mexico, from Benoit de St. Claire at Fort Charteres. (The latter post was built in 1717 on the left bank of the Mississippi approximately 25 miles above the Kaskaskia River and was the last post to be surrendered to the British following the defeat of the French in 1765.) Chapuis also received a passport from the commandant at Michilimackinac, which would allow him to return to Illinois after his trading expedition. Following these very necessary preliminaries Chapuis and Luis Feuilli set out via Fort Cavagnolle toward the southwest.

Along the route they traded with the Osages and the Kansas Indians. They left the latter tribe in March 1752, and moved on to the Pawnees and eventually reached the Comanches, who guided them to Santa Fe where they were imprisoned and their goods impounded. There is a rumor that they were taken to Spain as prisoners. I have been unable to verify the latter statement.

Many abuses crept into the trade. Both Indians and whites were at fault. In order to curb violence that might result from such bad faith, the French would deprive offending tribesmen from what had by now become a very necessary commerce. Offending whites were punished by losing their trading licenses as well as their trade goods. This eliminated some of the problems, but not all.

In 1754 the final phase of the French and Indian War broke out and as a result of their defeat by the British, the French as a nation were expelled from North America. Individual Frenchmen, however, remained and continued to be prominent in the fur trade.

The French as a nation had left an indelible mark on the fur trade of the Missouri and points southward. They had penetrated the trans-Mississippi West in general, and had explored most of the Mississippi-Missouri watershed. They had reached the Rockies in Canada and there is reason to believe that they had also done so in the present continental United States. They had explored the Missouri and nearly every major branch of this great river to the mountains and had traversed much of the country between the Mississippi and the Spanish territories to the southward. Maps made by them were fairly accurate in depicting the lower Louisiana areas. The Missouri River, as seen in their maps, had a tendency to flow from west to east much along the route of the present Platte River. It was surmised at that time that the headwaters of the Missouri were near the sources of the Rio Grande and this thinking was reflected in their maps.

Their expeditions had taken them among the Mandans, thus that region was well known to them, as was the area between those tribesmen and the Great Lakes area. They had advanced as far west as Calgary, Canada, where they had built a post named Fort Jonquerre. Despite their magnificent efforts, much remained to be explored in the upper Missouri country.

The Spanish took over, following the expulsion of the French, but by their own admission reported that they had not made much progress by the year 1774, when Pedro Piernas wrote that "the most distant natives of the Missouri" were the Mahas, Panis and Ottoes, and one tribe "recently discovered more in the interior than those mentioned," the Arikaras. He also protested bitterly that some renegade Frenchmen were circulating among the tribesmen of the upper Missouri fomenting trouble between the natives and some Spanish traders who ascended the river annually to trade with them.

A few chosen Frenchmen in high offices who had exclusive grants continued to trade with the natives. This system of giving exclusive trading grants to a selected few proved to be very unfair and unprofitable.

The grants were superseded and this led to the founding of St. Louis, Missouri. One of the grantees, a man named Laclede, had been given exclusive rights and control of the fur trade of the Missouri as far north as the St. Peters River. During one of his trips he was accompanied by a young boy named Auguste Choteau. They selected the junction of the Missouri and the Mississippi as the site for his headquarters post February 15, 1764. Of interest is the fact that Frenchmen gravitated to this place, which almost immediately became the center of the vast fur trade of the upper Mississippi and Missouri areas because of its strategic position on both of these main arteries of travel.

Laclede traded almost exclusively along the Missouri River, allowing private individuals and parties to trade in other areas. He also furnished merchandise for many private traders and as he grew, so did the city of St. Louis, which spread its influence as it burgeoned in size and importance.

Louis Saint Ange de Bellerive, another Frenchman, assumed control of the town for the Spanish who realized its key position in blocking expansion by the British who were moving steadily southward. An ambitious plan was devised in 1763, having two main features. First, they wanted to build a series of posts at measured intervals among the various tribes with whom they had commerce, to protect their northern and eastern district boundaries. (All enclosed by the Louisiana boundaries.) Secondly, the plan also included ten other forts that were to be built on the Mississippi River. Things did not go as planned.

The Spanish as a nation were afraid that the British would encroach on their lands, so they sent Captain Don Francisco Riu with instructions to build two forts at the mouth of the Missouri and plant a colony of Acadians there. One post was built, with Riu as it commandant. St. Ange was left in charge of St. Louis, the other post as well as having a free rein with the Indian trade. Rui's regime was not popular nor was he competent, but despite his seeming incompetence trade broadened and profits were huge.

J. Cecil Alter, author of several historical books including a biography of James Bridger, wrote that a fur trading company called a "Company of Explorers of the Upper Missouri" was organized in 1793. Fur trading expeditions under its aegis moved northward and joined the ever growing number of men to go upriver from St. Louis.

More and more famous names entered the rolls as the fur trade grew, and it would be difficult to mention all of them. However there are a few who were giants in the field that cannot be ignored. David Thompson was one of these. He was also a personage of great interest to us Northwesterners, being the first white trader to cross the Rocky Mountains into our own geographical haunts and report on same.

David Thompson, the famous cartographer and trader of the Northwest Company, came from the north to survey parts of the Missouri River. (He was doubtless one of the reasons for the Spanish program to place obstructions in the way of northern fur traders, but which was unsuccessful.)

Thompson had previously been employed by the Hudson's Bay Co. He left their employ because of a conflict of interests. The Hudson's Bay Company wanted him to work strictly as a fur trader with no time to be devoted to surveying. Thompson objected to this ruling by the old company because he felt, rightfully, that his surveying took very little time from his duties as a fur trader and added materially to knowledge of the areas over which he had travelled.

Because of this ridiculous ruling, Thompson resigned from the Hudson's Bay Co. and joined the ranks of their most bitter rival, the Northwest Company. It was during his first assignment with them that he was given the long desired opportunity to survey without the necessity of trading. His instructions read that he was to determine the position of the 49th parallel in the region of Red River, also to visit the Mandan villages on the Missouri River and to locate geographically the company's trading posts wherever he should visit.

It was while he was on this trip that he visited the Mandan Indians and reached one of their villages December 30, 1797. It was at this same place in 1804 that Lewis and Clark met Hugh McCracken and Rene Jessaume, both of whom were with Thompson of this particular trip. Jessaume was hired by the Lewis and Clark party to serve as their interpreter; the same position he held while with David Thompson.

While among the Mandan Indians, Thompson enumerated and described their villages and earthen structures as follows: The first village contained "thirty one Houses and seven Tents of Fall Indians . . . The village next below, is called the Great Village—, it contains eighty two Houses, is situated on the Turtle River, a short distance above its confluence with the Missisourie . . . The fourth Village was on the right bank of the Missisouri—40houses . . . The fifth and last Village contained one hundred and thirteen houses of Mandanes—."

Prior to this visit, several of Thompson's men had lived among them, and Rene Jessaume, his guide and interpreter, spoke the Mandan language fluently.

Thompson reported that there were very few guns among the natives because of the lack of powder and ball. His men traded seven of their own personal weapons to the Mandans and evidently supplied them with their supply of powder and ball, too. Thompson stated also that the Mandans had a few metal hoes, as well as some iron spear and arrow points and described the native materials used for the former as being made from "the shoulder blade bone of the Bison or deer—neatly fitted to a handle—which doe tolerably well in soft ground."

He did not mention specifically trading for beads as ornamentation, but other accounts did, so it is likely that Thompson's party must have done so, too. David did, however, mention that some of the women wore ornamented belts around their waists.

"The curse of the Mandanes," Thompson wrote, "is an almost total want of chastity—" and further statements by him prove it.

David described a nation of Indians which he called the Fall Indians who were confederated with the Mandans for protection although they spoke a distinctly different tongue. Thompson said that their previous homeland had been near the "Rapids of the Saskatchewan River, northward of the Eagle Hill;--." "Their reason for migrating to the Mandan country was due to the fact their neighbors 'the Nahathaways and the Stone Indians' who were allies attacked them and drove them southward."

Thompson headed northward January 10, 1798, via the Mouse River and Red River where Winnipeg now stands, to Cadotte's House which he reached March 24, 1798. (Thompson says he reached it on the 31st.) This post which had been built by J.B. Cadotte for the Northwest Co. the previous year was erected on the south bank of the Red Lake River (situated opposite the present town of Red Lake Falls, Minnesota.) The party headed for the headwaters of the Mississippi and eventually reached Turtle Lake, thinking it was the source of the MIssissippi. Thompson dated their arrival there, April 27th. Thompson was not far from the truth when he assumed that he had found the source of the great river because Turtle Lake is just a short distance from Lake Itaska, the true source of the Mississippi.

From this place, Thompson proceeded to the western end of Lake Superior, then moved southward surveying the south shore of the lake. He reached the Falls of Ste. Marie on May 28th. Here at Sault Ste. Marie, Thompson met Alexander Mackenzie and William McGillivray (both major owners an senior partners in the Northwest Co.) who were on their way to Grand Portage, where the annual meeting of the company was to take place. McGillivray told David that he had accomplished more in ten months than the Company had expected him to do in two years time! Both partners urged Thompson to survey Lake Superior around the east and north sides, to Grand Portage which at that time was the depot of the Company. Thompson and his men completed this job by the seventh of June, at which time he reached Grand Portage, having completed a survey of more than four thousand miles of practically uncharted lands in ten months time. This was an incredible feat because much of this work was done during the most difficult seasons of the year.

One and one half month later Thompson headed for the Churchill district surveying the country as he travelled. He visited several company posts enroute, making notes of their position with his crude surveying instruments.

At Lake La Biche, Thompson built a trading post and travelled with the natives of the area making astronomical observations. This post was located at the east end of Lake La Biche, tributary to the Athabaska River. La Biche River, outlet of the lake, flows into Athabaska River a few miles below Athabaska Landing. Thompson referred to the lake as Red Deer. (The French meaning for the word biche means deer. Ed.)

He left Lake La Biche during March 1799 on a surveying trip that took him to such widely divergent areas as the Saskatchewan River; Lesser Slave Lake; the Athabaska River, the Churchill River and eventually to Isle a la Crosse Lake which he reached May 20, 1799.

Here, at the Northwest Co. post which served the area, he found romance, because on June 10th he married Charlotte Small, daughter of Patrick Small, a lesser partner in the N.W. Co. and his Indian wife.

Thompson was twenty-nine years of age at the time of his marriage and his wife was only fourteen. Two years later to the very day their first child, a girl named Fanny, was born to bless their union at Rocky Mountain House, the first of their 15 children who were born many places west and east, where ever the Thompsons traveled. Soon he would accomplish his surveying of the entire Columbia River from source to mouth, but this takes us away from the topic of this paper.

A production of a map showing a part of the Missouri River may be found folded in the back of Volume 7 of the South Dakota Historical Collections. It was drawn by Perrin du Lac and is dated 1802. One area of this map traces the wanderings of one Jacques Machey during a trip that he made into the middle Missouri regions in 1796. It must have been a trading expedition, because during his travels he visited the villages of the Mahas (Omahas) and the Poncas.

On the same map mentioned above, Du Lac drew four figures on the Missouri River that look very much like musical notes and which he designated as being the "Ancien village de Ricaras" which obviously means the "Ancient village of the Arikaras." Other villages are shown on this same map nearly to the 47the parallel above. Still other areas of the lower Missouri are well drawn as far south as St. Louis. Tribal village areas of the Kansas Indians are depicted very clearly. Du Lac's map reflects knowledge of that period in history.

Pierre Antoine Tabeau, who wrote a narrative account of his

experiences on the Missouri River while he accompanied the Regis Loisel Expedition to that great river, had a great deal to say about the country and its people. He also wrote about the fur trade and stated that—"It was necessary to charge three piasters (Spanish or Mexican dollars with a value of 50 cents in U.S. coinage) for each knife and a hundred crowns for a pound of blue glass beads.—"

He stated that women did all of the work in the village. He also described some of the utensils that they used, and told how they skillfully improvised with available materials to make tools. To quote Tabeau— "Shoulder blades of cow or deer serve them with pick axes, reeds curved at the end, separated from each other by interlaced rods and bound in a bundle for a handle are their rakes; a sheet of tin drawn from old kettles furnishes them with knives with which they jerk their meat, cut the skins and other articles . . . By means of a buffalo horn, they split their wood, which the floods wash up on the bank . . . However, some are now provided with hatchets . . . They readily see their own abnormal servitude and the laziness of their husbands and say very often, if enough whites come, the Ricaras would have no women . . . A Spanish prisoner taught them how to melt our glass beads and to mould them into a shape that pleases them. This art which is as yet unknown to them is practiced only secretly and still passes for a supernatural and magical talent . . . They make a very hard but very coarse pottery which stands heat well and suffices for all their cooking."

For those who may not have believed Tabeau's statement about the manufacture of beads by the Mandans, we shall quote the great authority Frederick W. Hodge for verification. In his monumental volumes entitled *The Handbook of American Indians North of Mexico*, Volume 1 page 798, Hodge wrote:-(Mandans) "manufactured earthenware, the clay being tempered with flint or granite reduced to powder by the action of fire." He said also in the same volume on page 139 that "the Mandan and other Missouri tribes pounded and melted glass and molded it into beads."

Tabeau who was very outspoken in his journals, penned scathing denunciations of traders and trading methods that came under his direct observation. Among his remarks about the trade itself, he wrote about the great value of beads in the fur trade. We quote: "Those who are not versed in the Savage trade cannot imagine how important is the selection of articles and how far an individual, unfit or evilly-intentioned, can be harmful to the success of commerce and to good order . . . I shall not go into detail concerning the articles suitable for traffic with the Sioux and Ricaras . . . The articles for the former can be arranged with careful proportion to those for the Osages and Kans. (sic) Only there should be added many

blue glass beads, brass wire, iron for arrows, and spears . . . There is
no need, as I have already said, to consider for the Ricaras any object
the value of which exceeds that of a buffalo robe . . . They make great
use of vermillion—in trade . . . Intoxicating liquors would be merely
useless, up to the present among the Ricaras, who are not willing to
drink them unless they are paid."

Another reliable observer verified this. Maximillian Prince of
Weid, who made several trips into the early day West, remarked
while he was at Fort Clark, that he had never seen a Mandan under
the influence of liquor.

Tabeau, as was mentioned previously, was a great observer
and gave a beautiful word picture of what he saw. "The women are
covered with a skin of the cow or of the doe, bound around the middle of the body, sewed of the two sides, and ornamented with long
fringes at the bottom and down the seams. They cover the shoulders
and the upper part of the arms with two kinds of wings. From the
elbow to the wrist the sleeve is very narrow and is also ornamented
with threads which are everywhere a great adornment. The blue
bead, as precious here as the porcelain among the nations of the
Mississippi, is used to trim all the seams of these sacks called
Roman by some Frenchmen. The Sioux women are dressed almost
in the same fashion and are distinguished only by rolls of brass wire
in the ears and by huge locks of hair, covered with blue beads and
tied on the temples in the shape of cushions."

Tabeau, after remarking that the men also wore their hair as
ornamentation gave the following minute description of a Sioux
dandy: "He has shoes fully ornamented with a skunk skin trailing
at each heel and decorated with a piece of scarlet. The lower part of
the leg is bound with two narrow cords, trimmed with quills of the
porcupine. Leggings of very white antelope-skin, of which one has
a cut out fringe and the other streaked with black, are joined and
crossed above and are like Bavaroises. (Note: a type of trousers
worn about the time this journal was written, which had fore and aft
flaps that buttoned around the waist. Ed.) These fringes are ornamented with shells and with various spurs, the little clashes of
which are sonorous enough to attract attention. A long, wide
chemise of antelope-skin, all its edges fringed, perforated and fes-
tooned below with different figures, has two narrow points which
trail under the arms and is closed only from the elbows to the wrists
where there are wrought and pendent cuffs All this is trimmed with
little bells. Upon the shoulder straps, diverse shells are fixed, and a
band of fine leather, ornamented with porcupine quills and painted
with figures of different colors, covers the throat and the stomach.
Above it, is a collar of bear-claws, between which are little tassels of

blue beads. Triple rolls of brass wires are in the ears, which are also trimmed with a double row of shells and feathers. Upon the head are scattered, without order, little balls of swan's down The hair, separated into two tresses, covered with fine red leather, hangs very low in front. The face is daubed with white, blue, black and vermilion. In the left hand is a spear, of which the long handle, gay with rags and fine leather and ornamented with porcupine, is held in the middle and kept in countenance with a pouch of the pekan. The head and tail of this animal, being the most brilliant and ornamented parts, hang side by side. A chichikoi (rattle. Ed.) filled with small pebbles which make a noise, is attached to the left wrist. The other hand is reserved for gestures."

The man's garb described by Tabeau was no doubt the exception, rather than the rule, because it seems as though nothing was missing from his outfit that could have possibly been there. One might even classify him as what we term today as a primper, or it is possible that he was making a determined effort of dazzle some particular damsel that he wanted to court and marry. He must have been eye catching to say the least!

Tabeau did not forget to report graphically on the moral fibre of the Sioux women. He told how they were punished for infidelity in various ways. He mentioned, in passing, that the Sioux women were more reserved than Arikara women. Then, he further enlarged on this theme by saying that the Sioux women knew "the value of their favors, if their facility in granting them is any criterion. The most inflexible is not proof against a prize of vermillion and of twenty strands of blue beads. There are, nevertheless, a few prudes who greatly wish to pass for cautious ones: but who surrender themselves, moreover with discretion and secrecy."

Here, once again, Tabeau seems to be speaking with the voice of experience, and here we will leave him.

It is my feeling that this paper should end with mention of the Lewis and Clark expedition which had by this time reached the Mandan villages on their way into what was generally known then as "Terra Incognita."

Patrick Gass, the oldest man in the party and one of its Sergeants, wrote under date of (October) 27th (1804) his observations regarding the Mandans, as follows: "This village contains 40 or 50 lodges, built in the manner of those of the Rickarees—some of the children have fair hair."

On Sunday (the) 28th of October 1804—Clark mentioned that he "entertained Several of the Curious Chiefs whom, wished to see the Boat which was very curious to them viewing it as great medicine, as they also Viewed my black Servent—" As a note of explanation regarding these two remarks:-The boat that he wrote about was one that had been made with a metal frame in such a manner that it could be folded for ease in handling. The frame could be covered when needed. The latter gentleman was a negro man servant of Clark's named York. He was indeed a curiosity to these people who had never seen a negro . Many of the women asked to touch him so that they could determine whether his color would rub off.

We shall now view the Lewis and Clark party through the observant eyes of Francois Antoine Larocque, a clerk in the service of th Northwest Company. Larocque, accompanied by seven seasoned trappers and traders, left Fort Assinaboine, (on the south side of the Assinaboine River at the mouth of the Souris River) on a trading excursion, November 11, 1804. His ultimate goal was to be among the Missouri River tribes.

While among the Gros Ventres, while his men were trading for furs, Larocque inquired as to the whereabouts of Touissant Charbonneau and learned that he was downriver at one of the Mandan villages and that he had been engaged as interpreter by Lewis and Clark. He set out to locate Charbonneau and while enroute to the village met Meriwether Lewis. The meeting took place on November 25, 1804, and Francois described it as follows:-"On the road thither met with Captain Lewis, chief of the American party—with Jussiaume and Charbonneau—· had about a quarter of an hour's conversation with him, during which he invited me to his house and appeared very friendly."

Two days later Larocque met Lewis at the village of a Mandan chef named Black Cat. He "spoke to Charbonneau about helping as interpreter in the trade to the big Bellies: (The literal translation of Gros Ventres from the French, is Big Bellies. Ed.) he told me that being engaged to the Americans, he could not come without leave from Captain Lewis and desired me to speak to him, which I did. (Capt. Lewis told me that as he had no business for Charbonneau but at times during the winter, he had no objections to his helping me upon certain conditions which agreeing to, Charbonneau promised me he would come next morning."According to the above gentlemen's agreement Charbonneau was allowed to help the Larocque party several times during the winter, and both Lewis and William Clark, co-captain in this great expedition, had several opportunities to explain to Larocque and purpose of the expedition upon which they were launched. There was however some misunderstanding during the meeting on November 27th, because according to the remarks recorded by the two American journal, Baptiste Lafrance, one of the men who accompanied the Larocque party, made some disparaging remarks which can best be explained by the comments recorded at the time. "Seven Traders arrived from the Fort on the Ossinoboin from the NW. Company one of which Lafrance took upon himself to speak unfavourable of our intentions &c. the principal Mr. LaRock (& Mr. Mc. Kensey) was informed of the Conduct of their interpreter & the Consequences if they did not put a Stop to unfavourable f& ill founded assursions &c. &c."

During the several month's that the Larocque party was near the Lewis and Clark group there was several opportunities for visits during which there was greater understanding between the two parties.

Shortly after this, we learn through the journal of Sergeant John Ordway of the Lewis and Clark party that our good friend Antoine Tabeau is in the neighborhood and warns the party of a possible attack by the Sioux Indians. Ordway wrote "thursday 28th 1805. Mr. Tabbo a frenchman—Sent a letter up to the commanding officers & Mandan chiefs to keep a good lookout for he had heared the Sioux say that they should shurley come to war in the Spring against us and mandanes—." It seems as though things were getting crowded on the Missouri!

The enthralling story of the epoch-making trip of Lewis and Clark has been told many times and by far more eloquent writers than I, so there is no need to repeat it here. Their safe return to civilization with the single loss of a man is a feat seldom equaled. Of interest to us and also of great importance, is the fact that they travelled along and on the Missouri to it's very source, changing the map of terra incognita to a known area in the short space of two years. What is amazing about this is the fact that their explorations opened a stretch of the Missouri equally as long as that part of the lower river that had taken a century to explore—and for this as well as other things, we owe the Lewis and Clark party a great debt of gratitude--for giving the United States another solid foothold in the Northwest, which was the only area of the U.S. that was not purchased or taken by force from another nation.

Jerome Peltier is a founding member and past sheriff of the Spokane Westerners. He is the author of numerous books and articles dealing with the history of the American West, particularly the Fur Trade and the Pacific Northwest. His interest in original documents and accounts was a natural result of his many years in the antiquarian book trade in Spokane, Washington.

Vol. 40　　　　　No. 2　　　　　1996

Robert Franklin Cummins

"THE YOUNGEST 12 YEAR-OLD FREIGHTER IN WASHINGTON TERRITORY"

By Jerome Peltier

My introduction to Robert Franklin Cummins was when an article about him appeared in The Spokesman-Review newspaper, May 10, 1953. It's headline aroused my interest for it read "Early Day Freighter, Recalls Hardships in Making Trips" Besides covering what the headline intimated, the article stated that Mr. Cummins regretted that he had missed 11 years being able to observe the State of Washington, its territorial birthday (1853). It is true, that he was not around to celebrate that great event, but he maintained, proudly, that he grew up with the territory, and he saw it enter statehood in 1889.

The article brought to my attention many facts about him that I had failed to elicit from him through correspondence. I knew his address so I resolved to interview him in person if he was physically able to handle one.

Wash Board And Creeks

On Nov. 14, 1954, I was able to interview him as well as tape our interview with his permission. When asked about his early life, he stated that he had been born 7 miles from Walla Walla in 1864. He had lived in the state all of his life. He showed pardonable pride in Washington when he said," I calculate to live and die here, it's good enough for anyone". He described how his family came west as follows:

"My father came to Walla Walla by an ox team wagon train in 1862 from Iowa". He explained although many of the people in the party were young "no one brought buggies, they could only bring heavy wagons - I've heard my father say, that men would ride ahead of the wagon train to scout for water and grass". He also said "that the oxen were slow". (The normal day's travel at that time was 10 to 15 miles per day.) He recounted some of his parents hardships on the trail as follows:

"When the train would stop, the women would get out the wash boards and go to washing in the creeks. The men would all get out and go to setting the wagon tires". (Authors note: Tires were metal, on wooden wheels. Heat would shrink the wood.)

See page 8 "Farmers Federal Aid-1792" by Felix Entenmann

"The wheels would get so loose that they would roll up some canvas around the fellys. To tighten the tires, they would heat them and then wet them down and they would draw-up."   (Felly: curved pieces of wood forming rim of wheel).

Mr. Cummins talked of his family: "My Mother and Father were both from Ohio. They immigrated here with 4 boys and 1 girl. I was the first one born here - seven miles from Walla Walla, where my parents settled".

He described Walla Walla as a child "There was a blacksmith shop and very few houses (in Walla Walla) then. The old Nez Perce Trail went right through what is now the main street. All of my playmates at that time were Indians, as we were the only whites around there. We would talk in the old Chinook jargon which we both understood. (Note- the jargon used was a coastal fur trade language, which evolved out of Indian, French, English and a few other languages and which involved only a few hundred words.) "I could play with them in good shape. In those days you would see the Indians that always passed by. The bucks would never handle the pack horses, which were left with the squaws. The bucks would hunt for game to feed their people and would smoke pipes which contained tobacco and the red bark of what they called kinnikinnick. They would smoke about three puffs and pass the pipe on to the person next to them."

He continued: "When they would come to camp, the Indian (men) would let the squaws unpack the pack horses and prepare the meals while the bucks would care for the horses."

Robert Cummins recalled the difficult times the pioneer farmers confronted: "My father farmed down there at 'Tuschy" (Touchet Station) and there wasn't a threshing machine in the whole country - not even a reaper or mowing machine. We had to cut the grain with those old cradles. We'd haul it in and tramp it out and then wait for a windy day, because we didn't even have a fanning mill."

How To Make A Plow
When a windy day came the farmers of that day would toss the wheat into the air and the chaff would be blown away from it or would be separated from the grain which was then stored away in burlap bags or other containers until the next trip was made to town. Cummins said: "When we got the wheat, then we would take it to town and exchange it at about 1/3 for flour since there was a grist mill there." It would appear from this, that the miller could make a handsome profit from each deal. He could keep his family well fed and still have some flour for sale out of the 2/3rds of the grain left to him for his work and the use of his equipment.

"My dad told me when he first came here, there was no place to buy a plow and he wanted to do some plowing, so he went to the blacksmiths there and he got an upright piece and a wooden landslide, and the share made. They cost him $40. He got a wooden mold board and wooden handle and beams and he had his plow. The blacksmiths in those days had to order all of his (their) iron and then made the tools to sell," Cummins said.

"When I was a kid in the Walla Walla country, that was ten years before this town (Spokane) was taken up as a homestead, the population down there (Touchet) was mostly Indians and we were about the only family down there. I remember the adobe walls of the old Hudson Bay Camp. When I was in it, the top was all off, but the side walls built of sod, were still there."

142

A Snake Head

I have always been curious about Dr. Dorsey Baker's strap-iron-railroad as well as data given to me from an old Spckane County pioneer friend of mine named Albert Johnson, who had also lived in the area of the railroad and was a mutual friend of ours.

"I was here long before there were any railroads built in the state. The first railroad was a narrow guage built by Doc Baker, (which ran) from Walluly (Wallula) to Walla Walla. It was built on wooden rails, 4 x 6's x 16 feet long. When they got as far as "Tuschy" (Touchet) Station the first of the rails were worn out as they had to go back and reinforce the rails with iron strippers. These straps were about as wide as three fingers. By the time, they got up to Lydon's Station, which was past our place, that was all broken up, so they had to go back and rebuild and they put it on about 4 inch steel railing. They got a little "T" iron, laid it on a 2 x 6 wooden rail, to make it stronger to hold the little engines. Then they made it to Walla Walla. Doc Baker later sold out to the O.W. R and N and they widened it out into standard guage. Doc Baker then put his money into the Baker and Boyer Bank, a famous pioneer bank in Walla Walla."

"Albert Johnson once mentioned taking a ride when the strap iron curled up and ran into the floor of the car. The little engines had a little platform in front, just like a switch engine, and a man sat there with a hammer and would nail down the straps. They called him a "snake head". They sometimes had a shepherd dog sitting at his side, and he would run out and bark at the cattle to keep the road clear. Those little engines only had four drive wheels and the little cars they built only had four wheels, and they were all flat cars. They were sixteen feet long."

"The material for the railroad such as lumber was cut up in the Clearwater country, and was rafted down to Walluly. They had it sawed up in Walluly and then had the little train there to haul it out. I rode on the Baker road myself. We went on an excursion and sat there and grinned like we were really going some place. After it was sold to the O.W.R. and N. they built a branch line up through there and went over the Alto Hill and into Starbuck. The Union Pacific then bought it from O.W.R. & N. They couldn't pull a whole train up the hill at Starbuck, so they kept an engine there to pull the cars to the top of the hill. They put in a bumper set in order to double up the cars with bumpers on them, but they had to put it in the center of the train to shove and pull. Then they rebuilt on a water grade from Walluly."

Some Freighting Experiences

Robert Cummins, the father of our subject, ran a freight line from Touchet Station near Walla Walla to Spokane, Robert Franklin Cummins our narrator, said "He had two teams of four horses. I drove one and my brother Jesse drove the other. We ususally stayed close together when we drove the freight route so we could help each other in case we got stuck."

The route, when they drove together was from Touchet Station to Walla Walla, Waitsburg, Dayton, Colfax, Steptoe Butte and into Spokane. "It took a week to make the round trip", Cummins recalled.

"I started driving a team in freighting when I was 12 years old in 1886. The men would load my wagon for me and then I would drive the wagon. We would go down to Walluly, where we would get our loads, which had been hauled up that far by the river boats. Then we would come on up and stop at our place all night and we'd go on through Colfax and right on up to Spokane, coming out by Cash Up Davis. Colfax

143

was a kind of mining camp, with just a few settlers and it was kind of a trading point. We used to stop at Cash Up's because he had water there. He had a little store along the road just below Steptoe Butte. He was chunky and had a heavy beard - saved his money and wouldn't buy a razor. We never went down into the Big Bend country in my freighting days. We would haul into here (Spokane) and the people in the Big Bend used to go into Walla Walla for their provisions, which had been hauled from Walluly to Walla Walla by boat. That is where they cut across the Lyons Ferry. We did our crossing at Riparia at the Old Texas Ferry. We had a big hill from Tucannon over the top of the road there, and that's when we put on eight horses. We carried a 40 hundred pound load with 4 horses." Further questioning on my part brought out the fact that when he climbed out of the Snake River Canyon at Ripiaria, he needed help from a man who followed him with a team and wagon to that point. He told me that he and his helper, perhaps his brother - Jesse, unloaded half of his load at the bottom of the hill; pulled the remainder to the top of the hill with a double team, where they unloaded it. They drove down hill with an empty wagon; loaded the remaining half of the load on it and hauled that up to the top of the hill where they loaded the first half on the wagon.

From that point on, Robert said he could handle the rest of the trip to his destination, which he informed me was Spokane Bridge. At this delivery point, he said, "There were usually men available, who would help me unload my wagon."

I didn't have the presence of mind to ask him how he was given such an important job at such a young age nor to ask him to describe the village of Spokane Bridge.

Dent On Forehead
In recalling the Nez Perce Indian War of 1877, Mr. Cummins said: "I can't remember much about the Nez Perce Indian War, except that they took the women and children out on a barge in the middle of the Columbia River near Walluly and kept them there until they know Indians weren't coming that way."

"I can't remember much about the war but I got this the next year". With that remark he pointed to a dent in his forehead, which he got from the Indian uprising.

"We lived in Tuschy (Touchet) Station during the Bannock Indian War of 1878. When they sent the soldiers down to Walla Walla, I was commissioned by the commander to pilot the soldiers over into Tucannon, where there was fighting. It was about 4 miles right up through an elevated mountainous area and there was no route through there that the soldiers knew. I had lived in that country. Some soldiers and I had just 'clumb' (climbed) a hill and were overtaken by some Indians. Their horses were faster, and mine had just climbed the hill. We were separated from the main body of soldiers and taken to the Cayuse Indian camp. When we got there I found an old childhood friend called Lacouse. They got my horse out and I got out that night. During the fighting, a bullet glanced from my head and the Indians bandaged that before I was freed. You can offend an Indian as fast as you can a white man and they'll recollect you. If you are a friend of theirs, in time of trouble they'll stay right by you."

I think that Lacouse, while saving Cummins life must have gotten into trouble with his tribesman for his act of friendship, although Cummins said nothing of it.

Cummins continued: "I wasn't in on the fighting expedition against the Nez Perce Indians, but remember the people were all afraid. Fortifications were set up practically everywhere. On Havermale Island, in the Spokane River, a fort was set up. In the little towns there were barricades. Colfax had a small one."

From left: Robert Franklin Cummins, Woodson Cummins,
Nancy Cummins Jacobs, James Madison Cummins, William Henderson Cummins

From this somber note Robert Cummins told about schooling and what great changes that had taken place in the field of education:

"When I went to school I got on a cayuse and went three miles to a neighbor's house. About the time I'd get there to study, Dad would take me out to round up a herd of horses. There were no public schools and the teacher would get a dollar a day and would board with the parents of the kids. A group of people would get together and hire a teacher and then each person would pay a part of the tuition or cost for his children. I got more schooling after I got away from home and left school than I did at that time."

"I settled in St. John when I came into this area. That whole country was practically laid open for settlement. There were some homesteads to be taken then, but the railroad had secured (the) right of ways in there and they sold some of the odd sections, which were railroad property. I bought a piece of land from the railroad because I wanted to be near the road. I paid $7.25 an acre and now it's worth $200.00."

Robert Cummins described some of the hardships the pioneers had to undergo. He said: "I remember the winter of 1879-80. I was in St. John. A fellow by the name of Joe Carl had 200 head of cattle, which he had turned out in the spring of the year. The snow came in March when we thought the season was over. Over 2 feet of snow came. He came to my place and said 'Say, Big Bob, can you come down to my place an hep (help) me haul hay? I've got two carloads of hay at Lacrosse and I got a carload of grain at Winona and I can't get it to my cattle and they're dying. Come down with a span of horses'. I said "I can't go with a span of horses, but I can go down with 4 horses. Well, we hauled hay for 2 weeks and he still lost about half of his cattle. We'd feed cattle in the morning, then go to Lacrosse and then feed again in the afternoon. I recollect one night the wind blowed from the northeast and the cattle all went down in a low place where there was brush and laid down. Pretty near every 2 year old heifer that was going to bring a calf were walked on by other cattle. We lost about 60 cows that night".

Cattle Piled on Fences

I remember talking to Barney Fitzpatrick, son of the founder of Davenport, Washington, about one of the bad winters in the Big Bend Country. He told me that cattle piled up against fences and in low places, and died there. He also told me that some of the cattle became so hungry that they ate the hair off of fallen animals and died as a result.

During the nine years that Robert Cummins drove freight line for his father, he often drove into Spokane. He recalled: "At that time there were stumps on practically every street in Spokane and the road zig zagged through there. I used to go over the Monroe Street Bridge when it was like a beaver slide. It was a wooden structure and was quite short, just covering the width of the river, so we had to come down the banks and then climb the other side. There were only a few people then on the other side (north) living in the timber which had a road running through it."

In a Spokane Spokesman Review article dated March 10, 1953, Mr. Cummins told a reporter that he "hauled badly needed supplies into Spokane after the fire of 1889. (And) that the city was nothing but a charred ruin."

Cummins quit freighting after 9 years and went into farming at the age of 21 years. He farmed at St. John, Washington, until his retirement in 1935 at the age of 71, at which time he moved to Spokane, Washington. He was a 40 year member of the Christian Church at St. John.

Mr. Cummins died in Spokane shortly after Christmas in 1960 at the age of 96. He was survived by 71 direct descendents. Services were held at Hazen & Jaeger Valley Funeral Home, with the Rev. Edwin Martin of St. John officiating. Internment was at The Pines Cemetery, in Opportunity.

With the death of Robert Franklin Cummins, another large gap was left in the pioneer ranks of our State, for people like him, not well known, were the fabric that Owas woven into the cloth that made the tapestry which tells a picture story of the stirring history of our state.

RESUME ON JEROME PELTIER

Jerome Peltier's interest in western history started in 1925, the year he moved west with his family by train from Cloquet, Minn.

Indians performed tribal dances in full regalia on the train platforms. Cowboys on horses raced the departing trains - cowboy and indians to a young boy.

Graduating from Kinman Business University, Jerome held many positions with John W. Graham Co., before becoming their credit manager. After transferring to

146

Spokane Paper & Stationary, he and his wife, LaVerle purchased Clark's Old Book Store in 1950.

Jerome and LaVerle had been married in 1937 at the St. Paschal Church. They became parents of three children who helped in the running of the book store.

Selling the store in 1978, has allowed Jerome to spend more time with his collection of over 5000 volumes of Western Americana.

Having published 12 books and many oral histories, Jerome has contributed often to the Westerner's Quarterly.

The National President of AARP honored him for his public service after his 3rd term as president of the Spokane Valley Chapter of AARP.

Other memorable honors include meeting Father Cataldo, receiving the 1985 Distinguished Author of History award from the Eastern Washington State Historical Society and the "Living Legend #16" honor from the International Westerners. Glen Adams is currently working to publish a book of Jerome's many historical articles.

At the young age of 85, Jerome Peltier continues to collect history, especially oral histories and spend time teaching western history in the area schools.

Early Day Settler's Pie Recipe

This is an old-fashioned vinegar pie still made by grandchildren of early settlers.

1 cup brown sugar
2 cups water
1 cup vinegar
2 tablespoons butter
1/2 cup flour
Water

Plain pastry for 2 crust pie.

Combine sugar, water and vinegar and heat to boiling. Add butter and stir until it melts.

Mix flour until smooth with a little cold water. Add to boiling liquid slowly and stir

until thickened. Line pie plate with pastry; pour in filling and cover with strips

of pastry, lattice fashioned. Bake in a very hot oven (450 F.) 10 minutes; reduce heat

to moderate (350 F.) and bake about 25 minutes longer. Makes 1 (9 inch) pie.

From the collection of Ed & Betty Weilep

Index

COLOPHON

The Jerome Peltier book of Pacific Northwest history was printed in late November of 1996 in the workshop of Glen Adams which is located in the quiet country village of Fairfield, southern Spokane County in Washington state. Fairfield is a farming village on state highway 27 that runs between Opportunity and Tekoa, and is one township removed from the Idaho line. The Peltier book consists mostly of articles printed in the *Pacific Northwesterner,* which is the quarterly publication put out by the Spokane Corral of Westerners, one of a number of such corrals operating in the U.S. and beyond. The extra typesetting for this title was by Teresa Ruggles using a Compugraphic Editwriter 7300 computer photosetter. The photography/darkroom work was by Susan Paulson using a 24 inch Companica 660C vertical camera. Susan Paulson also stripped the film and made the printing plates as well as designing the colophon and title pages. The sheets were printed by Trevor Del Medico using a 28 inch Heidelberg press, model KORS. Folding was by Garry Adams on a 26x40 Baum Dial-O-Matic folding machine. Paper stock is 70 pound Crown Bright offset. Hard case binding was by Al Chidester, Arts & Crafts bindery at Oakesdale, Washington. Paper copies were bound by Glen and Garry Adams using a Sulby Mark II adhesive binding machine. This was a fun project. We had no special difficulty with the work. This is the 602nd title to come from Ye Galleon Press.